FAULT-TOLERANT
PARALLEL COMPUTATION

THE KLUWER INTERNATIONAL SERIES
IN ENGINEERING AND COMPUTER SCIENCE

T0137287

THE KLUWER INTERNATIONAL SERIES
IN ENGINEERING AND COMPUTER SCIENCE

FAULT-TOLERANT PARALLEL COMPUTATION

by

Paris Christos Kanellakis
Brown University
Providence, Rhode Island, USA

and

Alex Allister Shvartsman
Massachusetts Institute of Technology
Cambridge, Massachusetts, USA

KLUWER ACADEMIC PUBLISHERS
Boston / Dordrecht / London

Distributors for North America:
Kluwer Academic Publishers
101 Philip Drive
Assinippi Park
Norwell, Massachusetts 02061 USA

Distributors for all other countries:
Kluwer Academic Publishers Group
Distribution Centre
Post Office Box 322
3300 AH Dordrecht, THE NETHERLANDS

Library of Congress Cataloging-in-Publication Data

A C.I.P. Catalogue record for this book is available
from the Library of Congress.

ISBN 978-1-4419-5177-9

*The publisher offers discounts on this book when ordered in bulk quantities. For
more information contact: Sales Department, Kluwer Academic Publishers,
101 Philip Drive, Assinippi Park, Norwell, MA 02061*

Printed on acid-free paper.

Printed in the United States of America

I dedicate my work on this monograph
To the memory of my dear friend Paris

Στη μνήμη του αγαπητού μου φίλου Πάρι

Alex A. S

Paris Christos Kanellakis
1953–1995

CONTENTS

LIST OF FIGURES

LIST OF TABLES

LIST OF EXAMPLES AND REMARKS

LIST OF SYMBOLS

FOREWORD

The conventional perception is that, by extending a trend established at the dawn of the computer era, in the recent past we have experienced the same dramatic rate of improvement of parameters which has become the hallmark of computer technology. And indeed, the ubiquity of the computer, which has invaded and permeated every corner of present-day activity, can only reinforce such perception. The pattern of improvement has been so regular to be formulated as an empirical law of technological progress, the so-called Gordon Moore's Law. In addition, the process technology which has been fine-tuned in the last two decades has almost relegated to history the component unreliability that plagued the early developments of the digital field. Users have become accustomed to "faster and safer" machines, with no apparent end in sight. Therefore, it may be a little surprise to learn that over the past fifteen years the raw clock speed achieved in digital systems has not increased – as one may venture – by orders of magnitude, but by a mere factor between 3 and 4. Indeed, the interplay between the space of physical structures and the speed at which they are operated, has brought us to fully realize what an absolute limitation is represented by the finiteness of the speed of light. The very speed of light that the more modest technologies of yesteryear comfortably permitted us to take as infinite.

Although further progress at the circuit level is certainly to be expected, the consensus is that its rate will be excruciatingly low. The natural consequence of this state-of-affairs is that the ever increasing demands on performance can only be met by exchanging space for time, by resorting to machines with a large number of agents concurrently cooperating in the solution of the same problem, i.e., to parallelism. Despite some recent industrial failures in this area, and the ensuing ill-advised doomsday pronunciations, parallelism is undoubtedly the last frontier of computation.

As anybody, who has ventured into this field of research, knows, parallelism is fraught with enormous difficulties, which may explain its somewhat sluggish take-off in computing practice. The main difficulty is the absence of a "natural" model (analogous to the von Neumann machine) which would be crucial to the program portability that seems so natural in serial computing. Understandably, in this context most appealing is a model which dispenses with the idiosyncrasies of a specific network and represents a natural generalization of the von Neumann model. Such model is the well-known *parallel RAM* or P-RAM, in which there is a common (shared) memory each cell of which is equally accessible by all processors (rather than by just one). P-RAM algorithmics has been extensively studied over the past two decades, and a considerable body of techniques is available today. Moreover, since parallel machines are ultimately built as networks of processing elements, substantial attention has been devoted to the problem of simulating P-RAM behavior on realistic networks. But even such practice-oriented outlook always dealt with an idealized technology, where synchrony is guaranteed and equipment reliability is absolute.

This monograph by Kanellakis and Shvartsman squarely confronts the inadequacy of the prevailing approach to P-RAM computation. Massive parallel systems are the main focus of their study. As such systems become larger, even the fine technology of today cannot provide fault-free operation. Moreover, the increase in system size seriously weakens the assumption of synchrony. The authors therefore thoroughly investigate the problem of simulating a P-RAM step in the presence of failures, i.e., of simulating a step of a fault-free P-RAM by means of a fault-prone P-RAM. Their objective is to achieve fault-tolerance while maintaining efficiency, that is, to guarantee graceful degradation of performance as failures become more severe. This equilibrium of fault-tolerance and efficiency is denoted as *robust* computation. The authors consider a rich spectrum of failure models of increasing severity, from a static scenario (fabrication defects) to a most stringent situation, where an extremely powerful on-line adversary can induce the failures most prejudicial to the success of the simulation. As an excellent pedagogical device, they choose a particularly simple bench-mark, which they later show being essentially equivalent to the most general P-RAM step, the *Write-All* problem, i.e., the task of writing 1 in all cells of shared memory. Executing this task involves the assignment of processors to the writing of individual cells, while processors may fail during execution. As a consequence, careful bookkeeping of cell writing progress, of processor survival, and of processor assignment, are subtasks whose coordination is crucial to both the correctness and the efficiency of the process. A number of ingenious techniques are developed for a variety of failure scenarios, intended to capture precarious reliability and fault of synchrony. A special role in this theory is conferred to the CRCW P-RAM, the most powerful P-RAM variety that permits concurrent writes beside concurrent reads. In the fault-free environment, only logarithmic overhead separates the CRCW version from its weaker counterparts. Not so in the fault-prone world, where the authors show that efficiency and fault-tolerance cannot be reconciled except if concurrent writes are available. This phenomenon appears related to the fact that write-concurrency hides information from an omniscient adversary, and raises interesting questions in the realm of the thermodynamics of fault-prone parallel computing. Another interesting problem area will arise, and may stimulate several attentive readers, if one considers the problem of simulating a step of a fault-free P-RAM by means of a fault-prone network of processors, where the write-concurrency is no longer an assumed property of the model but a behavior to be algorithmically simulated. This monograph, with its rigorous approach, analysis, and results represents an indispensable background for such possible developments.

As a personal note, I first agreed to write a foreword to this welcome book in the summer of 1995, when my colleague and friend Paris Kanellakis graciously invited me. His office was two doors down the corridor from mine, and his periodic visits had become a welcome feature of my daily routine in the department. His conversation on the widest spectrum of subjects, from current events to deep questions in computer science, was always refreshing and stimulating. I was looking forward to some enlightening discussions as this project would evolve towards its conclusion. Suddenly, this projection was shattered. His tragic departure deprived the field of a brilliant contributor at the peak of his productivity, and we should all be grateful to Alex Shvartsman for disclosing and completing their unfinished work. Today, as a community we still mourn Paris. As a friend, I feel privileged I can add to his public image my personal remembrance of his frank and open smile, a breath of fresh air for all those who were touched by his presence.

Franco P. Preparata

AUTHOR'S PREFACE

Advances in computer technology made parallel machines a reality. Massively parallel systems use many general-purpose, inexpensive processing elements to attain computation speed-ups comparable to or better than those achieved by expensive, specialized machines with a small number of fast processors. Numerous efficient algorithms were developed for massively parallel machines. In the parallel setting however, the *independent failure* property expected of distributed systems is not inherently present. That is, when even one processor or its program fails, the entire computation either halts or produces incorrect results. This reliability bottleneck is among the fundamental problems in parallel computation.

In this monograph we pursue the goal of combining the reliability potential that comes with replicated processors in distributed computation, with the speed-up potential of parallel computation. The difficulty associated with combining fault-tolerance with efficiency is that the two have conflicting means: fault-tolerance is achieved by *introducing redundancy*, while efficiency is achieved by *removing redundancy*. We present recent advances in *algorithmic ways of introducing fault-tolerance in multiprocessors under the constraint of preserving efficiency*. The approach we develop is ultimately aimed at narrowing the gap between abstract models of parallel computation and realizable multiprocessors. The goal is to allow the parallel program development and analysis to be performed using a convenient high-level shared-memory model such as PRAM without any concern for fault-tolerance. Once a fault-free program is specified, it should be correctly and efficiently executed on parallel machines whose processors are subject to fail-stop processor errors and delays. We show that this is possible for certain models of parallel computation under a variety of fail-stop models of failure. We define the models and present key algorithmic techniques used in designing fault-tolerant and efficient programs for these models. We prove theoretical limitations on the possibility of combining fault-tolerance and efficiency. We present general fault-tolerant algorithm simulations and transformation techniques, and we conclude with a survey of relevant recent results for asynchronous and randomized computation, and for the message-passing model of computation.

A Roadmap for this Monograph

In the diagram below we show major dependencies among chapters and sections. Solid arrows indicate prerequisites and dashed arrows suggest a reading order where prerequisites are not indicated.

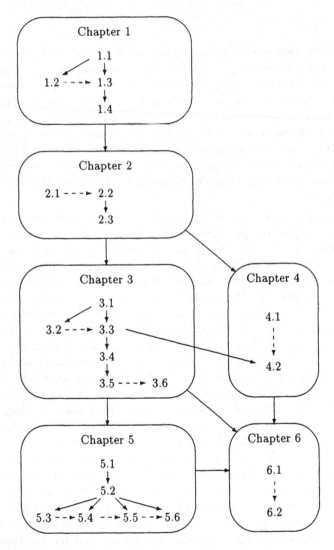

In Chapter 1 we overview inherent trade-offs between the goals of achieving efficiency through parallelism, and achieving fault-tolerance through distribution. We present a key primitive operation that we call *Write-All*; efficient algorithms for *Write-All* lead to efficient fault-tolerant parallel computation using shared memory. We include the summary of the main simulation results.

In Chapter 2 we present the parallel models we use in this work. We start with the basic PRAM model and its main variations. We then focus on the models and complexity measures that we use in the remainder of the monograph.

In Chapter 3 the algorithmic techniques used in developing deterministic solutions for the *Write-All* problem are presented. We preview techniques and data structures used for failure detection, processor allocation and load balancing and we present the most important deterministic algorithms for the failure models defined in Chapter 2.

In Chapter 4 we give the lower bounds for the *Write-All* problem for specific models of processor failures. We also consider computation using memory snapshots and approximate computation.

In Chapter 5 we present efficient deterministic and fault-tolerant simulations of synchronous shared-memory parallel algorithms on the fault-prone shared memory machines. We also examine closures with respect to fault-tolerant transformations of important classes of efficient parallel algorithms.

In Chapter 6 we overview results dealing with fault-tolerance and efficiency in shared-memory randomized parallel algorithms and in distributed-memory algorithms.

Bibliographic Notes

In each chapter we provide detailed bibliography dealing with the topics covered in that chapter. Here we give additional pointers to conferences, book chapters and books covering the various areas related to parallel computation and fault-tolerant algorithms.

In the past few years, many papers on these and closely related topics appeared in the annual symposia on Principles of Distributed Computing (PODC), Parallel Algorithms and Architectures (SPAA), Foundations of Computer Science (FOCS), Theory of Computing (STOC), and the annual workshop on Distributed Algorithms (WDAG). The interested reader is encouraged to consult the proceedings of these symposia for both the existing results and, in the future, for the new results in these areas. Many of the results have also now appeared in journals such as Distributed Computing, SIAM Journal of Computing, Information and Computation, Information Processing Letters, Journal of the ACM, Journal of Algorithms, Journal of Parallel and Distributed Computation, and Nordic Journal of Computing.

The Handbook of Theoretical Computer Science contains several chapters dealing with the foundations of parallel computation and parallel algorithms. The chapter by Karp and Ramachandran [60] deals with the fault-free PRAM models and algorithms. The chapter by Pippenger [101] covers theoretical foundations for networks used in interconnection of processors and memories. The chapter by Valiant [116] presents general purpose parallel architectures that use specific interconnection topologies.

A three-volume compilation of research results dealing with the foundations of ultradependable computing is edited by Koob and Lau: a volume covering Paradigms for Dependable Applications [65], a volume presenting Models and Frameworks for Dependable Systems [66], and a volume on System Implementation [67]. Another volume edited by Gibbons and Spirakis [45] includes several articles surveying important results in parallel computation, including reliable parallel computation.

Two additional books provide an encyclopædic coverage of key issues in decentralized computation. The book by Leighton [74] presents the foundations of parallel algorithms and architectures. The book by Lynch [80] presents a grand tour of distributed computation models, algorithms, issues of fault-tolerance, and impossibility results.

Acknowledgements

I thank Christos Papadimitriou and Franco Preparata for their advice and numerous insightful comments which substantially improved the clarity and organization of the presentation. I am grateful to Nancy Lynch for her support and encouragement during the production of this manuscript. Alan Fekete read some of the early chapter drafts and his thoughtful feedback is very much appreciated. I acknowledge with gratitude many helpful comments on various aspects of the monograph by Bogdan Chlebus, Vincent Cholvi, Maurice Herlihy, Roberto De Prisco, Volker Strumpen and Asaph Zemach. I had the opportunity to present parts of the monograph at the MIT Theory of Distributed Systems seminars. I thank the members of the TDS group for many questions and comments that prompted me to revise the monograph in several places. Thanks are also due to Carl Livadas and John Lygeros for help with typesetting, in LaTeX, of the Greek texts of the dedication and the concluding citation.

The material we present in this monograph includes some results of our colleagues who have contributed to the research in the field of fault-tolerant parallel computation. Any list of workers in this field will be incomplete without the names of Richard Anderson, Jonathan Buss, Richard Cole, Cynthia Dwork, Zvi Galil, Phillip Gibbons, Joe Halpern, Zvi Kedem, Chip Martel, Alan Mayer, Dimitrios Michailidis, Naomi Nishimura, Krishna Palem, Arvin Park, Michael Rabin, Prabhakar Ragde, Arvind Raghunathan, Paul Spirakis, Ramesh Subramonian, Orli Waarts, Heather Woll, Moti Yung and Ofer Zajicek.

Parts of this work were supported by the following contracts: ARPA N00014-92-J-4033 and F19628-95-C-0118, NSF 922124-CCR, and ONR-AFOSR F49620-94-1-01997.

Finally, I thank Scott Delman of Kluwer Academic Publishers, for his interest, participation and valuable assistance during the completion of this monograph.

$$\star \quad \star \quad \star$$

Paris Kanellakis and I began preparation of this monograph in 1994. By December of 1995 we had compiled most of the material and drafted four of the planned seven chapters. We were to complete the remaining work during the winter vacation. It was not to be. Tragically, my friend Paris, his wife Mate and their children Alexandra and Stephanos died in a plane crash on December 20th, 1995. This is a profound personal loss that I cannot express in words. Our book is now complete, but the loss remains. I miss you, my brother.

Alexander Allister Shvartsman
Cambridge, Massachusetts

1

INTRODUCTION

THIS study of fault-tolerant parallel computation uses models of computation based on the *parallel random access machine*, or PRAM. The PRAM model is generally accepted as a convenient abstraction useful for defining and analyzing parallel algorithms. However it makes some assumptions that call into question its practicality. The main such assumptions are global synchronization of processors, high-bandwidth concurrent access to shared memory, and infallibility of processors, interconnections and memory. In this monograph we pursue the goal of preserving the high-level PRAM abstraction that makes it attractive for programming parallel algorithms, while narrowing the gap between PRAMs and realizable parallel machines. Our primary focus is the removal of the assumption that the processors are failure-free. In some settings we also show how to relax the assumption of global synchrony and how to limit shared memory access concurrency in fault-tolerant algorithms while preserving their efficiency.

In this chapter we present the goals of achieving efficiency through parallelism and achieving fault-tolerance through distribution. Systems consisting of multiple processing elements are often used to speed up computation. The presence of multiple processing elements also constitutes a form of redundancy that can be exploited to introduce fault-tolerance. We overview the inherent trade-off involved in combining efficiency and fault-tolerance, and we present the primitive operation of *Write-All* that plays a central role in subsequent chapters. Efficient algorithms for this primitive lead to general results for efficient fault-tolerant parallel computation in the shared memory models. We introduce the main complexity measure used to gauge the efficiency of fault-tolerant algorithms. This measure takes into account the speed-up achievable in the absence of failures and the efficient use of resources (processors) whether or not any failures are encountered. We preview the failure models used in the remainder of the book and we summarize the main fault-tolerant simulation results.

1.1 COMPUTING WITH
MULTIPLE PROCESSORS

Multiple cooperating processors are often deployed to increase efficiency of computation according to the following criteria:

Increase system throughput by performing multiple loosely-coupled or unrelated tasks in parallel. This ranges from assigning processing elements to specific system tasks (e.g., augmenting central processors with dedicated input/output processors), to assigning general-purpose processors to specific application tasks (e.g., providing several processors in a time-sharing system so that multiple applications can be executed concurrently).

Reduce response time for a particular task by partitioning it into components that can be executed in parallel and assigning a dedicated processing element to each such component (e.g., searching a large file in parallel by assigning parts of the file to individual processors).

Systems meeting the first objective have for some time been available through integrated hardware and operating system software solutions. Working towards the second objective has proved more difficult, since discovering and developing efficient parallel algorithms is, in general, a very challenging task. In some cases existing sequential algorithms can be parallelized, but this is time-consuming and such techniques are difficult to generalize. Although general-purpose techniques, such as pipelining, are able to speed up the execution time of sequential algorithms, such speed-ups are constant and have little impact on the ability of the algorithm to be executed on multiple pipelined processors. Thus, speeding up a single large computational task by using multiple processors requires that there exist an efficient and faster-than-sequential parallel algorithm for that task.

Multiple processors can also be deployed to meet the goals of fault-tolerance:

Increase system availability by replicating the computation and/or computing resources so that even if some parts of a computations do not complete, or incorrectly complete due to a failure, then (given sufficient redundancy in the system) the overall computation is able to complete successfully.

Enable graceful degradation in the face of failures by eliminating single points of failure, by detecting and isolating faulty sub-components, and rescheduling tasks among the non-faulty processors.

Traditionally, research in the distributed computing field has concentrated on fault-tolerance, while parallel computing research has taken speed-up as its

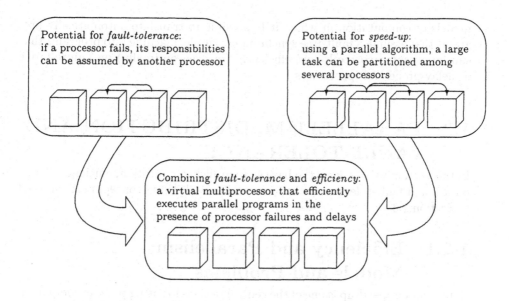

Figure 1.1   Combining fault-tolerance and efficiency.

main focus (here the terms *distributed* and *parallel* allude to the traditional research areas and do not refer to specific or necessarily distinct computation paradigms). A synthesis of these two directions yields an approach for computing with multiple processors whose goal is to obtain scalable parallel speed-up, while enabling graceful degradation in the face of failures (Figure 1.1). This goal is achieved by combining:

- the **reliability** potential that comes with replicated processors, with

- the **speed-up** potential of computing with multiple processors

The benefits of such a combination of speed-up with reliability are of course obvious, yet its feasibility is far from obvious. To combine efficiency with fault-tolerance, we need to resolve an inherent conflict present in the means of achieving fault-tolerance and efficiency:

- *fault-tolerance* is achieved by *introducing redundancy*, while

- *efficiency* is achieved by *eliminating redundancy*.

In this monograph we present algorithmic techniques for reconciling this conflict in the presence of processor failures, restarts and delays. We explore some

models of computation in which it is possible to translate automatically programs that assume a fault-free synchronous parallel machine into programs that
can be executed correctly and efficiently (or even optimally) on failure-prone
or delay-prone multiprocessors.

1.2 PARALLELISM, DISTRIBUTION AND FAULT-TOLERANCE

In this section we overview the basics of parallel computation, efficiency, distribution and fault-tolerance. Readers familiar with these concepts can proceed
to Section 1.3.

1.2.1 Efficiency and Parallelism: Models and Problems

Computation speed-up is one of the central reasons for using parallel computers.
If a task can be done in sequential time T using a uniprocessor, then ideally
we would like to perform the same task in parallel time $\tau = T/P$ using P
processors. Reaching such linear speed-up is an important goal of parallel
algorithm design.

In the setting where multiple processors cooperate on a common task, in order
to hope to achieve a speed-up almost linear in P, we need to assume that the
processors are operating either in synchrony, or at least at comparable speeds.
This assumption is in fact implemented in highly parallel computing devices
such as systolic arrays and SIMD (single-instruction, multiple-data) devices such
as vector processors. In the synchronous setting, where there are P processors
that operate in lock-step, the success of reaching the goal of efficient speed-up
can be directly quantified.

The *parallel work* of such algorithms can be expressed as the product of the
number of processors P and the parallel time τ. Parallel work measures the
total number of machine instructions executed by the processors during the
computation. This measure requires that we account for all available computing
resources by including all instructions of any idle processors.

For a particular problem, a parallel algorithm is considered *optimal* when the
parallel work is related by a multiplicative constant to the best known or best
achievable sequential time for the same problem (for uniprocessors, the notions
of *work* and *time* are equivalent). That is for optimal parallel computation we
require that $P \cdot \tau = O(T)$. Of course for the computation to be practical, the
constant must be small.

The number of processors P must also be scalable with the problem parameters. For achieving a meaningful better-than-constant speed-up, for an input of size N, we must be able to increase the number of processors P so that it is non-negligible compared to the input size N and/or to the best sequential time T. For example, it may be possible to achieve parallel time polylogarithmic in N, by deploying sufficiently many processors.

Note that using work as the main complexity measure is more strict than using parallel time alone. This is because the goal of minimizing parallel time is in some cases achieved by using a polynomial number of processors, e.g., quadratic in input size. Such an algorithm cannot be considered efficient if its work far exceeds the best sequential time for the same problem.

In the cases when optimality is not reached for whatever reason, a parallel algorithm is considered efficient, if it attains a near linear speed-up and when its work is increased by only a modest amount. This typically means that using P processors on inputs of size N, the parallel time achieved is within a multiplicative factor polylogarithmic in N of T/P, i.e., $\tau = \log^{O(1)} N \cdot T/P$. In this case the parallel work is also degraded by a polylog factor, $P \cdot \tau = \log^{O(1)} N \cdot T$. In some cases, the goal of achieving high speed-ups is worthwhile even when the work is within a small polynomial factor of the optimal work, i.e., when $P \cdot \tau = N^{\varepsilon} \cdot T$, where $\varepsilon < 1$.

We take the view that synchrony is an important component of achieving the promise of the massively-parallel efficient computation. When a system is not completely synchronous, then at least we must be able to make assumptions about the time it takes for a processor to perform a unit of work and to communicate. Such systems are sometimes called *timed-asynchronous*. In working towards the goal of efficient computation, it is reasonable to assume that the processors available to a computation are all equally powerful. It makes little sense to include, for example, processors that are much slower than the rest. In designing for parallelism in a synchronous or timed-asynchronous system, we count on the availability of sufficient computational resources whose behavior is within the designed parameters. Of course we need to be able to deal with processors with erratic timing behavior, but the computation need not be exclusively concerned with such "deviants" (provided of course the correctness can be maintained).

This brings us to another important point. In developing highly parallel algorithms, it is assumed that the processors are *willing* participants in a solution, that is the processors are there to cooperate and do not need to be coerced into cooperation. We must also be able to deal with unexpected deviations from such willing cooperation, but such cases are the exception, not the norm. In particular, we can rely on "good citizenship" of the cooperating processors not to exhibit arbitrary or malicious behavior.

To combine isolated processors and memories, there is a variety of interconnection topologies that yield models of computation and realizable architectures covering the spectra of paradigms from shared-memory to message-passing, and from tightly-coupled to loosely-coupled. For example, the PRAM (parallel random access machine) model can be viewed as a shared-memory, tightly-coupled model. Systolic array architectures are based on a message-passing, tightly-coupled model. Wide area networks fall into the message-passing, loosely-coupled model, while local area clusters of processors sharing disk storage belong to the shared-memory, loosely-coupled model. These are just few of the possible data points, and additional refinements can be made, for example, on the basis of the ability to perform fine- vs. coarse-grain computation. Note that the shared-memory/message-passing dichotomy alone is not sufficient to determine whether a decentralized machine constitutes a suitable parallel processing platform. For example, a collection of PCs sharing a file server is a shared-memory machine not very well-suited for solving finely-grained parallel problems, while a hypercube multiprocessor is a message-passing machine that is a basis for several contemporary parallel machines.

Here we consider the models of computation in the shared-memory, tightly-coupled paradigm which, in addition, are suited for fine-grain parallelism. The PRAM is a convenient abstraction of such models which has been successfully used in the development of efficient parallel algorithms. Several efficient simulations of such models in other parallel architectures have been developed (e.g., hypercubes), making many shared-memory algorithms transparently portable to such architectures. In other cases, an algorithm can be mapped directly onto another architecture. In the next chapter we discuss some of the advantages and disadvantages of the model we chose as the basis for our exposition.

Efficient or optimal parallel algorithms have been developed for many fundamental computation tasks.

Example 1.1 *Sorting*: Sorting is one of the most fundamental operations in computing and will serve as an illustration here and in the next section. In the domain of sequential computation, sorting N values requires $N \log N$ operations. Thus, in the parallel setting, the efficiency and speed-up goals are to be able to sort in polylogarithmic in N time using a linear in N number of processors. These goals have been achieved for several models of decentralized computation ranging from shared memory models to message passing fixed-degree network models. Optimal logarithmic time algorithms have also been discovered. □

1.2.2 Fault-Tolerance, Distribution and Redundancy

From an algorithmic standpoint, it appears that the promise of massively parallel efficient computation is within reach. But what about fault-tolerance? For a parallel machine with an extremely large number of processors, memories and interconnect components (even if we assume very high reliability of individual components) ensuring high reliability of the machine is still a challenge. Even when failures are infrequent, what happens when a failure does occur?

A system that is able to preserve its specified functionality despite certain faults in its subcomponents is called *fault-tolerant*. A *failure* of a system is its inability to perform its function. Note that the meaning of the terms *fault* and *failure* depends on the context and the level of abstraction of the terms' usage. From the system's standpoint, a *failure* of one of its subcomponents is a *fault*. Whether or not this fault will cause the system itself to fail depends on the fault-tolerance characteristics of the system and on whether or not the fault causes an *error* in the state of the system. For example, a failure of the memory location 177 is a fault that may never be noticed if no processor ever reads anything from this location.

An important goal of a fault-tolerant system is to prevent the failures of its sub-subsystems (i.e., the faults within the system) from causing the system to enter an incorrect state such that the system is unable to function according to its specification. For this goal to be meaningful, specifications must be given both for the system itself, and for the types of faults the system must be able to tolerate. Given the specification of the failure model $\mathcal{F}$, the system must conform to its specification for any failure pattern in $\mathcal{F}$. We address failure modeling in the next section.

To make a uniprocessor able to tolerate faults, *redundancy* is introduced. There are two common ways of increasing fault-tolerance through redundancy, one is called *time redundancy* and the other *space redundancy*.

Time redundancy increases the fault-tolerance of a computation by introducing additional computation steps that either check the results for correctness and/or repeat the same computation. This is normally done using different algorithms or distinct computation paths, and then either choosing the better result among those obtained according to some criteria, e.g., correctness checks, or by voting.

Space redundancy introduces additional hardware components so that the faults in one component can be masked by a spare component. There are available systems that use dual processors to provide a degree of processor fault-tolerance, or deploy *shadow* or *mirror* disks for seamless masking of disk failures. The *triple modular redundancy* (TMR) is another venerable method that uses triplicates of components, at least two of which are assumed to be correct, i.e., non-faulty.

There is a spectrum of techniques that have characteristics of both space redundancy and time redundancy. For example, error-correcting memories and RAID storage devices are made fault-tolerant by introducing additional physical components, while performing additional computation to encode data or to mask errors.

A major problem with the approaches above is that they are expensive. Consider the TMR technique, for example. If we deploy TMR in the space redundancy mode using triplicate processors, then we at least triple the cost of hardware while achieving some fault-tolerance, but realizing no gains (at best) in performance. If one deploys TMR in the software time redundancy mode, then we achieve some fault-tolerance while slowing down the system (at least) threefold.

A worthwhile objective for a fault-tolerant system with r-fold redundancy in processing elements designed to tolerate up to $r - 1$ element failures, is the r-fold increase in performance in the absence of processor faults. When there are indeed $r - 1$ failures, then the system's performance approximates the performance of a single processing element.

Similarly, consider a decentralized (parallel or distributed) system consisting of p processing elements designed to achieve up to p-fold speed-up. Such a system has an inherent redundancy, and there is no reason why we should not expect the system to tolerate up to $p - 1$ processor failures with graceful degradation in performance as the number of faults increases.

Example 1.2 *Robust sorting*: In the previous section, we cited sorting networks as examples of highly efficient parallel structures. One such example is a single-pass sorter based on shuffle-exchange network. The sorter uses $\Theta(N \log^2 N)$ processing elements and it sorts N inputs values in time $O(\log^2 N)$. It turns out that it is possible to construct an iterative version of the sorter whose performance degrades gracefully in the presence of certain patterns of failures. The sorter has depth $O(\log N)$ and it uses $(N \log N)/2$ elements. In the absence of processing element failures it sorts its inputs taking $O(\log N)$ iterations and time $O(\log^2 N)$. The network performance degrades gracefully when the faulty elements are simply by-passed (thus becoming "wires"). It is possible to identify N critical pairs of processing elements, such that when failures do not affect both members of such pairs, the sorter continues its operation correctly.   □

Such *robust* sorting network is a good example of synergy of fault-tolerance and efficiency in parallel computation. It is also an example of the technique known as *algorithm-based fault-tolerance*. Here fault-tolerance is achieved by taking advantage of the properties specific to the parallel algorithm and building into the algorithm certain checks that ensure that the tasks that have been incorrectly or incompletely performed due to failures are repeated until the algorithm terminates correctly. In the case of the sorting network, the data continues to be passed through the network until it is sorted.

Other examples of algorithm-based fault-tolerance include matrix operations, e.g., multiplication, where checksum columns and rows are used to perform redundant scalar operations so that faults (up to a certain maximal pattern) to either be corrected using checksums, or detected. In RAID devices, algorithm-based fault-tolerance is achieved by additional coding of the input data and retrieval results, using error-correcting schemes, so that if disk components fail (up to a certain maximum) then the data can be re-created.

Such techniques can be described as algorithm-specific, as they are particular to certain algorithmic domains. We are primarily interested in *algorithmic* techniques that are *general* and that are applicable to many classes of algorithms, although in some cases we are also interested in tailoring specific algorithms for fault-tolerance when this produces additional benefits in either the number of tolerated failures or in efficiency.

1.3 A TRADE-OFF BETWEEN FAULT-TOLERANCE AND EFFICIENCY

The quest for high speed-ups has led to efficient parallel algorithms that are very tightly designed, so that every processor is fully utilized doing something essential for resolving the input task. Thus, *parallel algorithm efficiency* implies a *minimization of redundancy* in the computation, leaving very little room for fault-tolerance. Most known efficient parallel algorithms either would not terminate correctly, or become inefficient when they are perturbed by simple processor errors. These perturbations are of course outside the original setting, but are nonetheless realistic and they underline the need for fault-tolerance.

Once processor failures are introduced into a parallel computation, the $\tau \cdot P$ work measure loses its meaning. This is because the computational resource is no longer under the control of the computation — it varies due to failures, and only limited resources may be available at any given time. The efficiency of fault-tolerant parallel computation is more appropriately measured in terms of the processor work-steps that are *available* to the computation.

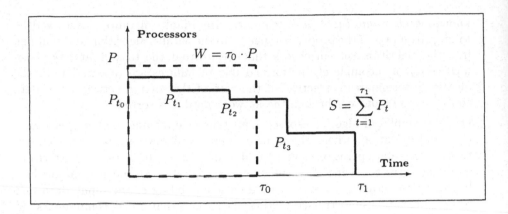

Figure 1.2   Work in the absence and the presence of processor failures.

Example 1.3 *Work subject to failures*: Consider a synchronous P-processor algorithm that terminates in time τ_0 in the absence of failures. The fault-free work $W = \tau_0 \cdot P$ is the area of the dashed rectangle in Figure 1.2. Due to failures the algorithm begins with $P_{t_0} < P_0$ processors, and then the number of active processors is reduced to P_{t_1}, P_{t_2} and P_{t_3} at times t_1, t_2 and t_3 respectively. The computation finally terminates at time τ_1. The work in the presence of these failures is more appropriately described by the area bounded by the "staircase" formed by the heavy solid lines and the two axes. $\square$

In the example, the shape of the "staircase" is determined by the *failure pattern* F, established by an adversary, that determines when and what processors fail-stop (and, in general, fail-stop or restart) during the execution. We now formally define the work in the presence of failures in terms of the *available processor steps*.

Definition 1.3.1 Consider a parallel computation with P initial processors that terminates in time τ according to an external clock, after completing its task on some input data I and in the presence of the failure pattern F. If $P_t = P_t(I, F) \leq P$ is the number of processors completing an instruction at time t, then we define the *available processor steps* as: $S(I, F, P) = \sum_{t=1}^{\tau} P_t$.
$\square$

We assume that the discrete time steps at which processors may be completing instructions are determined by internal clocks, local to the processors. The definition does not assume that there is a global clock that is available to the processors, but that the time at which instructions complete can be measured

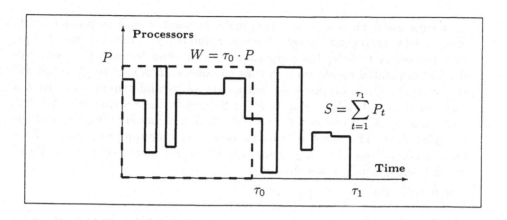

Figure 1.3 Work in the absence and the presence of failures and restarts.

on a discrete external clock which is fast enough to have clock-ticks that coincide with the internal clock-ticks at which instructions are completed.

In Example 1.3, we assumed synchronous parallel processors. In this case the internal clock-ticks are exactly the ticks of the external clock in the definition. The definition is general enough to capture the work of parallel computations where the clock rates can vary and/or fluctuate, and where processors can stop and later restart.

When the restarts are undetectable, the distinction between failure/restart pair of events, and asynchronous processor delays essentially vanishes. In the most general case, the shape of the "staircase" of Figure 1.2 will instead appear as a "comb" with an irregular pattern of short and missing "teeth", corresponding to the number of processors completing instructions at times determined by local clocks and by the pattern of failures and restarts as depicted in Figure 1.3. Note that we make no assumption about the duration of the individual instructions.

The parallel time of a fault-tolerant algorithm, unlike the parallel time of a fault-free synchronous algorithm, does not depend exclusively on the number of initial processors P and the size of the input. When failures occur, the parallel time depends also on the variations in the size of the available computing resources. If an adversary stops all but one processor, the time of the execution can be as large as the available processor steps S. Nevertheless, for some realistic failure patterns it is easy to estimate the upper bound on the parallel time of a fault-tolerant algorithm. For example, if the adversary allows a subset of processors, of size at least P', to complete their instructions during each time slot, then the time of the execution is at most S/P'.

As we discussed already, it is conceptually straightforward to provide fault-tolerance by taking advantage of space redundancy – one can use P fail-stop processors to solve the computational task, and let each processor run the best sequential algorithm with time complexity $T(N)$, where N is the size of the input. Such solution is as fast as any sequential computation using a single processor. It tolerates up to $P - 1$ failures (if there are no restarts), but its work in the worst case is $S = T(N) \cdot P$, which is achieved in the case without a single failure. This is not an efficient use of the computing resources — for a fault-tolerant P-processor algorithm to be efficient it must have work overhead which is substantially lower than P.

Our focus in this monograph is on:

(i) Providing as much fault-tolerance as is available using the naïve space redundancy approach, while

(ii) Enabling faster algorithms that approach the speed-up of best parallel algorithms when there are no failures, and

(iii) Achieving worst case work S that has overhead as small as possible (and at most sub-linear in P) relative to the work (i.e., time) of the best sequential algorithm for the same problem.

We now give a preview of the main definitions and results that are formally presented in later chapters.

The fault-tolerant algorithms and simulations of fault-free algorithms on fault-prone machines are classified by how well they meet the criteria (i), (ii) and (iii) above. For this purpose we define the notion of *robustness* that combines *fault-tolerance* and *efficiency*. Informally, if an algorithm meets all three criteria, we say that the algorithm is *polynomially robust*, i.e., it is fault-tolerant and it is polynomially efficient since its computational overhead is bounded by P^ε for some $0 \leq \varepsilon < 1$. If in addition the overhead is bounded above by $\log^{O(1)} P$, then we say the algorithm is *polylogarithmically robust* or simply *robust*. Finally, if the overhead is bounded by a constant, we say that the algorithm is *optimal*.

These definitions are extended to algorithm simulations by applying the three criteria to each simulated parallel step. In the context of a deterministic simulation, the basic problem to be solved is the *fault-tolerant and efficient* simulation of each parallel step of N fault-free processors using P fault-prone processors. A simulation is *polynomially robust* (respectively *robust*, *optimal*) if the computational overhead in simulating each parallel step of N processors is polynomial (respectively polylogarithmic, constant). Note that the definitions dealing with simulations do not require that the *simulated* algorithm be efficient.

Remark 1.4 *Amortized work*: A more sophisticated approach would be to amortize the work of simulating individual parallel steps over all steps of the computation. This approach is needed in simulations in which, for example, we make probabilistic assumptions about the completion of a particular step and proceed to the next. When the assumption is invalidated, the simulation must backtrack. Here we present simulations based on deterministic simulations of individual parallel steps — thus using an amortized efficiency measure is equivalent to the per-step efficiency measure we outlined. □

We consider five main models of failure-inducing adversaries. These form a hierarchy, based on their power. Each adversary is more powerful than the preceding, and, as we have already suggested, the case of undetectable restarts is essentially the case of *asynchronous* processors. Below are brief descriptions of the failure models. We define and discuss the models in detail in the next chapter.

Initial failures : adversary causes processor failures only prior to the start of the computation.

Fail-stop failures : adversary causes stop failures of the processors during the computation; there are no restarts.

Fail-stop failures, synchronous restarts : adversary causes stop failures; subsequently to a failure, the adversary might restart a processor, but only at well-known points during the computation.

Fail-stop failures, detectable restarts : adversary causes stop failures; subsequently to a failure, the adversary might restart a processor and a restarted processor "knows" of the restart.

Fail-stop failures, undetectable restarts : adversary causes stop failures and restarts; a restarted processor does not have the knowledge of the restart.

Except for the initial failures case where the adversary is necessarily off-line, the adversaries are omniscient and on-line. A major characteristic of these adversary models is that they are worst-case. An adversary has full information about the structure and the dynamic behavior of the algorithm whose execution it interferes with, while being completely unknown to the algorithm.

The main results for deterministic simulations are summarized in Table 1.1. These results are shown Chapter 5.

In the table we consider several models constrained by the adversary and memory access concurrency. For each model, we specify the type of robustness achieved by the simulation, the number P of the simulating processors as a

Model Constraints	Simulation Robustness	Using P Processors[a]	Memory Usage		$\|F\|$ per Step[c]
			Total[b]	Clear	
Initial fail-stop[d]	Robust	N	$\Theta(m)$	0	0
	Optimal	$N/\log N$	$\Theta(m)$	0	0
Fail-stop (with synchronous restarts)	Robust	N	$\Theta(m)$	$\Theta(P)$	$P-1$
	Optimal	$N\frac{\log\log N}{\log^2 N}$	$\Theta(m)$	$\Theta(P)$	$P-1$
	Optimal	$N\frac{(\log\log N)^2}{\log^3 N}$	$\Theta(m)$	0	$P-1$
Fail-stop with controlled memory access[e]	Robust	N	$\Theta(m)$	$\Theta(P)$	$P-1$
	Optimal	$N\frac{\log\log N}{\log^4 N}$	$\Theta(m)$	$\Theta(P)$	$P-1$
	Optimal	$N\frac{(\log\log N)^2}{\log^5 N}$	$\Theta(m)$	0	$P-1$
Fail-stop with detectable restarts	Polynomial	N	$\Theta(m)$	$\Theta(P)$	Any
	Optimal	$N/\log^2 N$	$\Theta(m)$	$\Theta(P)$	$P\log N$
Fail-stop with undetectable restarts[f]	Polynomial	N	$m\log^{O(1)}m$	$\Theta(P)$	Any

[a] Specifies the upper bound for P, the number of fault-prone processors used to simulate N fault-free processors.

[b] Where m is the memory used by the fault-free algorithm.

[c] The size of a failure (failure/restart) pattern F per simulated parallel step.

[d] Memory access is EREW (exclusive-read, exclusive-write).

[e] The concurrent memory access of the simulated algorithm is increased at most by the number of failures $|F|$ for writes and at most by $7|F|\log N$ for reads.

[f] Simulations of fast (polylog parallel time) algorithms.

Table 1.1   Summary of the deterministic simulation results.

function of the number of the simulated processors N, total memory requirements of the simulation, the part of the memory that needs to be initially clear, and finally the number of failures (or failures and restarts) allowed during the simulation of each N-processor parallel step.

For all dynamic failure models which do not allow processor restarts, the results also hold when the restarts, if any, can be synchronized with the start of the simulation of the next parallel step.

In many cases, the simulations can take advantage of processor *slackness* to achieve optimality, i.e., when the number of *simulating* processors P is smaller than the number of *simulated* processors N, then for certain ranges of $P < N$ the simulations become optimal and the available processor steps of the simulation is asymptotically equal to the parallel work of the simulated algorithm.

The details leading to the simulation results are presented in the subsequent chapters. A key role to achieving robust computation is played by solutions to a basic problem that we define next.

1.4   THE WRITE-ALL PRIMITIVE AND ROBUST COMPUTATION

To deal with failures that arise during a computation, it is necessary for the remaining active (non-faulty) processors to detect the failures and assume the responsibility for the work of the stopped (faulty) processors. Thus *failure detection* and *load balancing* are instrumental in the development of fault-tolerant algorithms. Furthermore, these two functions must be performed efficiently whether any failures occur or not. Naïve strategies for processor failure detection and load balancing are inadequate for our purposes, whether they are centralized (e.g., using a master control), or distributed (e.g., using clustering). A master control strategy is sensitive to particular patterns of simple failures. Clustering can degrade by a multiplicative factor linear in the number of processors in a cluster.

We now give an example that illustrates a key problem, solutions to which we develop and use in the chapters that follow.

Example 1.5 *Write-All*: One of the simplest tasks that can be performed by a PRAM is: *given a zero-valued array of N elements and P processors, write value 1 into each array location.* We call this task *Write-All*. When $P = N$ and in the absence of failures, this *Write-All* problem is trivially solved in constant time by the following optimal (PRAM) program.

```
{ true }
forall processors PID = 1..N parbegin
    shared integer array x[1..N];
    x[PID] := 1
parend
{ x[i] = 1 (i = 1, ..., N) }
```

However, even a single processor failure prevents the establishment of the postcondition $\{x[i]=1 \ (i=1, \ldots, N)\}$.

Simple fixes are available that will make the above program more fault-tolerant. For example, for a small number of failures up to k, consider the clustering algorithm that introduces $(k + 1)$-fold redundancy:

```
forall processors PID = 1..N parbegin
    shared integer array x[1..N];
    for i = PID to PID + k do
        if i ≤ N then x[i] := 1 else x[i − N] := 1 fi
    od
parend
```

This algorithm performs well for dynamic failure patterns with few errors, but poorly when there are many failures. For example, if k is fixed and N variable then the algorithm cannot handle a linear in N number of failures, and if k is allowed to grow to, for example $N/2$, then the overall work becomes quadratic in N.   □

We will show in Chapter 5 that efficient and fault-tolerant solutions for the *Write-All* problem of Example 1.5 can be used as a basis for efficient and fault-tolerant computation in general. For example, in the model admitting arbitrary patterns of dynamic stop-failures we show the existence of an N-processor CRCW PRAM algorithm for the *Write-All* problem for which $S = O(N \log^2 N / \log \log N)$. This, in turn, leads to the ability to execute (or simulate) any synchronous parallel program developed for the fault-free environment on a CRCW PRAM whose processors are subject to fail-stop failures. Such executions use *Write-All* algorithms as *primitive operations* to simulate each synchronous parallel step. Since a *Write-All* algorithm is to be invoked a small fixed number of times per simulated parallel step, the cost of each such step is the same as the work performed by the *Write-All* algorithm used. In effect, we reduce the problem of simulating a single parallel step to solving the *Write-All* problem.

The *Write-All* problem captures the computational progress that can be naturally accomplished in unit time by N synchronous processors in the absence of failures. Because our techniques for achieving fault-tolerant and efficient computation are based on solutions for the *Write-All* problem, we grace it with its own definition:

Definition 1.4.1 Given a zero-valued array of N elements and P fail-stop processors, the *Write-All* problem is to set each element of the array to 1.   □

Remark 1.6 *Certified Write-All*: A variation of the *Write-All* problem, known as the *Certified-Write-All* occurs in the literature. It is defined by requiring that a particular shared memory location, *done*, that is initially 0, is set to 1 after the *Write-All* array is set to 1. We will not be making a distinction between the two problem definitions, since for all algorithms we present in the subsequent chapters, there is some well-defined memory location that can be used in lieu of the *done* flag to indicate that the *Write-All* array is set to 1. □

Write-All should not be thought of as initializing an array of N elements, but transforming, in parallel, the contents of shared memory from one state to another, and ultimately executing *any* PRAM step in the presence of failures. En route to developing robust simulation techniques, we will illustrate the techniques using solutions for the *Write-All* problem and another basic problem that we call *general parallel assignment* or *GPA*:

Definition 1.4.2 Given an array $y[1..N]$ of initial values $a_1, a_2 \ldots, a_N$ from some set A, and P fail-stop processors, the *general parallel assignment* problem is to store in each $y[i]$ $(1 \leq i \leq N)$ the result of computing $f(i, \langle a_1, \ldots, a_N \rangle)$, where f is a constant time computable function $f : \{1, \ldots, N\} \times A^N \to A$. □

We will show that the complexities of solving the *Write-All* problem and the *GPA* problem are identical. The techniques used to develop robust *GPA* algorithms directly lead to robust simulations of any PRAM algorithms. The reader can get a glimpse of some of the simulation details by observing the similarity between the array y and the function f on one hand, and the shared memory of a PRAM and the machine instructions executed by the individual processors on the other. We defer further discussion until Chapter 5.

1.5   BIBLIOGRAPHIC NOTES

For a surveys of parallel algorithms, speed-up, complexity, interconnection networks and parallel architectures we refer the reader to chapters by Karp and Ramachandran [60], Pippenger [101] and Valiant [116] in the Handbook of Theoretical Computer Science, and to the book by Leighton [74] already mentioned in the Preface. The parallel random access machine (PRAM) is formalized by Fortune and Wyllie [42]. An exposition of PRAM algorithms can be found in [30].

Systolic arrays, as special purpose programmable parallel architectures, were introduced by Kung and Leiserson [70]. A good overview of systolic arrays was contributed by them as Section 8.3 in a book by Mead and Conway [89]. The systolic model of computation, systolic algorithms and algorithms for a variety of parallel processing architectures are covered in detail by Leighton [74]. Patterson and Hennessy [96] give an introduction to pipelining vector processors. The now venerable classification of computing systems that includes the

SIMD (single-instruction, multiple data) and MIMD (multiple-instruction, multiple data) models was introduced by Flynn [41]. This classification is discussed by Patterson and Hennessy [96]. Sorting networks are presented by Knuth in [64, Section 5.3.4]. The robust sorting network we used as an example of synergy between parallelism and fault-tolerance is due to Rudolph [106].

For a survey of principles of fault-tolerance in distributed systems see an article by Cristian [31]. Dealing with failures in the context of consensus problems is covered in depth by Lynch in [80], where the most important results can be found. Some of the key original results dealing with the upper and lower bounds on the number of processors for consensus problem are by Pease, Shostak and Lamport [97], and Lamport, Shostak and Pease [73]. The seminal impossibility result for consensus in the asynchronous setting even with a single stopping failure is due to Fischer, Lynch and Paterson [40]. See also the survey by Lynch [81].

Failure types such as Byzantine, omission failures, fail-stop failures, etc., have been studied for a long time. For an overview, see the survey chapter by Lamport and Lynch [72]. Schlichting and Schneider [108] showed how to construct correct algorithms for fail-stop processors by using a formal methodology and an appropriate programming language framework.

In the context of parallel computation, off-line adversaries were used by Martel, Subramonian and Park [87]. In this context, the probabilistically limited adversaries were used by Kedem, Palem and Spirakis [63]. The *Write-All* problem was formulated by Kanellakis and Shvartsman in [56] originally for on-line omniscient adversaries. The general parallel assignment problem is also defined there. An amortized approach to achieving robust simulations is taken by Kedem, Palem, Raghunathan and Spirakis [62].

2

MODELS FOR
ROBUST COMPUTATION

F ORMULATING suitable models of parallel computation and processor failures goes hand in hand with the study of algorithms and their complexity. In this chapter we revisit and formally define the models of computation that are the subject of our presentation, the models of failures that we are addressing, and the major variations of the fail-stop parallel random access machine. We define and discuss the complexity measures that we use to characterize the efficiency of algorithms for the models selected and in the context of particular failure models. We introduce the high-level programming notation used to specify algorithms and we discuss the implementation and architectural issues related to the abstract models we study.

2.1 FAULT-FREE PRAMS AND THEIR VARIANTS

In the study of algorithms for the tightly-coupled synchronous shared memory multiprocessors one abstract model attracted significant amount of attention. This model is the Parallel Random Access Machine or PRAM. The PRAM model was formulated for the setting where the processors need to cooperate in working towards a common computational goal. The PRAM combines the simplicity of a single processor RAM (Random Access Machine) model with the power of parallelism.

The PRAM model is used widely in parallel algorithms research. It is a convenient and elegant model, and a wealth of efficient algorithms have been and are continually being developed for this model.

2.1.1   The Basic PRAM Model

Since there are several standard variants of the model, we start by describing the general characteristics of the PRAM family.

Common features of PRAM models

A PRAM is defined as a set of synchronous processors that can concurrently access shared memory:

- There are P serial (RAM) processors with unique identifiers (PID) in a compact range, e.g., in the range $1, \ldots, P$. Each processor has access to its PID, and the number of processors P.

- The global memory is accessible by all processors and is denoted as **shared**; the P processors can concurrently access the shared locations and memory access takes unit time.

- There are Q shared memory cells, and the input of size $N \leq Q$ is stored in the first N cells. Except for the cells holding the input, all other memory cells are cleared, i.e., contain zeroes. The processors have access to the input size N.

- Each processor has local memory denoted as **private**. The local memory is not accessible to other processors.

- All memory cells are capable of storing $\Theta(\log \max\{N, P\})$ bits.

It is usually also assumed that the size of the shared memory Q is polynomial in the number of processors P, and the size of the input N, and that the private memory is relatively small, e.g., polylogarithmic in P or even constant.

The PRAM instruction set is essentially that of a conventional RAM. The instructions executed by the processors are defined in terms of three synchronous cycles:

Read cycle : a processor reads a value from a location in shared memory into its private memory,

Compute cycle : a processor performs a computation using the contents of its private memory,

Write cycle : a processor writes a value from a location in private memory to a location in shared memory.

PRAM variants

There are several variants of the basic model, each defining the allowable patterns of shared memory access. There are three main variants:

EREW, the *exclusive-read, exclusive-write* variant allows no concurrent access by more than one processor to the same memory location.

CREW, the *concurrent-read, exclusive-write* variant allows arbitrary concurrent read access to a memory location, but no concurrent write access to the same location.

CRCW, the *concurrent-read, concurrent-write* variant allows arbitrary concurrent read and write access to the same memory location. With the concurrent writes enabled, the following three write policies are distinguished:

(1) COMMON CRCW in which all concurrently writing processors must write the same value,

(2) ARBITRARY CRCW in which the write of a single processor is arbitrarily chosen to succeed, and

(3) PRIORITY CRCW in which the processor with the highest PID succeeds in writing its value.

Among these variants, the EREW is the weakest and the PRIORITY CRCW is the strongest PRAM variant. Any algorithm for the weaker variant also works in the stronger variant. The converse is not true, but stronger variants can be simulated by the weaker variants at a cost. In particular, it can be shown that a PRIORITY PRAM can be simulated on an EREW PRAM with a slowdown that is logarithmic in the number of processors.

Finally, when showing lower bounds, an impractically strong model, called the IDEAL PRAM, is sometimes used. In this model there are no limits on the sizes of the private and shared memories, and a processor can perform arbitrary computation on its private memory in unit time. The IDEAL PRAMs are also classified as EREW, CREW and CRCW IDEAL PRAMs. Such IDEAL PRAMs were used in showing lower bounds results for the settings without failures. When proving some of the lower bounds for the fault-prone models, we consider a powerful PRAM model in which processors are able to read and locally process the entire shared memory at unit cost. We call such models the *memory snapshot* models.

In much of the exposition, we use the concurrent-read, concurrent-write (CRCW) PRAM. In the algorithms we present, all concurrently writing processors write the same value making our approach independent of the CRCW conventions for concurrent writes. In the cases where we deal with other than the CRCW variant, we will explicitly point this out.

2.1.2   Advantages and Limitations of the PRAM Model

To understand why the PRAM model is widely adopted for algorithmic study, we take a brief look at the PRAM's sequential ancestor, the RAM. The reasons for the success of the RAM model of computation have been summarized by Valiant:

> The phenomenon of general purpose computation in the sequential domain is both specific and powerful. We take the view here that it can be characterized by the simultaneous satisfaction of three requirements. First there exists at least one high-level language U that humans find satisfactory for expressing arbitrary complex algorithms. Second there exists a machine architecture M, in this case the von Neumann model, that can be implemented efficiently in existing technologies. Finally there exists a compilation algorithm A that can transform arbitrary programs in U to run on M efficiently.

The same harmony is yet to be achieved in the domain of decentralized (parallel and distributed) computation. There is no universally accepted high-level programming paradigm U, while there are several feasible but dissimilar machines M that dictate a particular style of programming that suits specific compilation algorithms A.

At the abstract level, however, the PRAM model comes close to satisfying the three requirements. In the next section we discuss a high-level programming language notation for the model. Other notations used in the literature differ essentially at the syntactic level. These notations have been widely accepted and used for specifying PRAM programs. Likewise, techniques exist for efficient compilation of such high-level language programs for execution on the abstract PRAM. The problem of course is that implementations of general synchronous shared memory machines using extant technologies are scalable only to modest ranges of processors and memory. However efficient simulations of PRAMs on some realizable parallel architectures exist (e.g. hypercube), and where general simulations are not available, some PRAM algorithms have been mapped onto the target architecture. It is worthwhile to pursue the study of PRAM computations since improvements in PRAM algorithms in many cases result in improvements in algorithms for practical architectures.

Finally, lower bounds are also informative. The computing folklore states that "one can always slow down programs by using real hardware." In other words, theoretically provable inefficiencies for parallel computation are usually amplified in practice.

We now review the main idealized assumptions in the PRAM model:

Memory access concurrency: processors can read from (in the CREW and CRCW variant) and write to (in the CRCW variant) the same shared memory cell concurrently. In the extreme case all processors are able to access a given cell concurrently.

Memory access bandwidth: processors can access shared memory in parallel and such access takes unit time.

Global synchronization of processors: processors proceed in lock-step and an observer outside the PRAM can associate a "global time" with every event, i.e., although the processors do not have access to "global time" and the PRAM does not provide a "global clock", processors can keep accurate local clocks by counting their steps and communicating through shared memory.

Fault-free execution environment: the processors, memory and processor/memory communication are free of faults.

Each of the above assumptions increase the attractiveness of the PRAM model as the target of parallel algorithm development. At the same time, these assumptions make it difficult for the PRAM to be implemented as a scalable architecture (and decrease the significance of PRAM results). The challenges of synchronizing subcomponents, providing constant length access paths to memory cells, communicating between components at a high bandwidth, and of masking failures are present even in uniprocessors. Because of the large number of processors in the parallel setting, the physical limitations encountered in meeting these challenges in a scalable fashion become problematic much sooner.

There are a number of proposals that address the above assumptions (see Bibliographic Comments). In this book our main goal is to relax the assumption that the computing resources are fault-free. For some failure models we also either eliminate concurrent memory access or control the memory access concurrency in terms of the number of failures encountered during the computation. We also relax the strict synchronization requirements in some cases. However, recalling the discussion in the previous chapter, we consider synchrony to be a desirable enabling property of fault-tolerant parallel computation. Completely removing the assumption of synchrony undermines the very goal of parallel computation – the goal whose objective is to achieve a predictable P-fold speed-up as compared to the best sequential algorithms. For this reason, we treat asynchrony as a deviation from the intended parallel computation paradigm, i.e., *we treat it as a fault.*

We thus proceed with the assumption that the synchronous shared-memory parallelism is a valuable abstraction because it yields a model with a widely acceptable programming paradigm that makes the specific speed-up goals directly quantifiable. It is therefore important to continue projecting this abstraction externally, while hiding the less-than-perfect reality in a transparent and an efficient way.

Synchronous parallelism with concurrent memory access	Asynchronous concurrency with interleaved memory access
$\{x = 0\}$ **parbegin** $\quad x := \langle x + 1 \rangle$ $/\!/ \quad x := \langle x + 1 \rangle$ **parend** $\{x = 1\}$	$\{x = 0\}$ **cobegin** $\quad x := \langle x + 1 \rangle$ $/\!/ \quad x := \langle x + 1 \rangle$ **coend** $\{x = 1 \vee x = 2\}$

Figure 2.1 Synchronous parallel and asynchronous concurrent executions.

2.1.3   A Programming Notation

PRAM algorithms are usually presented as high level programs that can be compiled into assembly-level PRAM instructions using conventional techniques. The programs are described in a model independent fashion using block-structured notation with the **parbegin-parend** construct specifying parallelism, and other conventional control structures such as **if-then-else** and **while-do** to control the flow of execution within a single processor. In reading the parallel code, it is important to keep in mind that the semantics of programs in the synchronous parallel model differ from the semantics of programs in the asynchronous concurrent shared memory model.

The most striking difference between the asynchronous concurrent model with interleaved memory access and the parallel model is observed for the synchronous CRCW memory access discipline. In the synchronous case, we have concurrent execution and assignment, while in the asynchronous case, the atomic actions that make up the program elements are interleaved in some order.

Consider the two program fragments in Figure 2.1, each executed by two processors. We use the **parbegin-parend** brackets in this monograph to denote parallel execution with memory access concurrency.   In this example we use the accepted **cobegin-coend** brackets to denote concurrent execution with interleaving. The statements or statement blocks separated by $/\!/$ are executed concurrently. The expressions in braces describe the state of the computation and the angled brackets are used to denote atomic actions.

For the synchronous program, the value of x is deterministically computed to be 1, that is the synchronous program is equivalent to a single multiple assignment "$x, x := x + 1, x + 1$". In the asynchronous case the value of x is either 1 or 2 which is caused by interference due to possible interleavings within the program. Even if we do not require the atomic evaluation of $x + 1$, then

$\{x = 1\}$ still holds in the synchronous case, while the results are essentially undefined for the asynchronous program.

These differences illustrate the "unusual" feature of the CRCW PRAM: synchronous parallel read/write to the same memory location. When two processors execute the program segment, both processors read x simultaneously, and store the incremented value to x simultaneously establishing $\{x = 1\}$. As we will show in the discussion of the lower bounds for the *Write-All* problem, it is the concurrent assignment that, by providing memory write redundancy, allows for fault-tolerance to be combined with efficiency in some models, even when subjected to the most powerful adversaries.

In order to reason about the synchronous parallel programs, one needs to specify precisely the relative timing of all the commands and statements. It may be intuitively understood that the parallel assignments in Figure 2.1 are synchronized, since they have identical timing characteristics. However, if the right hand side of the second assignment was changed to a more complicated expression that takes longer, or a different number of instructions, to evaluate then, to synchronize the assignment, we would have to specify that the evaluations of the right-hand-side expressions are performed first, followed by the parallel assignments.

In most cases we are dealing with, the programs executed by the individual PRAM processors are identical, but the processors have their own instruction counters and they may be working on different data. Such model is called the *single-program multiple-data* model, or SPMD. The SPMD programs, where the number of processors and their PIDs are known can be expressed as follows:

> **forall processors** $PID = 1..P$ **parbegin**
>   Program(PID)
> **parend**

Each processor executes the sequential "Program(PID)" based on its processor identifier. This can be equivalently expressed as:

> **parbegin**
>   Program(1) $/\!/$ Program(2) $/\!/ \ldots /\!/$ Program(P)
> **parend**

The SPMD model can be viewed as a generalization of the SIMD (single-instruction, multiple-data) model when, in the SIMD case, each processor can either execute the current instruction or perform on a no-op based on certain criteria. On the other hand, SPMD can also be viewed as a restriction of the MIMD (multiple-instruction, multiple-data) model by providing means of synchronization. The asynchronous shared memory model, in its general form, is essentially the MIMD model.

Special care must be taken when constructing SPMD parallel programs consisting of the **parbegin-parend** constructs above and the conventionally-looking **if-then-else** and **while-do** blocks. For example, in the following program,

> **forall processors** $PID = 1..2$ **parbegin**
>   **if** expression(PID)
>   **then** block1
>   **else** block2 **fi**
> **parend**

the specific timing of operations performed by the two processors, if each takes a different branch in the **if**, need to be precisely defined for the program to make sense. A similar situation exists with the "**while** guard **do**" loop construct when some of the processors exit the construct after evaluating the guard expression and some continue executing the loop.

A number of techniques exist for unambiguously compiling these constructs into machine language instructions. These techniques typically use processor masking approaches and ensure synchrony by "padding" the shorter execution paths by an appropriate number of no-op instructions. Such transformations affect only the lexical structure of the program text and do not affect the computational complexity of algorithms. Examining this in more detail is outside our scope. In our algorithms, we avoid the ambiguity and enforce synchrony by using the **while** loops in which the guard expressions are evaluated identically by all processors and in which the **if-then-else** branches consist of simple assignments whose meaning and timing is made clear by the program text.

For example, in the program such as the one below, we always evaluate the right-hand side expressions first, and then perform the assignment, all in parallel, so that the pre- and post-conditions hold. To ensure this at compile time, the number of machine instructions in the right-hand side evaluation of the first, more complicated, assignment is counted. This number is used to determine the number of no-ops necessary to append to the second assignment's right-hand side evaluation to ensure that both evaluation consist of the same number of instructions (for simplicity assuming identical timing for all instructions).

> $\{x = 1 \wedge y = 2\}$
> **forall processors** $PID = 1..2$ **parbegin**
>   **if** $PID = 1$
>   **then** $x := y * y + x$
>   **else** $y := 0$ **fi**
> **parend**
> $\{x = 5 \wedge y = 0\}$

The programming notation we overviewed is generally easy to work with and reason about. While in the asynchronous concurrent model one needs to worry about the interleavings of, and the interference among, the threads of execution, in the synchronous parallel model we have an essentially mechanical process of understanding the deterministic timing characteristics of the programs' lexical structure.

We will be using such notation in presenting algorithms for fault-prone multi-processors. The interpretation of programs will of course depend on whether the processors may stop, restart at arbitrary or the well-defined synchronization points, or experience unpredictable delays corresponding to failures and undetectable restarts.

2.2   FAULT-PRONE PRAMS

We build our models of fail-stop PRAMs as progressive extensions of the basic PRAM model given in Section 2.1.1. In all models processors that are subject to failures stop without affecting the shared memory, that is the processors are *fail-stop*. Depending on the model, failed processors may be restarted.

Failures and restarts (where allowed) are formally specified in terms of failure patterns as follows.

Definition 2.2.1 A *failure pattern* F is a set of triples $\langle event, \text{PID}, t \rangle$ where *event* can be failure indicating processor failure, or it can be restart(*type*) indicating a processor restart, where *type* can be synchronous, detectable or undetectable; PID is the processor identifier; and integer t is the time indicating when the processor stops or restarts. This time is a global time, that is assigned by an adversary (and visible to an observer outside the machine). The *size* of the failure pattern F is defined as the cardinality $|F|$, where $|F| \leq M$ for some parameter M.   □

In the definition above, we are concerned with the failures and restarts caused by an adversary, but also with the *magnitude* of failures, that is the with the cardinality of the set representing the failure pattern.   For failure patterns without restarts, $|F| \leq M < P$, and when restarts are allowed, then $|F|$ can be very large relative to P. The efficiency of some algorithms will depend on the size of the failure patterns.

In the rest of this section we formally define and explain the measures of efficiency which we use to characterize the fault-tolerant algorithms and we detail a hierarchy of fail-prone models of parallel computation. We will then discuss the variations of the processor, memory, and network interconnect parts of our models.

2.2.1   Complexity Measures

We now formally define the complexity measure of *available processor steps S*. The measure generalizes the *Parallel-time × Processors* product. Our definition is based on Definition 1.3.1, which describes the work $S(I, F, P)$ of a particular execution of an algorithm. Here, the work of an execution depends on the input I, the number of processors P, and the failure pattern F belonging to a failure model $\mathcal{F}$. Recall that $S(I, F, P)$ measures the work of an algorithm when the number of processors performing the work fluctuates due to failures and restarts (or delays), and it does not charge for time steps during which a processor was unavailable due to a failure (recall Figures 1.2 and 1.3).

Definition 2.2.2 The *available processor steps* of a P-processor PRAM algorithm on any input data I of size $|I| = N$ and in the presence of any failure pattern F of size $|F| \leq M$ in the failure model $\mathcal{F}$ is defined as $S = S_{N,M,P} = \max_{I,F}\{S(I, F, P)\}$.   □

In some cases we need to maximize S also over all failure pattern sizes M. In such cases we use the notation $S_{N,P}$, and it is defined as $\max_M\{S_{N,M,P}\}$.

The available steps measure S is used in turn to define the notion of algorithm *robustness* that combines fault-tolerance and efficiency:

Definition 2.2.3 Let $T(N)$ be the best sequential (RAM) time bound known for N-size instances of a problem. If a parallel algorithm for this problem completes its task with $S = S_{N,M,P}$ for any input of size N, and for any number of initial processors P $(1 \leq P \leq N)$, and for any failure pattern size M, in the failure model $\mathcal{F}$ then we say that the parallel algorithm is:

- *Optimally robust* when $S \leq c\,T(N)$, for a fixed c.

- *Polylogarithmically robust* when $S \leq c'\,T(N)\log^c N$, for fixed c and c'.

- *Polynomially robust* when $S \leq c\,T(N)\cdot N^\varepsilon$, for a fixed c and $\varepsilon < 1$.   □

When it is clear from the context, we use the term *optimal* to describe the optimally robust algorithm and we use the term *robust* only to describe algorithms whose multiplicative overhead for work is at most polylogarithmic. When the achieved robustness is polynomial, we explicitly denote it as such. Recall that straightforward N-fold space redundancy approach yields solutions with $\varepsilon = 1$. Thus the goal is to have $\varepsilon \ll 1$.

By the definition of S, for a given algorithm, we maximize $S(I, F, P)$ over inputs I of size N and failure patterns F of size $|F| \leq M$. For some failure models, it may be the case that S is not only a function of N and P, but also a function of M. When M can be large relative to P and N, using the the work measure S alone may not be sufficient to distinguish between the efficiencies of different algorithms, since M is not a parameter under the control of the algorithm.

The ultimate performance goal is to perform the required computation at a work cost as close as possible to the work performed by the best sequential algorithm known. Unfortunately, this goal is not attainable when an adversary succeeds in causing too many processor failures during a computation, e.g., a number of failures quadratic in N or P.

Example 2.1 *Work and large number of failures*: Consider a *Write-All* solution, where it takes a processor one instruction to recover from a failure. If an adversary is able to establish a failure pattern F with $|F| = \Omega(N^2)$, then work will be $\Omega(N^2)$ regardless of how efficient the algorithm is in recovering from failures. □

Therefore, for some algorithms, the measure S alone is not that meaningful when the size of the failure patterns is very large. To enable us to compare the efficiency of fault-tolerant algorithms, and to be able to contrast this efficiency with the efficiency of the best sequential algorithms, we introduce the *overhead ratio* σ that is a function of M. This ratio amortizes the work of an algorithm over the essential work and the size of the failure pattern:

Definition 2.2.4 A P-processor PRAM algorithm solving a problem for any input data I of size $|I| = N$ and in the presence of any pattern F of failures and restarts of size $|F| \leq M$ has *overhead ratio* $\sigma = \sigma_{N,M,P} = \max_{I,F} \left\{ \frac{S(I,F,P)}{T(|I|)+|F|} \right\}$, where $T(|I|)$ is the time complexity of the best known sequential solution for the problem. □

Such ratio is justified because any algorithm must do *something* for each step in $T(|I|)$ and for each triple in F.

Remark 2.2 *Overhead ratio for Write-All and linear-time sequential algorithms*: One of our objectives, is the development of efficient *Write-All* algorithms. For these algorithms, using the parameters of the definition above, $T(|I|) = |I| = N$, since the best sequential solution takes N time to solve the *Write-All* problem. Thus σ can be specialized for algorithms with linear sequential time complexity in terms of $\frac{S(I,F,P)}{|I|+|F|}$. For example, this applies also to any algorithm that is able to simulate a single PRAM step in the presence of failures. □

We also define the *competitive* overhead ratio σ' for comparisons of fault-tolerant parallel algorithms with their fault-free counterparts:

Definition 2.2.5 A P-processor PRAM algorithm solving a problem for any input data I of size $|I| = N$ and in the presence of any pattern F of failures and restarts of size $|F| \leq M$ has *competitive overhead ratio* $\sigma' = \sigma'_{N,M,P} =$ $\max_{I,F} \left\{ \frac{S(I,F,P)}{\tau(|I|) \cdot P + |F|} \right\}$, where $\tau(|I|)$ is the time complexity of the best known P-processor parallel solution for the problem.   □

If for a given problem there is a known optimal parallel solution, then for any fault-tolerant solution for the same problem the definitions of σ and σ' are equivalent and we have $\sigma = \sigma'$. We use σ' in Section 5.6 to assess closures of parallel complexity classes with respect to fault-tolerant algorithm transformations.

Of course, the goal is to make the overhead ratios σ and σ' as low as possible, and in general to be at most polylogarithmic in N and P. For small failure patterns, for example when $M = O(P)$, as in the case of the stop failures without restarts, S alone meaningfully describes the algorithm efficiency, and σ is simply $O(\frac{S_{N,M,P}}{N})$. When F can be large relative to N and P, as in the case with restarts enabled, σ provides a better reflection of the efficiency of fault-tolerant algorithms.

So far we have concentrated on the characterization of computation in terms of the number of processors, and time and work complexities. Later in this chapter we address the issues of memory access concurrency in the presence of failures, and memory initialization and access atomicity. For memory access we define measures of access concurrency which we use to design algorithms that control read/write concurrency in terms of the size of the failure pattern encountered during the computation.

2.2.2   Models of Processor Failures

Significant research is being devoted to the study of fault-tolerant, distributed computation in the presence of failures. The considered failures range from crash and omission failures to even malicious (the so-called *byzantine*) failures. Failures are extensively studied in the context of distributed algorithms for the *consensus* or *agreement* problem requiring that a set of processes, starting each with one initial private value, agree on one of these values.

For the synchronous message-passing model, the results are generally negative, implying that the number of processor failures must be less than a third of the total number of processors and that the connectivity of the network graph must be greater than twice the number of processor failures. The resources required by a solution are also substantial as the minimum number of synchronous communication rounds is at least linear in the number of failures.

In the case of asynchronous message-passing and shared-memory models, the results are even worse: the basic consensus problem cannot be solved at all. The above results are for deterministic algorithms, and they provide additional intuition for why synchrony is important not only for efficiency in the absence of failures, but also for efficiency (or even solvability) in the presence of failures.

Dimensions of failure models

In considering failure models for parallel computation, we identify the following dimensions of failure models.

Failures types: Byzantine failures, omission failures and fail-stop (or crash) failures have been long studied in the context of consensus and related problems as distributed algorithms able to deal with these failures were being developed. In the area of parallel computation, where processors are more tightly coupled as compared to a distributed environment, failures need to be classified further with an emphasis on the more benign fail-stop case. In state-of-the-art technology, processing elements are designed with built-in diagnostics capabilities. Upon detecting failures, such processors can isolate themselves from the rest of the computing environment without harmful effects. Such processors are modeled as fail-stop processors. We will show that it is possible to construct efficient and fault-tolerant algorithms for certain classes of parallel fail-stop processors. Thus in the context of tightly-coupled parallel computation the fail-stop failure model is both desirable and tractable.

Adversary types: The notion of adversary is useful for deriving lower bounds for specific failure models. An adversary determines which processors fail at what step of the computation and which errors are caused by the failures. When the adversary is *omniscient*, it has complete knowledge of the algorithm it is going to affect adversely. An *oblivious adversary* is limited in its knowledge about the computation it is affecting. An adversary can be limited in *time* or *space* either regarding its ability to select its own actions, or regarding the knowledge of the algorithm. Alternatively, an oblivious adversary may be restricted to causing failures at random.

An adversary can also be *on-line* or *off-line*. On-line adversaries are also called *dynamic* or *adaptive*. An on-line adversary decides during the computation which processors are subject to failure (or delay) and when the failure (or delay) is to occur. When the adversary is off-line, all failure decisions are made prior to the start of a computation. For deterministic algorithms, when the input is determined at the outset, there is no distinction between on-line and off-line omniscient adversaries, since an omniscient adversary is able to predict the exact behavior of the deterministic algorithm. The difference between on-line and off-line adversaries is most notable in the case of randomized algorithms and oblivious adversaries that have no insight into the outcome of the randomized choices. Such an off-line adversary is much weaker than the on-line adversary because the on-line oblivious adversary has the knowledge of the behavior of the algorithm in the past. Finally, an adversary might be limited probabilistically so that failures can caused only with a certain probability. We will deal primarily with the omniscient on-line adversaries. Although such adversaries are very strong, we will see that it is nevertheless possible to achieve fault-tolerance *and* efficiency for the the models we consider.

Granularity of failures: Whereas there is a fair amount of analysis based on types of failures and kinds of adversaries, there has been less attention paid to granularity of failures. Failure granularity defines the extent to which subsystem failures affect the overall system. Granularity also defines the smallest system components, such that a failure within the component is either completely masked by the component or causes the failure of the entire component. We will be dealing with the failures at the granularity level of a single processor.

Magnitude of failures: Many hardware oriented fault-tolerance techniques provide fault masking up to a pre-determined limit. In a distributed setting, some algorithms can handle processor failures when the number of failures does not exceed a certain fraction of the total number of processors. It is important, where possible, to develop techniques that can deal with *any* number of failures; however such techniques should be efficient when the number of failures is relatively small. The efficiency of a fault-tolerant solution may depend on the maximum allowable number of failures, but it is imperative that computations remain correct for any number of failures (as long as one or more processors remains operative).

Recovery and restarts: In some models it is reasonable to assume that faulty processors never recover. For example, fabrication defects may permanently disable some of the systolic array processors, while the array remains functional when equipped with on-board fault-tolerance. It is reasonable in other settings for processors to recover at some point and rejoin a computation in progress. Failures may be quantified by the duration of a processor's absence from a computation, and by the synchronization of processor restarts. We consider both the models without restarts and models with restarts.

Frequency of failures: A final but significant dimension is the frequency and timing pattern of failures. We believe that a fault-tolerant algorithm must show graceful degradation of performance so that when the failures are infrequent the algorithms must be near the peak of its efficiency. Here we consider models that place no restriction on the frequency of failures or time duration between failures. Of course when failures (and recoveries) are very frequent, the computational progress of an algorithm can be severely affected.

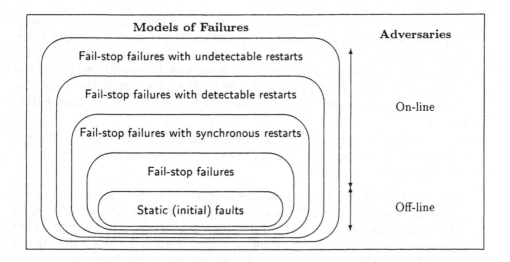

Figure 2.2 Adversaries and the processor failure hierarchy.

We now define the specific models of failure for which we develop algorithms in the next chapter.

The hierarchy of failure models

Recall our main failure models: static (initial) faults, fail-stop failures (without restarts), fail-stop failures with synchronous restarts, fail-stop failures with detectable restarts, and fail-stop failures with undetectable restarts. These form a hierarchy (see Figure 2.2), based on the power of the adversaries inducing the specific failure patterns. Except for the initial static failures case, the adversaries we consider here are worst case, omniscient and on-line.

Static faults: The adversary causes processor failures only prior to the start of the computation. That is, the failure pattern contains only triples of the form ⟨failure, PID, 0⟩. The failure pattern is otherwise arbitrary and the adversary has the ability to predict the behavior of the algorithm designed to cope with the failures. Once the failures are determined, the remaining active processors execute synchronously as in the standard PRAM model. Although this is not a very interesting failure model, it accurately reflects the possible failures due to permanent fabrication defects. Not surprisingly, highly efficient algorithms can be constructed in this model.

Fail-stop failures without restarts: The adversary causes fail-stop processor failures during the computation and there are no restarts. The active processors all execute synchronously as in the standard PRAM model. Processors that are subject to failures, stop without affecting the shared memory. Moreover, writes to shared memory are atomic. If a processor is stopped during a write, then the write either is not performed leaving the old value in the memory cell untouched, or the new value is successfully written (we revisit this atomicity assumption later in this chapter). The adversary is the worst case adversary that is omniscient and on-line (as is the case for the models that follow).

For this failure model, the failure patterns contain only the triples of the type $\langle$failure, PID, $t\rangle$, where $t \geq 0$ – only failures are allowed, and at any time during the computation.

Fail-stop failures with synchronous restarts: This is a simple extension of the model without restarts. Here restarts are allowed, but only at well-defined points during an execution of algorithm. Such points may coincide with a start of a particular stage of an algorithm. A failure pattern for this failure model may include triples with event types failure and restart(synchronous).

We will not be considering this model separately, since algorithms for the fail-stop no-restart model can be almost trivially extended for the model with synchronous restarts. Algorithms and simulations in the non-restartable model remain correct, and their efficiency is normally preserved when processor restarts can be synchronized with the start of the simulation of a particular parallel step.

Fail-stop failures with detectable restarts: The adversary causes fail-stop processor failures; subsequently to a failure, the adversary might restart a processor and the recovered processor has no knowledge of the restart. The processors restart in a known *restart* state and consequently are able to perform recovery actions as defined by the particular algorithm. It is assumed that failures do not cause the processors to lose their computation context[1].

As in the model without restarts, active processors execute synchronous instructions, however failures are able to introduce arbitrary delays between any two successfully executed instructions in any processor.

For this failure model, any of the failure pattern of the model with synchronous restarts are allowed, and in addition, the failure patterns containing the triples with events restart(detectable).

---

[1]It is also possible to consider the failure model with detectable restarts where processors lose the values stored in their private memory (registers) after failures. Some algorithms for the model with failures and detectable restarts can be adapted for the "memory loss" model. This is done with the help of well-defined segments of non-volatile shared memory that are read by processors after each detectable restart. We will briefly comment on that further in the next chapter.

Failures and undetectable restarts: In this failure model, the adversary causes processor failures and restarts such that the processors have no direct means of detecting that failures occur. In particular, when a processor is restarted, it does not necessarily "know" of the restart. Thus a failure followed by an undetectable restart can be viewed as an introduction of an arbitrary delay between two instructions. In other words, such model is identical to the model of the standard PRAMs with delay failures, i.e., the adversary is able to make processor execute no-ops between synchronous PRAM steps.

For this failure model, any of the failure pattern of the model with detectable restarts are allowed, and in addition, the failure patterns containing the triples with events restart(undetectable).

On undetectable restarts and asynchrony

When the restarts are undetectable, the adversary can additionally introduce sufficient delays between failures and restarts of processors, so that at no time during the computation are there two processors concurrently reading or writing. In this case the access to memory is never concurrent, and we have essentially an asynchronous system where the accesses to memory are interleaved with the interleaving imposed by an adversary.

Recall that we consider arbitrary asynchrony to be a form of a failure. This choice is motivated, in part, by problems typically encountered in asynchronous shared memory computations where it is impossible for a processor to distinguish a faulty processor from a processor that is very slow.

Containment of failure models

We say that the failure model $\mathcal{F}_1$ is *contained* in the failure model $\mathcal{F}_2$ if any failure pattern in $\mathcal{F}_1$ is also a failure pattern in $\mathcal{F}_2$. The containment of the models depicted in Figure 2.2 can be confirmed by observing that the set of the adversary behaviors of the higher-level models is a superset of the adversary behaviors of any of the lower-level models. This directly follows from the definition of failure patterns for each model. For any $\mathcal{F}_1$ and $\mathcal{F}_2$ that are depicted as $\mathcal{F}_1$ being contained in $\mathcal{F}_2$, we have that for all failure patterns $F \in \mathcal{F}_1$ it is also the case that $F \in \mathcal{F}_2$, from which $\mathcal{F}_1 \subseteq \mathcal{F}_2$. That the subset is proper is also easy to see from the possible failure event types as presented in sections above.

Suppose we have $\mathcal{F}_1 \subseteq \mathcal{F}_2$, then a lower bound for $\mathcal{F}_1$ is automatically a lower bound for $\mathcal{F}_2$. Also any fault-tolerant algorithm designed for $\mathcal{F}_2$ tolerates any pattern of failures from $\mathcal{F}_1$. This confirms the intuition that it is more difficult to develop efficient fault-tolerant algorithms for higher-level models in Figure 2.2.

Remark 2.3 *Alternative definition of failure models*: There is an interesting uniform approach for alternatively realizing these models of failure by modifying the finite state control of the fault-prone processors. Each machine instruction can have two parts, a *green* and a *red* part. The green part gets executed under normal conditions. If a processor fails then the red part is executed instead of the green part. The models are then defined as follows: For initial static failures, the adversary, prior to the start of the computation, selects a subset of the processors and stores the HALT instruction in the green and red parts of all instructions of such processors. For stop-failures without restarts, the adversary stores *halt* instructions into all red parts, and then causes the processors to fail dynamically during the computation. For stop-failures with synchronous restarts, the adversary can restart processors. Immediately prior to the restart, the adversary stores in the appropriate red instruction a code of the jump instruction that sends the processor to one of the synchronization points defined by the algorithm. For stop failures with detectable restarts, the adversary can cause arbitrary failures and restarts, but is not allowed to tamper with the green and red instruction parts. Finally, for undetectable restarts, the adversary paints the red instructions green!   □

2.3   IMPLEMENTATION AND EFFICIENCY ISSUES

We now discuss how our results can be implemented on a class of realizable multiprocessor systems, by directly mapping our algorithmic techniques for robust parallel computation onto a specific multiprocessor architecture. We present the architecture and discuss several design, efficiency and algorithmic issues dealing with robust computation in this and similar architectures.

2.3.1   Towards a Fault-Tolerant Parallel Architecture

Here we show an example of a realizable system that is consistent with the models in our scope. The main purpose in presenting the system's architecture is to show the type of a physical machine for which the techniques and algorithms we later develop are well-suited.

A Machine for fault-tolerant parallel computation

In our system the processors communicate with the shared memory using a network. A *combining* interconnection network is perfectly suited for implementing synchronous concurrent reads and writes. The combining properties are used

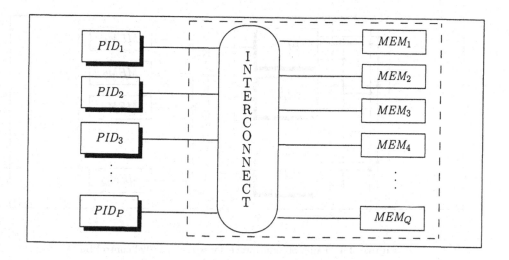

Figure 2.3 An architecture for a fail-stop multiprocessor.

in their *simplest* form – only to implement concurrent access to memory. The processors in the system are the fail-stop processors. Although a perfect fail-stop processor cannot be constructed using finite amount of hardware (consider the design of a circuit responsible for shutting down the processor upon an unrecoverable failure), the techniques we described above can be used to build a close approximation.

Our abstract model is realized as the architecture in Figure 2.3 as follows:

1. There are P *fail-stop* processors, each with a unique address and some amount of local memory. Processors are unreliable and are subject to failures at any point during the computation.

2. There are Q addressable shared memory cells. The input of size $N \leq Q$ is stored in shared memory. This memory is assumed to be reliable.

3. Interconnection of processors and memory is provided by a network whose external specification is that of a complete bipartite graph. For synchronous computation there are several fixed-degree topologies implementing such network. To implement concurrent memory access, the network also provides minimal combining properties. This network is aslo assumed to provide a reliable interconnect. For undetectable restarts the network need not be synchronous.

With this architecture, the algorithmic techniques we will develop become completely applicable. Specifically, when the underlying hardware components are

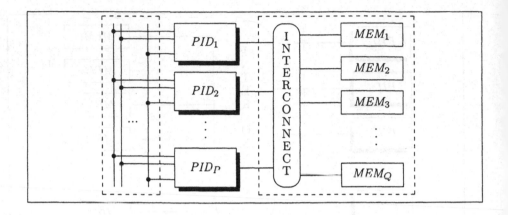

Figure 2.4   Fail-stop multiprocessor with a parallel control bus.

subject to failures within their individual design parameters, the algorithms we develop work correctly, and within the specified complexity bounds. In other words, when the processors are subject to stop-failures, and when the components in the dashed box in Figure 2.3 are able to mask their internal failures, then the algorithms for each of our models are able to tolerate any pattern of processor failures.

Some multiprocessors come equipped with additional control connections used for processor synchronization and broadcast signaling. Our architecture can be augmented with such control structures in a way that takes advantage of the *Write-All* algorithmic paradigm. Consider the architecture in Figure 2.4. Here we separate the interconnect into two parts. One still serves to interconnect the processors and the memory, while the other is a parallel bus structure consisting of P lines, with each processor connected to each of the lines. Each line serves to represent either a 0 or 1 in a way that corresponds to the *Write-All* array locations (assuming array $x[1..P]$). When $x[i] = 0$, then line i is driven low, and when $x[i] = 1$, it is driven high. Although such parallel interconnect does not scale well (since each processor must now be able to support P connections), its operations are extremely simple, and it is reasonable for a moderate number of processors. For high number of processors multiplexing can be used to reduce the number of physical lines (although it complicates the processing).

With this architecture, it becomes possible for each processor to test locally the truth of the predicate $\{x[i] = 1$ for $1 \le i \le P\}$ by checking that all P lines are high. With this in mind, *Write-All* algorithms can use a decentralized approach for processor allocation with the above local test used for termination. (We continue the discussion of algorithmic techniques in the next chapter.)

This approach can also dramatically simplify the requirements for the processor-memory interconnect when the tasks that the processors need to perform can be stored either in processor local memory or be localized in shared memory.

Other technology for fault-tolerance

We now cite additional technological approaches used to implement parallel systems that are able to operate correctly when they are subjected to certain failures. We have already discussed the general approaches to fault-tolerance based on space and time redundancy. The specific methods and technologies summarized below are instrumental in providing the basic hardware fault-tolerance on which the algorithmic and software fault-tolerance can be built.

Processor failures: Approaches using VLSI-level reconfiguration are used when permanent faults (due to fabrication defects) are the primary concern and when the transient faults can be detected. Components are manufactured with spare modules, such that some failures can be tolerated by detecting faulty modules and either bypassing them or automatically replacing them with the spare modules. When there are no available spare modules, the entire system is gracefully shut down (when possible). Such techniques are used to approximate fail-stop processor behavior.

Robust interconnection networks: Interconnection networks are used in multiprocessor systems to provide communication among processors, memory modules and other devices. The networks are made more reliable by employing redundancy. Replicated components are introduced into an interconnect network at different levels of granularity. By replicating the routing elements and some point-to-point links, some faults can be masked without altering the interconnect topology. When multiple distinct paths exist between certain sources and destinations, the loss of some of such paths alter the network topology, and then the routing logic becomes responsible for avoiding the lost paths. Schemes also exist that enable fast routing by allowing for some messages to be lost, while sending multiple encoded messages so that the intended message can be reconstructed even if some messages are lost. Finally, approaches exist that maximize the use of a faulty component if the components is partially functional, for example, a switch may be able to receive and send messages using a subset of its input and output ports. Our models of computation assume that a robust medium interconnecting the processors and the memories is available.

Fault-tolerant memories: Semiconductor memories are the essential components of processors and of shared memory parallel systems. These memories are being routinely manufactured with built-in fault-tolerance. Three main techniques are used in providing fault-tolerance: (1) Coding: in addition to the bits being stored, this technique utilizes additional (parity) bits in conjunction with various error detecting and/or correcting codes. (2) Replication or shadowing: two or more copies of the memory are maintained with either the majority vote being taken, or the faulty units being shut off in a hybrid approach. (3) Reconfiguration: spare memories are used to replace faulty units by reconfiguring memory units. These techniques make memory more reliable without appreciably degrading its performance.

2.3.2   Design and efficiency issues

We now discuss additional design issues that are relevant to the implementation of efficient algorithms using the failure models we defined on this architecture.

Processor failure issues

We have chosen to consider only the failure models where the processors do not write any erroneous or maliciously incorrect values to shared memory. While malicious processor behavior is often considered in conjunction with message passing systems, it makes less sense in tightly-coupled shared memory systems. This is because in a parallel system all processors are normally "trusted" agents, and so the issues of security are not applicable.

The default assumption we make is that throughout the computation at least one processor is fault-free. When comparing the time complexity of fault-free and failure-prone computation we will make a stronger assumption that a constant fraction of the processors are fault-free. For the models with restarts one can use the weaker survivability assumption that at each global clock tick at least one processor step executes to completion.

The fail-stop model with undetectable restarts and omniscient on-line adversaries is the most general fault model we deal with. It can be viewed as a model of parallel computation with arbitrary asynchrony.

The cost of the interconnect

In the algorithm design and analysis we assume that parallel memory access has fixed cost (and time). This assumption can be removed without affecting the correctness of the algorithms and of the analysis. If there is a cost L associated with reading or writing a single shared memory cell, then the work complexity of the algorithms and the simulations that we present increase by the factor L. For several interconnection networks such cost is polylogarithmic.

Memory access concurrency and redundancy

The choice of CRCW (concurrent read, concurrent write) model used here is justified because of a lower bound (that we present in Chapter 4) that shows that the CREW (concurrent read, exclusive write) model does not admit fault-tolerant and efficient algorithms. However we still would like to control memory

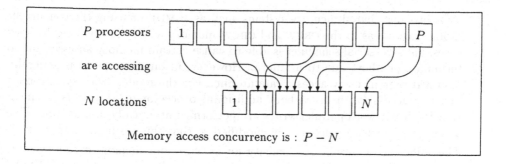

P processors

are accessing

N locations

Memory access concurrency is : $P - N$

Figure 2.5 Memory access concurrency.

access concurrency in order to minimize it. If P processors are accessing (i.e., reading or writing) N memory locations in a certain step of a computation, then $P - N$ concurrent memory accesses are "redundant" in the sense that the processors collectively do not obtain additional information by reading more than once from a single memory location, see Figure 2.5. We define measures that gauge the concurrent memory accesses of a computation.

Definition 2.3.1 Consider a parallel computation with P initial processors that terminates in time τ after completing its task on some input data I of size N in the presence of fail-stop error pattern F. If at time i $(1 \leq i \leq \tau)$, P_i^R processors perform reads from N_i^R shared memory locations and P_i^W processors perform writes to N_i^W locations, then we define:

(i) the *read concurrency* ρ as: $\rho = \rho_{I,F,P} = \sum_{i=1}^{\tau} \left(P_i^R - N_i^R \right)$, and

(ii) the *write concurrency* ω as: $\omega = \omega_{I,F,P} = \sum_{i=1}^{\tau} \left(P_i^W - N_i^W \right)$. □

For a single read from (write to) a particular memory location, the read (write) concurrency ρ (ω) for that location is simply the number of readers (writers) minus one. For example, if only one processor reads from (writes to) a location, then ρ (ω) is 0, i.e., no concurrency is involved. Also note that the concurrency measures ρ and ω are cumulative over a computation.

Our measures of memory access concurrency accurately capture the key distinctions among the EREW, CREW and CRCW memory access disciplines:

For the algorithms in the EREW model, $\rho = \omega = 0$.

For the algorithms in the CREW model, $\omega = 0$.

Memory atomicity

In the models we have discussed, the shared memory access is modeled either using the interleaving of the individual processors' memory access (as in the asynchronous shared-memory systems such as MIMD), or using the concurrent atomic access (as in the CREW and CRCW memory access disciplines). In both cases, an adversarial scheduler is able to cause certain memory accesses not to terminate or abort due to a failure. However, in our context, it is generally assumed that memory accesses are atomic. For the models with synchronous memory access (with or without additional processor delays), it is assumed that $\log N$-bit word parallel writes are performed atomically in unit time. The algorithms in such models can be modified so that this assumption is relaxed.

The sufficient definition of atomicity for synchronous memory access systems is: (1) $\log N$-size words are written using $\log N$ bit write cycles, and (2) the adversary can cause arbitrary fail-stop errors either before or after the *single bit write cycle* of the PRAM, but not during the bit write cycle.

The algorithms that assume word atomicity can be automatically compiled into algorithms that assume only the bit atomicity as stated above. This is done by storing a $(\log N)$-bit atomic word in two non-atomic words of the same size and using a single atomic toggle bit that points to the non-atomic word that contains the current value. When writes are performed, the non-current word is written first, and then the atomic bit is toggled. It is not difficult to see that this implementation is equivalent to having atomic words.

Memory initialization

A much more important assumption in many *Write-All* solutions is the initial state of additional auxiliary memory used (typically of $\Omega(P)$ size). The basic assumption is that: *The $\Omega(P)$ auxiliary shared memory is cleared or initialized to some known value.*

The assumption of clear shared memory is, in theory, a natural, even if unstated assumption for PRAMs (recall the definition in Section 2.1.1) and RAMs (cf., Turing Machine auxiliary tapes are initially blank). However, given the definition of *Write-All* this dependence on clear space raises a legitimate "chicken-or-egg" objection. In practice, memory locations typically contain unpredictable values, and processes that need to use large blocks of memory cannot assume that it is cleared or is initialized to a known value. In fact operating systems usually provide explicit services that allocate clear memory (cf. `calloc()` in standard C libraries). Such allocation is predictably much more time consuming, even in the absence of failures.

Therefore, while the clear memory assumption is consistent with standard definitions of PRAM, it is nevertheless a requirement that fault-tolerant systems ought to be able to do without. We will present an efficient deterministic procedure for the fail-stop models that solves the *Write-All* problem even when the shared memory is *contaminated*, i.e., contains arbitrary values.

Remark 2.4 *Determinism and randomization*: In our presentation the focus is on deterministic algorithms. We concentrate on determinism because we consider it important to provide deterministic guarantees, but also because many effective techniques exist for the problems of interest. Deterministic algorithms can be designed to deal with the most powerful adversaries we have defined. These adversaries are on-line, thus able to make decisions by observing the actions of the algorithm, and omniscient, meaning that the adversary knows everything about the algorithm, and is able to predict the future actions of the algorithm. Although such adversaries are very powerful, we demonstrate that efficient and even optimal deterministic algorithms and simulations can be constructed in many cases. Randomized solutions offer high efficiency for oblivious adversaries, while the worst case concerns addressed by the deterministic algorithms may be unnecessarily pessimistic in practical terms. Where deterministic algorithms come short of meeting the performance requirements, randomization offers a powerful alternative. Future developments in asynchronous parallel computation will employ randomization as well as the array of deterministic techniques we present here. In Section 6.1 we overview progress in randomized shared memory algorithms for models that closely relate to the models we consider here. □

2.4 BIBLIOGRAPHIC NOTES

The PRAM model of parallel computation was formalized by Fortune and Wyllie [42]. Computation on PRAMs was explored in Wyllie's thesis [119]. We use the PRAM definition as it appears in the survey of Karp and Ramachandran in [60]. The survey of Eppstein and Galil [37] and the survey [60] discuss the rationale behind the PRAM model and present many important PRAM algorithms and algorithmic techniques. A current assessment of the PRAM model is given by Vishkin in Chapter 1 of the book edited by Gibbons and Spirakis [45]. For IDEAL PRAMs see the papers by Beame and Håstad [15], and Li and Yesha [76], and for most important lower bounds, see [60]. The quote by Valiant on page 22 is from [116].

The notation for concurrent programs using the **cobegin-coend** construct was introduced by Owicki and Gries [94]. Programming notations for PRAM and compilation techniques are discussed by Wyllie [119] and Schwartz [109].

Kanellakis and Shvartsman introduced the notion of *robustness* and the measure of work in the presence of failures as available processor steps S [56], the definition of failure patterns and the overhead ratio σ. Martel, Subramonian and Park [87] extended the available processor steps measure to general applications using asynchronous PRAMs.

A complexity measure similar to the overhead ratio σ and the competitive overhead ratio σ' is used by Ajtai, Aspnes, Dwork and Waarts to formulate a framework for systematic competitive analysis of distributed algorithms [7]. The definitions of memory access concurrency are due to Kanellakis, Michailidis and Shvartsman [54]. The *Write-All* problem was proposed by Kanellakis and Shvartsman [56].

Given the desirable attributes of the PRAM model, a number of directions were proposed by researchers to compensate for its idealized nature. A number of proposals deal with the introduction of asynchrony into PRAM models. The work of Cole and Zajicek [26, 27], Gibbons [44], Martel, Subramonian and Park [87, 84], and Nishimura [93] formalized a variety of asynchronous parallel models and showed that efficient parallel computation is possible on such models for some definitions of scheduling adversaries. Different proposals explored the implications of memory access latency in parallel computation, including the work Papadimitriou and Yannakakis [95], and Aggarwal, Chandra and Snir [6]. Martel and Raghunathan [85] study pipelined memory reads and writes with a bound on the delay for memory access completion. Some of the algorithmics in the above settings are also appropriate in the fault-prone setting. This is the case when an algorithm can tolerate the presence of infinitely slow processors or when memory latency could be infinite. For example, the algorithms by Martel, Park and Subramonian [87, 84], although developed with asynchrony in mind, are able to tolerate processor failures. Other models, for example the BSP model by Valiant [117], and the LogP model by Culler, Karp, Patterson, Sahay, Schauser, Santos, Subramonian and van Eicken [32], forcefully address the idealized features of PRAMs and present sound foundations for realistic fault-free computation. Unfortunately, these models are not well-suited for fault-tolerant shared memory computation and would require significant refinement to enable fault-tolerant computation. In particular, the distributed-memory feature of LogP means that significant resources need to be expended on memory replication and consistency to compensate for potential losses of processors and associated memories.

Technologies for implementing components and systems which operate correctly when subjected to certain failures are surveyed by Cristian [31], and in a special *IEEE Computer* issue [52]. The general *fail-stop* processor behavior is formally studied by Schlichting and Schneider [108]. Interconnection networks are used in a multiprocessor system to provide communication among processors, memory modules and other devices, e.g., as in the *ultracomputers* by Schwartz [109]. An encyclopædic survey of the interconnection networks is given by Almasi and Gottlieb in [8, Chapter 8]. Theoretical foundations for such networks are summarized by Pippenger in [101]. The fault-tolerance of interconnection networks has been the subject of much work in its own turn, see the survey by Adams, Agrawal, and Seigel [3].

Providing memory management schemes suitable for memory access patterns of parallel algorithms has been a subject of much recent research. Mehlhorn and Vishkin proposed using replication to improve memory access [90]. Upfal and Widgerson used a quorum-like approach to reduce the overhead of replica management [115]. An efficient deterministic scheme using a constant memory overhead is described by Pietracaprina and Preparata [98]. Increased memory overhead requirements of replication can be controlled using information dispersal techniques, such as that of Rabin [104] and the discrete holography of Preparata [103].

Achieving VLSI-level fault-tolerance through reconfiguration is a subject of a comprehensive work by Negrini, Sami and Stefanelli [92]. A grand tour of coding techniques used in memory error detection and correction is presented by McEliece [88]. The survey of Sarrazin and Malek [107] covers additional techniques that are used to make memory reliable without degrading its performance. The architecture in Figure 2.4 on page 38 is given by Yen, Leiss and Bastiani [120].

The surveys of Abraham, Banerjee, Chen, Fuchs, Kuo and Narasimha Reddy [2] and of Chean and Fortes [21] overview the algorithm-based fault-tolerance in systolic arrays. Relevant theoretical bounds are given by Kaklamanis, Karlin, Leighton, Milenkovic, Raghavan, Rao, Thomborson, Tsantilas [53].

3

THE WRITE-ALL PROBLEM: ALGORITHMS

D EMONSTRATING the existence of robust algorithms for the *Write-All* problem given in Definition 1.4.1 is essential for developing the approach to algorithm simulations and transformations we present in Chapter 5. Here we describe and analyze several key algorithms for the *Write-All* problem using three different algorithmic paradigms. We begin overviewing the paradigms, and the basic algorithmic techniques and data structures used in solving the *Write-All* problem. In presenting the algorithms we normally give the complexity results in terms of N, the size of the *Write-All* array, and P, the number of initially available processors.

3.1 ALGORITHMIC PARADIGMS AND TECHNIQUES

Load balancing and processor allocation subsequent to processor failures are often the key problems to be solved in developing efficient algorithms. The *Write-All* algorithms can be classified in terms of the algorithmic paradigms for balancing and allocation. There are also several algorithmic techniques and data structures that are frequently found in *Write-All* algorithms.

3.1.1 Paradigms for Solving Write-All

We consider three algorithmic paradigms for load balancing and processor allocation used in constructing robust solutions for the *Write-All* problem in a variety of failure models. The paradigms differ in the type and the extent of knowledge used by the processors in allocating themselves to unfinished tasks in a balanced fashion.

Global allocation paradigm

In the global allocation paradigm processors are allocated using knowledge about the *global* state of the computation. The processors compute and reduce the information that is in turn used to synchronize and allocate processors. The global allocation paradigm is best suited for algorithms assuming high degree of processor synchrony, since to take advantage of the global view of the computation, a processor needs to know that the view is not going to be changed drastically through the actions of faster processors. The goal in the global allocation paradigm is to achieve processor allocation that is as close as possible to the ideal allocation that could be implemented if processors were endowed with the ability to perform *memory snapshots*. This is the ability to read the entire shared memory in unit time. Although memory snapshots are too powerful to be assumed realistic, in some algorithms we are able to approximate memory snapshots in logarithmic time. We also use memory snapshots as a tool for proving lower bounds for *Write-All* in Chapter 4.

Local allocation paradigm

Here processors make allocation decisions based on the information that is *local* to the processors, or the information that can be available to a processor from the shared data structures in a constant number of shared memory accesses. Because no global synchronization of processors is assumed, local allocation algorithms are good candidates for use in the fail-stop no-restart, the restartable, and the asynchronous (restartable without knowledge) models. The local allocation paradigm algorithms attempt to approximate the knowledge available to the processors in the global allocation paradigm algorithms through the use of appropriate data structures. The local paradigm is well suited for both deterministic and randomized algorithms (we present a deterministic algorithm later in this chapter). Because this paradigm is often used when processors are subject to delays or are asynchronous, the algorithmic techniques here necessarily differ from the techniques used in the global allocation algorithms that assume synchronous processors.

Hashed allocation paradigm

Here processors are allocated in a hashed fashion, either according to a randomized scheme or using a deterministic scheme that approximates a particular randomized scheme. Hashed allocation algorithms can be used in both restartable and non-restartable failure models, but they are most effective when the processors are asynchronous or are subject to delays. The hashed allocation was used for the first time in the context of randomized algorithms or algorithms that rely on information generated at random. Hashed allocation algorithms

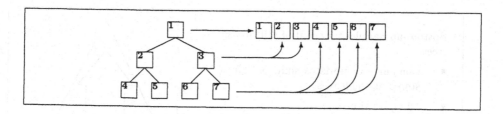

Figure 3.1   Storing a maintenance-free binary tree in an array.

are either motivated by randomized solutions or are arrived at by derandomization.

3.1.2   Algorithmic Techniques for Write-All

We have noted earlier that load balancing and processor allocation are often the key problems to be solved in developing efficient algorithms. Balancing and allocation are even more crucial in the fault-prone setting where processor failures and restarts make precise load balancing and processor allocation difficult if not impossible. Accurate failure detection is needed to guarantee eventual processor allocation to tasks that were not completed and to avoid allocating processors to tasks that were completed. The allocation needs to balance the processor loads according to appropriate criteria.

We now illustrate the main techniques used in solving the *Write-All* problem. The techniques deal with failure detection, processor enumeration, progress estimation and load balancing. The algorithms often use full binary trees for the purposes of accumulation and utilization of the global knowledge about the computation (such algorithms are well suited for solutions in the global allocation paradigm). Once the utility of such trees for synchronous algorithms is clear, their use by algorithms with asynchronous or restartable processor will be easy to understand.

The tree structures must be resilient to processor failures, and if possible, not require any maintenance of the topology. Fortunately this is easily accomplished by storing a full binary tree in a linear array with implicit tree structure as follows (Figure 3.1): the root of the tree is the first element of the array, and any non-leaf element i has the element $2i$ as its left child and the element $2i + 1$ as its right child. This scheme is readily generalized to trees other than binary.

The algorithms use either the bottom-up or top-down traversal of such full binary trees. The number of leaves is normally equal to, or proportional to the number of work elements N, and the height of the tree is logarithmic in N. The bottom-up traversals implement parallel summation algorithms and

Bottom-up parallel traversal of full binary trees:

- Computes or updates sums of values stored at the leaves
- $O(\log N)$ time
- $O(P \log N)$ work
- Used for error detection and progress estimation

Top-down parallel traversal of full binary trees:

- Divide-and-conquer according to the hierarchy specified by the tree
- $O(\log N)$ time
- $O(P \log N)$ work
- Used for error recovery and load balancing

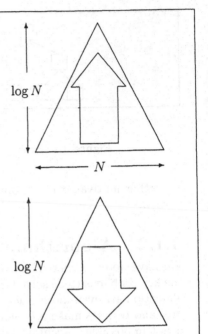

Figure 3.2 Synchronous bottom-up and top-down tree traversals.

the top-down traversal implement a divide-and-conquer processor allocation strategy using a hierarchy, see Figure 3.2.

The traversals take logarithmic time and the computations on the trees are *approximate* in the sense that the values computed are estimates. The formal properties of the traversals are established in the algorithm analysis sections of this chapter. In this section we give a few intuition-building examples.

It is easy to see how the traversals of binary trees can be generalized to logarithmic (to base q) traversals of full q-ary trees for some constant q. For most algorithms the best performance is achieved with binary trees, but in some algorithms the trees can be parameterized so that the desired performance bounds are achieved when the trees are not binary.

Here is an illustration of the use of top-down traversal to estimate the number of active processors. This estimate is taken to be the number of active processors who may have reached the root of the tree:

Example 3.1 *Processor enumeration*: Consider a processor counting tree with $N = 4$ leaves. The tree is stored in the array $c[1..7]$. There are four processors with PIDs 1, 2, 3, and 4, that start at the leaves and traverse the tree towards its root. At each step, a processor writes into the node corresponding to its location in the tree, the sum of the two child locations. If processor 1 failed prior to the start of the traversal, processor 3 failed immediately after writing 1 into its leaf $c[6]$, and processor 4 failed after calculating $c[3] = 2$ as the sum of the contributions recorded in $c[6]$ and $c[7]$, then the tree will look like this after the completion of the phase.

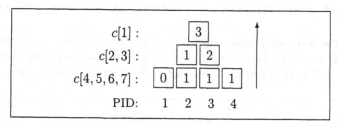

Observe that the root $c[1]$ has the value 3, yet the actual number of active processors is 1. The traversal computed an overestimate of the number of active processors. In fact this will always be so. The root value is exact only when there are no failures during the traversal. □

The following example illustrates the construction of the progress tree used in the divide-and-conquer processor allocation. Here we estimate the number of completed tasks based on the information brought to the root of the tree by surviving processors:

Example 3.2 *Progress estimation*: Consider the progress tree with four leaves ($N = 4$) stored in the array $d[1..7]$. There are 4 processors with PIDs 1, 2, 3, and 4, that begin at the leaves and traverse the tree towards the root. Each processor begins by writing into its leaf an indication (1) that it finished its task. Then each parent gets the sum of its children. If, during the bottom-up traversal of the progress tree d, processor 4 failes prior to the start of the traversal, and processor 3 fails after the first step of the traversal having written 1 into the leaf $d[6]$, then the tree d will look like this after the completion of the phase.

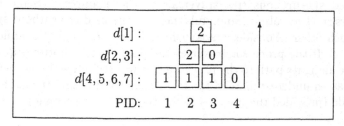

Note that each of the processors may have completed its tasks associated with the leaves of the progress tree prior to the start of the traversal. Yet the value of the root $d[1]$ is 2. This indicates that not all tasks were completed, since $d[1] = 2 < 4 = N$. This illustrates why the value at the root of the tree will normally be an underestimate of the actual number of completed tasks.   □

In the load balancing top-down traversal, we assume that the progress tree is an exact summation tree (i.e, the value at each internal node is the sum of the values at its two children), and the processors are allocated at each non-leaf node of the tree in proportion to the number of remaining tasks in each subtree.

Example 3.3 *Load balancing*: Consider the progress tree with four leaves ($N = 4$) stored in the array $a[1..7]$. There are two surviving processors with PIDs 1 and 2, that begin at the root and traverse the tree towards the leaves.

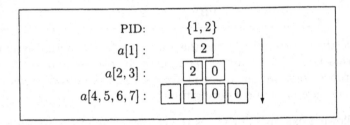

At the root, both processors will be sent to the right subtree. This is because out of the two tasks in the left subtree, both have been completed, and none of the tasks in the right subtree are completed. At the internal node $a[3]$, the two processors will be equally divided between the left ($a[6]$) and the right ($a[7]$) subtrees since equal number of unfinished tasks exists in each of the two subtrees.   □

Note that the progress-estimation traversal in Example 3.2 is not guaranteed to yield the exact summation tree needed by the load balancing traversal in Example 3.3 above. Algorithms that assume this property must be able to deal with such situations.

We used synchronous tree traversals in the examples. Some traversals of progress trees are also meaningful when processors do so without synchronizing with each other. Consider an asynchronous processor that completes its work on a leaf. If the processor traverses the progress tree bottom-up and updates the tree along its path to the root, the tree will still have the property that each node has an underestimate of the tasks completed within the subtree rooted at the node (provided the updates of the tree nodes are atomic).

Algorithms in this chapter

In the description of algorithms we assume, unless stated otherwise, that N is a power of 2. Nonpowers of 2 can be handled using conventional padding techniques. The expression "log" refers to logarithms to the base 2, all other bases will be explicitly shown; **div** stands for integer division with truncation.

In this chapter we present the following algorithms (in parenthesis we give etymology of these algorithms' names):

Algorithm E (<u>E</u>xclusive-read, <u>E</u>xclusive-write algorithm) : this is a deterministic algorithm that for the initial failures model has $S = O(N + P' \log P)$, where the number of initial failures is $P - P'$.

Algorithm W (historically the first <u>W</u>rite-All algorithm) : this is a deterministic fail-stop no restart algorithm for which $S = O(N + P \log^2 N / \log \log N)$.

Algorithm V (this is a simplified <u>V</u>ersion of algorithm W) : this is a deterministic algorithm that for the model with stop failures without restarts has $S = O(N + P \log^2 N)$, and for the fail-stop model with detectable restarts it has $S = O(N \log^2 N + M \log N)$, where $M = |F|$, the size of the failure/restart pattern.

Algorithms W and V assume that a linear segment of the shared memory is initialized to 0 prior to the start of the computation. We also give an algorithm that, for the models without restarts, requires no memory initialization:

Algorithm Z (it <u>Z</u>eroes its auxiliary memory) : this is a deterministic algorithm in the fail-stop model that has $S = O(N + P \frac{\log^3 N}{(\log \log N)^2})$ without any memory initialization assumption. We also describe *algorithm* Z^{-1} that "cleans up" shared memory after itself.

The algorithms above make heavy use of memory access concurrency. The following algorithms control this concurrency:

Algorithm $W_{CR/W}$ (it is based on algorithm <u>W</u> and it <u>C</u>ontrols concurrent <u>R</u>eads and <u>W</u>rites)] : this is a deterministic robust algorithm in the fail-stop model with $S = O(N \log N \log P + P \log P \log^2 N / \log \log N)$ where $1 \leq P \leq N$. This algorithm is able to control memory access concurrency as follows: it has read concurrency $\rho \leq 7|F| \log N$, and write concurrency $\omega \leq |F|$. We also present an optimal parameterization of this algorithm called *algorithm* $W_{CR/W}^{opt}$.

Algorithm W_{ave} (it uses *Wave*s of processors) : is a related robust algorithm which limits the maximum memory access concurrency per each synchronous parallel computation step.

Algorithm $Z_{CR/W}$ (it is based on algorithm *Z* and it *C*ontrols concurrent *R*eads and *W*rites) : this is a deterministic algorithm in the fail-stop model with $S = O(N + P \log^2 P \log^3 N/(\log \log N)^2)$ where $1 \leq P \leq N$, and without any memory initialization assumption. It has read concurrency $\rho \leq 7|F| \log N$, and write concurrency $\omega \leq |F|$.

The remaining algorithms are designed for the models allowing asynchronous restarts (and they can be used of course in all failure models we defined):

Algorithm X (there is no etymological e*X*planation) : this is a deterministic algorithm that can be used in both the fail-stop and restartable models, as well as in completely asynchronous settings. For the models with restarts and/or asynchrony this algorithm has $S = O(N^{1.59})$. We also give a version of this algorithm, called *algorithm X'*, for the case when $P < N$.

Algortihm AW (an *A*synchronous *W*rite-All algorithm) : this is a robust randomized *Write-All* algorithm. The processors are allocated to tasks based on schedules that are generated as random permutations. The expected work of the algorithm is $O(N \log P)$ for the range of processors $1 \leq P \leq \sqrt{N}$.

Algortihm AW^T (it uses *AW* at each interior node of its progress *T*ree) : this is a polynomially robust *Write-All* algorithm. The processors are allocated according to hybrid local and hashed allocation paradigms. The work of the algorithm is $O(N \cdot P^\varepsilon)$ for any $\varepsilon < 1$ and for the range of processors $1 \leq P \leq N$.

Algorithm Y (because historically *Y* followed algorithm X) : this is an efficient derandomization of algorithm *AW*. Experimental work suggests that the algorithm is efficient. The analysis of algorithm Y as an open problem that shows an interesting connection between group theory, combinatorics and multi-processor scheduling.

We now present these algorithms in detail. In Sections 3.2 to 3.5 we give the algorithm in the order of failure model containment (from static failures to undetectable restarts), and in Section 3.6 we consider algorithms which control memory access concurrency. (Algorithm E in the section below is relatively complex, but the rest of the chapter does not depend on it, and the reader may want to skip Section 3.2 on first reading.)

```
01   forall processors PID=1..P parbegin
02      Phase E1: Use non-oblivious parallel prefix to compute rank_PID and P'
03      Phase E2: Set x[(rank_PID − 1) · N/P' ... (rank_PID · N/P') − 1] to 1
04   parend
```

Figure 3.3   A high level view of algorithm E.

3.2   STATIC WRITE-ALL: ALGORITHM E

The failure models we are generally considering allow arbitrary dynamic processor failures. Such models do not admit efficient solutions without concurrent memory accesses. . In this section we consider the weaker model of static (initial) failures. Such failures can only occur prior to the start of an algorithm. We show that simple and efficient solutions are possible in this model without requiring concurrent accesses, i.e., suitable for EREW memory,access, and without any need to initialize the shared memory.

We assume that the size of the *Write-All* instance is N and that we have P processors, $P' \leq P$ of which are alive at the beginning of the algorithm. We do not know P' *a priori* or which of the processors are faulty.

The EREW algorithm E consists of two phases E1 and E2. In phase E1, processors enumerate themselves and compute the total number of live processors. With this information in phase E2, the processors partition the input array so that each processor is responsible for setting to 1 all the entries in its partition (see Figure 3.3).

The enumeration phase E1 is a simple non-oblivious EREW enumeration algorithm based on parallel prefix computation that does not assume a known number of processors and that produces correct results for any pattern of static failures.

A detailed description of phase E1 is given in Figure 3.4. The phase uses a full binary tree of height $\log P$ for enumeration. The tree is denoted by T in the figure. The processors begin at the leaves and with the initial rank 1. The processors then start moving up toward the root in synchrony. The algorithm ensures that at each interior node of the tree, at most one processor moves up. If two processors reach sibling nodes within the tree, one of them has to wait at the current level to avoid concurrent accesses at the parent. By convention, the processor that is allowed to continue is the one coming from the right. That other processor stays behind and waits for the rank information to be supplied to it.

Each processor P_i that continues needs to be able to communicate with the processors that have stopped at lower levels of the subtree rooted at the current

```
01 current_rank := 1 -- each processor starts with initial rank 1
02 left_child := nil -- no left children yet
03 stopped := false -- initially all processors can move up
04 pos := P + PID − 2 -- initial position in the tree
05 for i := 1.. log P do
06    if not stopped then -- processor can still move
07       T[sibling(pos)].val := 0 -- probe sibling sibling node
08       T[pos].val := current_rank
09       rank_sib := T[sibling(pos)].val
10       if rank_sib = 0 then -- no one there
11          pos := ⌊pos/2⌋ -- move to parent node
12       else if current node is a left child then
13          stopped := true; T[pos].val := 0 -- let the sibling continue
14       else -- current node is a right child; processor continues
15          current_rank := current_rank + rank_sib
16          T[left_child].val := rank_sib -- propagate rank update
17          T[sibling(pos)].right_child := left_child -- modify trees
18          left_child := T[sibling(pos)]
19          pos := ⌊pos/2⌋ -- move to parent node
20       fi
21    else -- processor has suspended; just propagate rank updates
22       if T[pos].val > 0 then -- there's a rank update to propagate
23          current_rank := current_rank + T[pos].val -- update own rank
24          T[T[pos].right_child].val := T[pos].val -- update right child
25          T[pos].val := 0 -- get ready for the next iteration
26    fi fi
27 od
28 -- complete rank updates and broadcast the number of live processors
29 for i := 1.. log P do
30    if not stopped then -- this is the processor that reached the root
31       T[left_child].val := −current_rank
32    else -- stopped processors just propagate the values they receive
33       if T[pos].val > 0 then -- there's a rank update to propagate
34          current_rank := current_rank + T[pos].val -- update own rank
35          T[T[pos].right_child].val := T[pos].val -- update right child
36          T[pos].val := 0 -- get ready for the next iteration
37       else if T[pos].val < 0 then -- this is the number of live processors
38       -- propagate to both children
39          T[left_child].val := T[T[pos].right_child].val := T[pos].val
40          alive := −T[pos].val -- alive is the number of live processors
41    fi fi
42 od
```

Figure 3.4   A detailed description of phase E1.

location of P_i so that it can "broadcast" rank updates to them. To this end, the waiting processors in P_i's subtree form a *diffusion tree* whose root is the processor that most recently encountered P_i. Each processor in this tree is waiting because it encountered either P_i or some other processor in the tree. P_i can broadcast a value to the processors in the diffusion tree by passing the value to the root of the tree and then having each processor pass the value to its children.

To do this, phase E1 algorithm in Figure 3.4 assumes that each node of T has two fields: *val*, which is used for broadcasting, and *right_child*, which points to the root of the right subtree of waiting processors. We also use *left_child* to point to the left subtree. Note that *left_child* is a private variable, whereas *right_child* is a node field; this is because a waiting processor P_j determines its left subtree by itself while its right subtree is determined by the processor that caused P_j to wait.

When a processor moves up, it checks whether there is any processor at the sibling node by using a "probing" scheme. The processor writes 0 to its sibling node, then writes its current rank at its own node and then reads the sibling node (lines 07–09). If it is 0, then there is no processor at the sibling node, otherwise the value read is the number of processors in the subtree rooted at the sibling. As in the standard parallel prefix the processor that comes from the right adds this value to its rank (line 15). In our case, the right processor also initiates the broadcasting of this value to the processors in its tree of stopped processors by writing the value to the root of this tree (line 16).

The trees of the two processors that meet are merged. This is done by creating a new tree with its root being the processor that came from the left, its left subtree the tree of the left processor and its right subtree the tree of the right processor (lines 17–18). An illustration of this process is provided in Figure 3.5 for $P = 8$.

When the rightmost live processor gets to the root its rank is the number of live processors P' and this value is propagated through the tree down to the other processors (lines 29–41). In phase E1 algorithm in Figure 3.4 we broadcast this value as a negative number to distinguish it from the rank updates which are positive. The whole process takes $2 \log P$ steps.

The algorithm can be made to work in place by collapsing the levels of the tree into a single linear array. In addition, because of the probing scheme, the initial values of the tree are irrelevant and so the algorithm works even in the presence of initial memory faults.

In phase E2, knowing the number of live processors and their ranks, processors partition the input and each sets to 1 the entries in its own part.

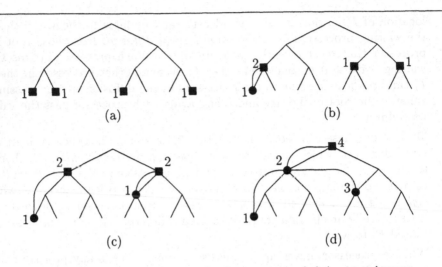

The heavy dots denote processors that have to suspend their ascent because of encounters with other live processors. The boxes denote processors that continue their upward movement. The numbers beside the processors indicate their ranks at each stage of the algorithm. The archs show the structure of the broadcast tree links.

Figure 3.5 An illustration of phase E1 with 8 processors of which 4 have failed.

Theorem 3.2.1 The *Write-All* problem with initial processor and memory faults can be solved in place with $S = O(N + P' \log P)$ on an EREW PRAM, where $1 \leq P \leq N$ and $P - P'$ is the number of initial faults.

It can be shown that this performance of algorithm E is the best possible for the EREW PRAM model.

3.3   NO RESTART WRITE-ALL: ALGORITHMS W AND Z

In this section we define and analyze a robust parallel algorithm for the *Write-All* problem in the fail-stop no-restart model. We call it algorithm W. The algorithm is robust for any dynamic pattern of failures with at least one surviving processor. Recall we have no knowledge of how many, when, or which processors will fail. Algorithm W requires a clear segment of the shared memory. We also develop a robust "bootstrap" procedure that clears its own shared memory and which uses W as a subroutine.

3.3.1 Algorithm W

Algorithm W consists of the parallel *loop* through four phases: (1) a failure detecting phase, (2) a load rescheduling phase, (3) a work phase where assignments $(x[i]:=1)$ are performed, and (4) a phase that estimates the work remaining and controls the parallel loop.

The entire algorithm is moderately involved, but fairly modular. Phases 1 and 4 involve bottom-up traversal of two different trees and phase 2 involves a top-down traversal of these trees.

This solution captures certain engineering intuitions such as failure detection, resource rebalancing and rescheduling using a divide-and-conquer strategy. The algorithm can be readily specified to a great level of detail. We give the complete description of the code in Figures 3.7 to 3.10.

Following the algorithm's definition, we prove its robustness by showing that, for any initial number of processors $P \leq N$ (where N is the size of the input array), and for any failure pattern, the algorithm terminates with work $S = O(N \log^2 N / \log \log N)$. We show that by parameterizing the data structures of algorithm W in terms of P and N, we can choose P such that the algorithm solves the *Write-All* problem optimally with $S = O(N)$.

For simplicity of presentation, in the rest of this section we assume that the initial number of processors P is N, where N is the input size. The result immediately extends to any P in the range $1, \ldots, N$ by assuming that the algorithm starts with N processors, and that $N - P$ processors fail prior to the first step of the algorithm.

Algorithm W definition

We define algorithm W in terms of its inputs, outputs, data structures and control flow.

Input: Shared array $x[1..N]$; $x[i] = 0$ for $1 \leq i \leq N$.

Output: Shared array $x[1..N]$; $x[i] = 1$ for $1 \leq i \leq N$.

Data structures: The algorithm uses full binary trees to (1) enumerate surviving processors, (2) allocate processors, (3) perform work ($x[i] := 1$), and (4) measure progress. There are four full binary trees, each of size $2N - 1$, stored as linear arrays in shared memory.

The trees are $c[1..2N - 1]$ (for processor counting and allocation), $cs[1..2N - 1]$ (for counting step numbers), $d[1..2N-1]$ (for progress counting) and $a[1..2N-1]$ (for top-down auxiliary accounting). They are initially 0.

```
01 forall processors PID=1..N parbegin
02    Phase W3: Perform work on the input data at leaves based on PID
03    Phase W4: Traverse the d tree bottom up to measure progress
04    while the root of the d tree is not N do
05        Phase W1: Traverse trees c and cs bottom-up to enumerate processors
06        Phase W2: Traverse trees d, a, c top-down to reschedule work
07        Phase W3: Perform rescheduled work on the input data
08        Phase W4: Traverse the d tree bottom up to measure progress
09    od
10 parend.
```

Figure 3.6 A high level view of algorithm W

The input is in a shared array $x[1..N]$, where the N elements of this array are associated with the leaves of the trees d and a. Element $x[i]$ is associated with $d[i+N-1]$ and $a[i+N-1]$, where $1 \leq i \leq N$. Similarly processors are initially associated with the leaves of the tree c, such that processor PID is associated with $c[\text{PID}+N-1]$.

Each processor uses some constant amount of local memory. For example, this local memory may be used to perform some simple arithmetic computations. Important local variables are PID, containing the initial processor identifier, and pn, containing a dynamically changing processor number. Note that PID's do not change but pn's do.

The total memory used is $O(N + P)$.

Control flow: Due to the omniscience of the adversary, we employ an oblivious iterative approach in the sense that the pool of the available processors is treated uniformly and is assigned evenly to the tasks that need to be done. The basic idea of the *loop* is: (a) For *failure detection* use bottom-up, fast parallel summation to estimate the surviving processors and to estimate the progress they have made. (b) For *load rescheduling* use a top down, divide-and-conquer strategy based on the estimate of progress made.

The algorithm consists of the parallel *loop* given in Figure 3.6. This loop is performed synchronously by all processors that have not stopped. It consists of four phases of steps, and the first time only part of it is executed (phases W3 and W4). Of course, processors can fail-stop at any time during the algorithm. We next proceed with a high level description of the phases, and then provide additional details with examples.

Phase W1 – *failure detection via processor enumeration*: The processors traverse bottom-up a full binary tree used for processor counting starting with the leaves associated with processor identifiers (PIDs) and finishing at the root. Processor counting is implemented as a version of the standard logarithmic time parallel summation algorithm.

Phase W2 – *failure recovery via balanced processor reallocation*: The processors use the full binary tree that represents the progress of the algorithm, and traverse it starting with the root and finishing at the leaves associated with the unfinished work. The processors are allocated in a divide-and-conquer fashion according to the hierarchy of the progress tree.

Phase W3 – *the work phase*: The processors now perform work they find at the leaves they reached in phase W2. (This work is a simple assignment in the case of *Write-All*, and other specific tasks when the algorithm is used for robust simulations or transformations.)

Phase W4 – *the progress measurement phase*: The processors begin at the leaves of the progress tree where they ended phase W3 and traversebottom-up it to the root to estimate the progress of the algorithm. The counting of the number of leaves where the work of phase W3 was successfully done is implemented as a version of the standard parallel summation algorithm.

Algorithm W technical details

In **phase W1** each processor PID traverses trees c and cs bottom-up from the location $\text{PID}+N-1$. The $O(\log N)$-node path of this traversal is the same (static) for all the loop iterations. As processors perform this traversal they calculate an overestimate of the surviving processors. This is done using a standard $O(\log N)$ time version of a CRCW parallel summation algorithm. Tree c holds the sums and tree cs the time-stamps (or step numbers) for the current *loop* iteration. This allows reusing c without having to initialize it each time. During this traversal surviving processors also calculate new processor numbers pn for themselves, based on the same sums. Detailed code for this procedure is given in Figure 3.8. Phase W1 is similar to, but much simpler than phase E1 of algorithm E because it is oblivious (static) and because memory access concurrency is taken advantage of.

Each processor PID starts by writing a 1 in the leaf $c[\text{PID}+N-1]$ of the tree c. If a processor fails *before* it writes 1 then its action will not contribute to the overall count. If a processor fails *after* it writes 1 then this number can still contribute to the overall sum if one or more processors were active at a sibling tree node and remained active as they moved to the ancestor tree node.

The main algorithm *W loop* consists of the four phases outlined in Section 3.3.1. Processor counting and enumeration is implemented as a static bottom-up traversal in procedure W1() in Figure 3.8, work assignment is done in a dynamic top-down traversal in procedure W2() in Figure 3.9, the work itself is phase W3 assignment "x[k]:=1", and the progress is measured via a dynamic bottom-up traversal in procedure W4() given in Figure 3.10. Parameter passing is by reference.

Algorithm W :

```
forall processors PID=1..N parbegin
  shared integer array
    x[1..N], -- input array
    c[1..2N-1], -- processor counts
    cs[1..2N-1], -- count step numbers
    d[1..2N-1], -- progress/done tree
    a[1..2N-1]; -- accounted tree
  private integer
    pn, -- dynamic processor no.
    k, -- array index for PID to work on
    step; -- processor counting time-stamp


  step := 0; -- initial time-stamp
  k := PID; -- initial work item for PID
  W3: x[k] := 1; -- do work: visit leaf
  W4(k); -- measure progress

  -- Main loop
  while d[1] ≠ N do

    W1(PID,step,pn); -- enumerate
    W2(pn,k); -- assign work
    W3: x[k] := 1; -- do work: visit leaf
    W4(k); -- measure progress

  od
parend.
```

Figure 3.7 Algorithm *W* code.

Static bottom-up traversal of the tree c to compute the overestimate of the number of processors in c[1]. Each processor computes its enumerated number in pn. The tree cs is used to synchronize counting across calls.

```
procedure W1( -- Processor enumeration
  integer PID, -- processor id
  integer step, -- time-stamp
  integer pn) -- enumerated id
shared integer array
  c[1..2N-1], -- processor counts
  cs[1..2N-1]; -- associated time-stampts
private integer
  j1, j2, -- sibling indices
  t; -- parent of j1 and j2

step := step + 1; -- new time-stamp
j1 := PID + (N-1); -- tree-leaf init
pn := 1; -- assume this PID is no. 1
c[j1] := 1; -- count PID once
cs[j1] := step; -- update time-stamp

-- Traverse the tree from leaf to root
for 1..log(N) do
  t := j1 div 2; -- parent of j1 and j2
  if 2*t = j1 -- j1 came from . . .
  then j2 := j1 + 1 -- left subtree
  else j2 := j1-1 fi -- right subtree
  if cs[j1] = cs[j2] -- active sibling?
  then c[t] := c[j1] + c[j2] -- yes
    if j1 > j2 -- j1 came from right
    then pn := pn + c[j2] fi
  else c[t] := c[j1] -- all siblings failed
  fi
  cs[t] := step; -- time stamp, and
  j1 := t -- advance up the tree
od
end.
```

Figure 3.8 Phase W1 code.

The same observation applies to counts written subsequently at internal nodes, which are the sums of the counts of the children nodes in tree *c*.

It is easy to show that phase W1 will always compute in $c[1]$ an *overestimate* of the number of processors, which are surviving at the time of its completion (see Example 3.1 for intuition and see Lemma 3.3.1 for formal argument).

We also need to enumerate the surviving processors. This is accomplished by each processor assuming that it is the only one, and then adding the number of the surviving processors it estimates to its left. This enumeration creates the dynamic processor number pn.

Finally, in phase W1 we must be able to reuse our tree during several iterations of the main loop. This presents a problem. For example, if a processor had written 1 into its tree leaf and then failed then, the value 1 will remain there for the duration of the computation, thus preventing us from computing monotonically tighter estimates of the number of surviving processors. This is corrected by associating a step number with each node of the count tree c and storing it in tree cs, thus time-stamping valid data. The count step is initially zero, and during each successive *loop* iteration, gets incremented by each surviving processor. Failed processors will not increment their step numbers, thus enabling the surviving processors to detect counts that are out-of-date and treat them as zeroes.

We need not worry about time-stamping overflow, since we have words of $O(\log N)$ bits and in the worst case of a single live processor the *loop* iterates N times (see Lemma 3.3.3).

In **phase W2** all surviving processors start at the root of the progress tree d. In $d[i]$ there is an underestimate of the work already performed in the subtree defined by i. Now the processors traverse d top-down and get rescheduled dynamically according to the work remaining to be done in the subtrees of i, see Figure 3.9.

It is essential to balance the work loads of the surviving processors. In the next section, we formally show that the algorithm meets the goal of balancing (Lemma 3.3.2). Although the divide-and-conquer idea based on d is sound, some care has to be put into its implementation.

In the remaining discussion of phase W2 we explain our implementation, which is based on *auxiliary progress tree a*. The values in a are *defined* from the values in d. All values in a are defined given d, although only part of a is actually *computed*. The important points are that (i) a represents the progress made *and* fully recorded from leaves to the root, and (ii) the value of each $a[i]$ is defined based only on the values of d seen along the unique path from the root to the node i.

At each internal node i, the processors are divided between the left and right subtrees in proportion to the leaves that either have not been visited *or* whose visitation was not fully recorded in d. This is accomplished by computing

Top-down traversal of trees c and d. Tree a is used to traverse paths to the *unaccounted* leaves using the information in the progress tree d. Tree c is used to balance the processors in proportion to the remaining work.

```
procedure W2( -- Divide-and-conquer
    integer pn -- dynamic processor no.
    integer k) -- data item index
    shared integer array
        c[1..2N-1], -- processor counts
        d[1..2N-1], -- progress/done tree
        a[1..2N-1]; -- accounted tree
    private integer
        j, j1, j2; -- current/left/right indices
    j := 1; -- start at the root
    size := N; -- the whole tree is visible
    a[1] := d[1]; -- no. of accounted nodes
    -- Traverse from root to leaf
    while size ≠ 1 do
        j1 := 2*j; j2 := j1 + 1; -- left/right
        -- compute accounted node values
        if d[j1]+d[j2] = 0 then a[j1] := 0
        else a[j1] := a[j]*d[j1]
                     div (d[j1]+d[j2]) fi
        a[j2] := a[j]-a[j1];
        -- processor alloc. to left/right sub-trees
        c[j1] := c[j]*(size/2-a[j1])
                     div (size-a[j]);
        c[j2] := c[j] - c[j1];
        -- go left/right based on proc. no.
        if pn ≤ c[j1] then j := j1
        else j := j2; pn := pn - c[j1] fi
        size := size div 2 -- half of leaves
    od ;
    k := j - (N-1) -- assign based on j
parend.
```

Figure 3.9 Phase W2 code.

Bottom-up traversal of the progress tree d. Tree d is maintained to contain the under-estimates for the number of leaves visited in each subtree, with $d[1]$ containing the underestimate of the total number of leaves visited. This number is used in terminating the overall program (when $d[1] = N$).

```
procedure W4( -- Progress estimation
    integer k -- current leaf
    )
    shared integer array
        d[1..2N-1]; -- done/progress tree
    private integer
        i1, -- left sibling index
        i2, -- right sibling index
        t; -- parent of i1 and i2
    -- mark the leaf done
    i1 := k + (N-1); -- leaf index
    d[i1] := 1; -- done!
    -- traverse the tree from leaf to root
    for 1..log(N) do
        -- the parent index of i1 and i2
        t := i1 div 2
        -- compute left/right indices
        if 2*t = i1 -- i1 came from . . .
        then i2 := i1 + 1 -- from left
        else i2 := i1 - 1 -- from right
        fi
        -- update progress tree and advance
        d[t] := d[i1] + d[i2]; -- update
        i1 := t -- advance to parent
    od
end.
```

Figure 3.10 Phase W4 code.

$a[2i], a[2i+1]$ and using these values instead of $d[2i], d[2i+1]$ in order to discard partially recorded progress (caused by failures and recorded by the processors in the dynamic bottom up traversal of d only part way to the root).

We detect partially recorded progress in d when a value of an internal node in d is less than the sum of the values of its two descendants. Thus, at i, after computing the values $a[2i]$, $a[2i + 1]$, the scheduling of work is done using divide-and-conquer according to the values $N - a[2i]$ and $N - a[2i + 1]$.

Formally, the nonnegative integer values in a are constrained top down as follows:

The root value is $a[1] = d[1]$.

For the children of an interior node i ($1 \leq i \leq N - 1$) we have $a[2i] \leq d[2i]$, $a[2i + 1] \leq d[2i + 1]$, and $a[2i] + a[2i + 1] = a[i]$.

These constraints do not uniquely define a. However, we realize a unique definition by making $a[2i]$ and $a[2i + 1]$ proportional (up to round-off) to the values $d[2i]$ and $d[2i + 1]$. Thus, our dynamic top-down traversal (given in detail in Figure 3.9) implements one way of uniquely defining the values of a satisfying these constraints.

The constraints on the values of a assure that (i) there are exactly $d[1] = a[1]$ number of leaves whose d and a values are 1 — such leaves are called *accounted*, and no processor will reach these leaves, and (ii) the processors reach leaves with the a values of 0 — such leaves are called *unaccounted*. Also see Example 3.5 below for additional intuition on a.

Remark 3.4 *Reducing shared memory requirement for algorithm W:* Strictly speaking, the auxiliary progress tree a need not be represented as a shared structure. Since the values of the a tree are computable from the d tree, it is sufficient for each processor to have three local scalar variables to represent a node and its two descendants as a "window" into the virtual tree a. However it is convenient to use a as defined above in the proofs of the next section. In any case, a linear amount of storage is used. □

In **phase W3** all processors are at the leaves reached in phase W2. Phase W3 is where the work of the original non-robust algorithm gets done. Each processor writes 1 in the array element associated with the leaf it has been rescheduled to. Prior to the start of the first iteration of the *loop* each processor PID tries to write in location $x[\text{PID}]$. This phase is contained within the main procedure in Figure 3.7.

In **phase W4** the processors record the progress made by traversing the d tree bottom up and using the standard summation method. The $O(\log N)$ paths (dynamically) traversed by processors can differ in each *loop* iteration, since processors start from the leaves where they were in phase W3. What is computed each time is an underestimate of the progress made. No time-stamps are needed here because the progress recorded increases monotonically. This dynamic bottom up traversal is given in Figure 3.10.

Phase W4 is a simple variant of phase W1, except for the fact that the path traversed bottom up is dynamically determined. One can show that the progress recorded in $d[1]$ by phase W4 increases *monotonically* and it *underestimates* the actual progress (see Lemma 3.3.3). This guarantees that the algorithm terminates after at most N iterations, since $d[1] \neq N$ is the guard that controls the main *loop*.

The following example illustrates phase W4, and provides intuition for why the tree a is used in phase W2 and why it is needed by the proof framework presented in the next section.

Example 3.5 *Progress estimation vs load balancing*: Consider phase W4 for $N = 4$, $P = 4$, and the progress tree stored in the array $d[1..7]$. Consider further the exact scenario that was described in Example 3.2 leading to the following progress tree:

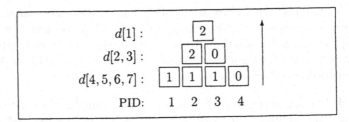

Let $P' = 2$ be the number of surviving processors. As before, $d[1] = 2$ is an underestimate of the actual number (at least 3 and most 4), of visited leaves. If the d tree is used directly in phase W2 to allocate processors to the unvisited leaves, then the leaf associated with d[7] will be allocated all P' surviving processors. On the other hand, by knowing the (overestimate) number of surviving processors P' and the (underestimate) of the visited leaves $d[1]$, we would like to prove that the allocation is balanced, and that no leaf is allocated more than $\lceil P'/(N - d[1]) \rceil = 1$ processors. We use the tree a in phase W2, where the surviving processors compute $a[6] = a[7] = 0$, with each reaching a distinct leaf thus assuring balanced processor allocation (exactly as in Example 3.3).   □

Analysis of algorithm W

We now outline the proof of robustness for algorithm W. Lemma 3.3.1 shows that in each loop iteration, the algorithm computes (over)estimates of the remaining processors. In Lemma 3.3.2 we prove that processors are only allocated to the unaccounted leaves, and that all such leaves are allocated a balanced number of processors. Lemma 3.3.3 assures monotonic progress of the computation, and thus its termination. In Lemma 3.3.4 we develop an upper bound on the work performed by the processors in terms of logarithmic block-steps.

Lemmas 3.3.1 and 3.3.3 are proved using simple inductions on the structure of the trees used by the algorithm. Lemma 3.3.2 is shown by using an invariant for the algorithm of phase W2. Lemma 3.3.4 involves a case analysis in estimating the block-steps of the algorithm.

These lemmas are used to show the main Theorem 3.3.5. We then parameterize the algorithm and exploit parallel slackness to obtain the optimality result Theorem 3.3.7.

We first introduce additional conventions. Let us consider the i-th iteration of the *loop* $(1 \leq i \leq N)$. Note that the first iteration consists only of phases W3 and W4. Define: (1) U_i to be the estimated remaining work, the value of $N - d[1]$ right before the iteration starts, i.e., right after phase W4 of the previous iteration (U_1 is N); (2) P_i to be the real number of surviving processors, right before the iteration starts, i.e., right after phase W4 of the previous iteration (P_1 is P); (3) R_i to be the estimated number of surviving processors, that is the value of $c[1]$ right after phase W1 of the i-th iteration (R_1 is P). The following is shown by straightforward induction on tree c.

Lemma 3.3.1 In algorithm W, for all loop-iterations i we have: $P_i \geq R_i \geq P_{i+1}$, as long as at least one processor survives.

Proof: The basis $P = P_1 = R_1 \geq P_2$ is obvious. P_i is the number of processors active prior to the first PRAM instruction of the phase W1 algorithm for static bottom-up traversal. By the definition of the model, we immediately have $P_i \geq P_{i+1}$. We will first show that $P_i \geq R_i \geq P_{i+1}$ by induction on the structure of the c tree after the completion of the phase W1 static bottom-up traversal. For simplicity we will treat the values of the c tree with incorrect cs version numbers as virtual zeroes, and not involve cs tree further in this proof. The proof will involve two inductions: one to show the first part of the inequality, and one for the second part.

(1) *Inequality $P_i \geq R_i$:* Let $s(t)$ denote the number of processors that *initiated* phase W1 of the algorithm in the subtree of the c tree rooted at node t. Clearly, we have that $s(1) = P_i$.

Basis: For all subtrees of height 0 rooted at t, $c[t] \leq s(t)$, because some processors may have stop-failed after the initiation of phase W1, but before the initialization of the leaves of c tree.

Inductive hypothesis: assume that for all subtrees of height h rooted at nodes t, we have $c[t] \leq s(t)$.

Inductive step: consider nodes t of height $h + 1$. By the inductive hypothesis: $c[2t] \leq s(2t)$ and $c[2t + 1] \leq s(2t + 1)$. If any processor reached a node t, then $c[t] = c[2t] + c[2t + 1] \leq s(2t) + s(2t + 1) = s(t)$. If no processors reached the node t, then $c[t] = 0 \leq s(t)$.

The induction stops at $t = 1$ where $R_i = c[1] \leq s(1) = P_i$, and so $P_i \geq R_i$.

(2) *Inequality $R_i \geq P_{i+1}$*: This can be shown using similar induction, but instead of $s(t)$ we define $r(t)$, to be the number of processors that initiated phase W1 in the subtree of the node t and that *completed* the phase W1 traversal. $r(1)$ is the upper bound for P_{i+1}, and the induction will show that $r(1) \leq c[1]$.
∎

In the dividing done during the dynamic top down traversal in W, we will allocate processors to tasks that either have not been completed, or have been completed, but not yet accounted for at the root $d[1]$. Recall that a leaf of d is *accounted* if it has value 1 and if the corresponding defined value in the leaf of tree a is also 1 (there are exactly $d[1]$ accounted leaves). In Algorithm W, the processors get allocated in a balanced fashion to the *unaccounted* leaves, i.e. the leaves whose associated (defined and) computed value in tree a is 0. The next lemma shows that the processor allocation to the unaccounted leaves is balanced. We give a proof sketch here and we leave the formal proof as an exercise to the reader (the only difficulty is the careful evaluation of expressions involving round-offs).

Lemma 3.3.2 In phase W2 of each loop-iteration i of algorithm W: (1) processors are only allocated to unaccounted leaves, and (2) no leaf is allocated more than $\lceil R_i/U_i \rceil$ processors.

Proof sketch: The lemma is shown by proving an invariant for the phase W2 algorithm. For each active processor, the main assertions of the invariant are that during the top down traversal, at each node j of the progress tree d and the auxiliary progress tree a: (1) $a[j]$ is strictly less than the number of leaves in the subtree of node j, and $a[j] \leq d[j]$, and (2) the maximum number of active processors allocated to the progress subtree of node j is equal (up to a round-off) to R_i/U_i times the number of unaccounted leaves in that subtree. When the surviving processors reach the leaves, it follows from the invariant that $a[j] = 0$, i.e., the leaf is unaccounted, and that the number of processors at that leaf is no more than $\lceil R_i/U_i \rceil$.   □

The following lemma shows that for each loop-iteration, the number of unvisited leaves is decreasing monotonically, thus assuring termination of the main loop after at most N iterations. The worst case of exactly N iterations corresponds to a single processor surviving at the outset of the algorithm.

Lemma 3.3.3 In algorithm W, for all loop-iterations i we have: $U_i > U_{i+1}$, as long as at least one processor survives.

Proof: To prove this, we define $a_i[1..2N\text{-}1]$ and $d_i[1..2N\text{-}1]$ to be the values of trees a and d after the completion of iteration i. $d_0[1..2N\text{-}1]$ are the initial zero values. We first show that if an iteration $i+1$ is started with tree d satisfying $d_i[t] \leq d_i[2t] + d_i[2t+1]$ $(1 \leq t < N)$, then after the termination of loop-iteration $i+1$, tree d will satisfy $d_{i+1}[t] \leq d_{i+1}[2t] + d_{i+1}[2t+1]$ $(1 \leq t < N)$, and along a path completely traversed from leaf to root by a processor in phase W4: $a_i[t] < d_{i+1}[t]$ $(1 \leq t < 2N$, t along the path traversed).

This can be shown using straightforward induction on the structure of the tree d and the loop-iteration number i. From this, since $U_i = N - d_i[1] = N - a_i[1]$ and $U_{i+1} = N - d_{i+1}[1]$, we have $N - U_i < N - U_{i+1}$ which leads to the desired result. ∎

We now come to the main lemma. We will treat the three $\log N$ time tree traversals performed by a single processor during each phase of the algorithm as a single *block-step* of cost $O(\log N)$. We will charge each processor for each such block step, regardless of whether the processor actually completes the traversals or whether it fail-stops somewhere in-between. This coarseness will not distort our results; since we can have at most P processor failures it amounts to a one time overcharge of $O(P \log N)$.

Lemma 3.3.4 For any failure pattern with at least one surviving processor, algorithm W completes all remaining work. Its total number of block-steps B is less than or equal to $U + P \log U / \log \log U$,[1] where P is the initial number of processors and U is the initial number of unvisited elements.

Proof: Consider the ith iteration of the main *loop* of algorithm W.

At the beginning of the iteration, P_i is the overestimate of active processors, and U_i is the estimated remaining unvisited leaves. At the end of the ith iteration (i.e., at the beginning of the $i+1^{st}$ iteration, the corresponding values are P_{i+1} and U_{i+1}. From Lemmas 3.3.1 and 3.3.3 we know that $P_i \geq P_{i+1}$ and $U_i > U_{i+1}$. Let also $P_1 = P$ and $U_1 = U$.

Let τ be the final iteration of the algorithm, i.e., $U_\tau \geq 0$ and the number of unvisited elements after the iteration τ is $U_{\tau+1} = 0$. We examine the following two major cases:

Case 1: Consider *all* block steps in which $P_i < U_i$:

By the balanced processor allocation Lemma 3.3.2, each leaf will be assigned no more than 1 processor, therefore the number of block steps B_1 accounted in

---

[1] The motivation for why does the expression $\log U / \log \log U$ occur in the theorem statement will need to wait until Chapter 4 where we give an adversarial strategy which has $\log U / \log \log U$ steps and which ultimately leads to the worst-case scenario for algorithm W.

this case will be no more than

$$B_1 \leq \sum_{i=1}^{\tau}(U_i - U_{i+1}) = U_1 - U_{t+1} = U - 0 = U.$$

Case 2: We now account for *all* block-steps in which $P_i \geq U_i$ in the following two subcases:

(2.a) Consider all block steps after which $U_{i+1} < \frac{U_i}{\log U/\log\log U}$:

This could occur no more than $O(\frac{\log U}{\log\log U})$ times since $U_{i+1} < U_1 = U$. No more than P processors complete such block-steps, therefore the total number of blocks $B_{2.a}$ accounted for here is

$$B_{2.a} = O(P\frac{\log U}{\log\log U}).$$

(2.b) Finally consider block steps such that $P_i \geq U_i$ and $U_{i+1} \geq \frac{U_i}{\log U/\log\log U}$:

Consider a particular iteration i. By Lemma 3.3.2, at most $\lceil\frac{P_i}{U_i}\rceil$ but no less than $\lfloor\frac{P_i}{U_i}\rfloor$ processors were assigned to each of the U_i unvisited leaves. Therefore, the number of failed processors is at least

$$U_{i+1}\left\lfloor\frac{P_i}{U_i}\right\rfloor \geq \frac{U_i}{\log U/\log\log U} \cdot \frac{P_i}{2U_i} \geq \frac{P_i}{2\log U/\log\log U}.$$

This can happen no more than τ times. The number of processors completing step i is no more than $P_i(1 - \frac{1}{2\frac{\log U}{\log\log U}})$.

In general, for P initial processors, the number of processors completing j^{th} occurrence of case (2.b) will be no more than $P(1 - \frac{1}{2\frac{\log U}{\log\log U}})^j$.

Therefore the number of block-steps $B_{2.b}$ accounted for here is bounded by:

$$B_{2.b} \leq \sum_{j=1}^{\tau} P\left(1 - \frac{1}{2\frac{\log U}{\log\log U}}\right)^j \leq P\sum_{j=1}^{\infty}\left(1 - \frac{1}{2\frac{\log U}{\log\log U}}\right)^j$$

$$= P\frac{1}{1 - (1 - \frac{1}{2\frac{\log U}{\log\log U}})} = P\cdot 2\frac{\log U}{\log\log U} = O\left(P\frac{\log U}{\log\log U}\right).$$

The total number of block steps B of all cases considered is:

$$B = B_1 + B_{2.a} + B_{2.b} = O(U + P\frac{\log U}{\log\log U}) \cdot \qquad\blacksquare$$

Theorem 3.3.5 Algorithm W is a robust parallel algorithm for the *Write-All* problem with $S = O(N\log^2 N/\log\log N)$, where N is the input array size, and the initial number of processors P is between 1 and N.

Proof: This follows from Definition 2.2.3 and Lemmas 3.3.1-3.3.4. Note that although we assumed N processors in Algorithm W, we only used the fact that $P \leq N$ in the lemmas. In fact, as indicated earlier, we accommodate $P < N$ processors by considering that $N - P$ processors failed prior to the beginning of the algorithm. This contributes a single charge of $O(N - P)$ to the cost, and does not distort the asymptotic result.

The result consists of the product of the total block-steps B, performed by the algorithm since and inclusive of the first iteration of the algorithm, times the cost of a single block-step. When $1 \leq P \leq N$, each block-step is performed in $O(\log N)$ time with one array element at each leaf. Therefore, using Lemma 3.3.4 with $U = N$, we obtain the needed result:

$$
\begin{aligned}
S \;&=\; & B \cdot O(\log N) \qquad &=\; O(U + P\tfrac{\log U}{\log \log U}) \cdot O(\log N) \\
&=\; & O(U \log N + P\tfrac{\log U \log N}{\log \log U}) \qquad &=\; O(N \log N + P\tfrac{\log^2 N}{\log \log N}). \qquad \blacksquare
\end{aligned}
$$

Optimal parameterization of algorithm W

One immediate observation based on the proof is that fewer processor steps will be expended by the algorithm if it is started with less than N processors. For example we reach a $S = O(N \log N)$ bound when using $P = N/\log N$ processors. A question can be posed: could an optimal algorithm for the *Write-All* problem be constructed using a non-trivial number of processors? This question is positively answered below.

We first observe that each block-step takes $\Theta(\log N)$ time and therefore each processor can be asked to perform $\Theta(\log N)$ processing steps in phase W3 without affecting the asymptotic complexity. We now parameterize algorithm W in a way that makes it possible to balance the time spent by each processor in tree traversals and the time spent working on the input (see Figure 3.11):

1. Let N be the size of the input.

2. Let $H \leq N$ be the instance size, and also the number of leaves in the progress tree, for the (non-parameterized) algorithm. Thus the height of the progress tree is $\log H$.

3. Let $G = N/H$ be the number of the input array elements mapped to each leaf of the progress tree. Each processor reaching a leaf will work not on one, but on G input elements.

4. Let $P \leq H$ be the initial number of processors (and the number of leaves in the processor tree).

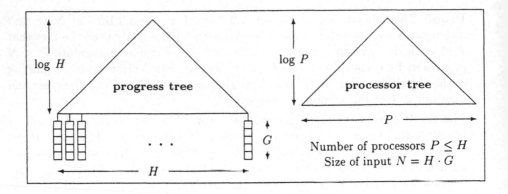

Figure 3.11 Parameterized data structures for algorithm W.

With these data structures, the performance of the parameterized algorithm W is described by the following lemma:

Lemma 3.3.6 Parameterized lgorithm W with P processors, with the progress tree with H leaves ($P \leq H$) and G input array elements at each leaf, performs work $S = O((H + P \log H) \cdot (\log P + \log H + G))$ for any pattern of stop failures.

Proof: The cost of a single block-step C_B consists of the time $O(\log P)$ of processor enumeration, time $O(\log H)$ of divide-and-conquer and progress measurement, and time $O(G)$ of work on the input data for a total of $O(\log P + \log H + G)$ [$= O(\log H + N/H)$]. By Lemma 3.3.4 the algorithm will verifiably visit all leaves of the progress tree after spending $B = U_1 + P_1 \log U_1 / \log \log U_1 = H + P \log H / \log \log H$ block-steps. Therefore $S = B \cdot C_B$, and so:

$$S = O(H + P \log H / \log \log H) \cdot O(\log P + \log H + N/H)$$
$$[\, = O(H \log H + P \log^2 H / \log \log H + N + PG \tfrac{\log H}{\log \log H})\,]. \qquad \blacksquare$$

To achieve work optimality, we would like to choose the parameters in the lemma so that $S = O(N)$. While the exact solution is involved, we observe that the following values for parameters G, H and P suffice to produce the desired result:

$G = \log N$

$H = N / \log N$ and

$P = N \log \log N / \log^2 N$.

Thus by exploiting parallel slackness, we achieve work optimality using a number of processors smaller than N (Figure 3.12):

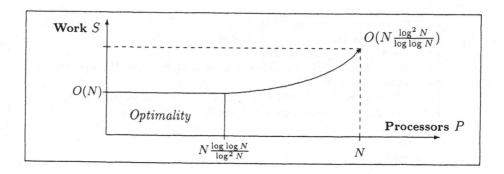

Figure 3.12   Work S of algorithm W.

Theorem 3.3.7 Parameterized algorithm W with $\log N$ array elements mapped to each leaf of the progress tree is a robust parallel algorithm that solves the *Write-All* problem of size N with $S = O(N)$, when $P \leq N \log \log N / \log^2 N$.

However, as we show in the chapter on lower bounds, no optimal N-processor algorithm exists for *Write-All*. We also show there that our upper bound for algorithm W is tight

The parameterized algorithm W, as in the last theorem above, can be used with any number of processors P such that $1 \leq P \leq N$. When using P processors such that $P > \frac{N}{\log N}$, it is sufficient for each processor to take its PID modulo $\frac{N}{\log N}$ to assure a uniform initial assignment of at least $\lfloor P / \frac{N}{\log N} \rfloor$ and no more than $\lceil P / \frac{N}{\log N} \rceil$ processors to a work element. Subsequent uniform assignment is similarly accomplished by using the enumerated processor numbers computed in phase W1.

3.3.2   Initialization: Algorithm Z

The *Write-All* algorithms and simulations (such as the one later covered in detail in Chapter 5) normally assume that a portion of shared memory, linear either in the size of the problem or the number of processors, is either cleared or is initialized to known values. Starting with the initialized portion of memory, these algorithms perform their computation by "consuming" the clear memory, and concurrently or subsequently clearing segments of memory needed for future iterations.

Here we describe an efficient *Write-All* algorithm which is tolerant of any (initial) shared memory *contamination*, i.e., which works even when the memory initially contains arbitrary values. The algorithm uses a *bootstrap* approach

```
00 - - Use P processors to clear N memory
01 forall processors PID=0..P − 1 parbegin
02    i := 0  - - Stage iteration counter
03    Clear a block of N₀ = K₀ elements sequentially using P processors
04    while Nᵢ < N do
05       Use Write-All solution WA(Nᵢ₊₁, P, Nᵢ) with data structures
06       of size Nᵢ to clear memory of size Nᵢ₊₁ = Nᵢ · Kᵢ₊₁
07       i := i + 1
08    od
09 parend.
```

Figure 3.13 A high level view of the bootstrap algorithm Z.

and makes "subroutine calls" to algorithm W. Our result is that for any failure pattern F (no-restart, $|F| < P$), it has work $O(N + P\frac{\log^3 N}{(\log\log N)^2})$ *without any initialization assumption.*

A Bootstrap procedure

We use the notation "WA(N, P, L)" to characterize the fault-tolerant *Write-All* algorithm that uses P processors and *clear* auxiliary memory of size L to initialize to 1 an array of size N.

We formulate a *bootstrap* approach to the design of fault-tolerant *Write-All* algorithms, to work with auxiliary memory which is initially contaminated. The bootstrapping proceeds in stages, where in each stage, in addition to solving *Write-All*, a segment of shared memory is also cleared:

In stage 1, all P processors clear an initial segment of N_0 locations in the auxiliary memory. In stage i we use P processors to clear N_{i+1} memory locations using N_i memory locations that were cleared in the stage $i - 1$. If $N_{i+1} > N_i$ and $N_0 \geq 1$, then this procedure will clear the required N memory location in at most N stages. Say τ is the final stage number, i.e., $N_\tau = N$. Let P_i be the number of active processors that initiate phase i, and define $N_{-1} = 0$. The cost of such a procedure is: $S_{boot} = \sum_{i=1}^{\tau} S_i(N_i, P_i, N_{i-1})$ where S_i is the cost of the WA(N_i, P_i, N_{i-1}) algorithm used in stage i.

The efficiency of the resulting algorithm depends on the choices of the particular *Write-All* solution(s) used in each stage and the parameters N_i. One specific approach is to define a series of multipliers $K_0, K_1, \ldots, K_\tau$ such that $N_i = \prod_{j=0}^{i} K_j$. The high level view of such an algorithm is given in Figure 3.13. The algorithm consists of an initialization (lines 02-03) and a parallel loop (lines 04-08).

Algorithm Z and its analysis

We call *algorithm Z* the algorithm that results from using algorithm W in each phase of the bootstrap procedure and. In the analysis we are using Lemma 3.3.6 from the previous section.

We analyze algorithm Z for the following parameters: we use $N_0 = \log N$ and $K_i = \log N$, thus $N_i = N_{i-1} \log N$ (for $i > 0$). In the initialization, all P processors traverse a list of size K_0 sequentially and clear it. Then, iteratively, the processors use algorithm W to clear increasingly larger sections of memory using the auxiliary memory cleared in the previous iteration for its trees (Figure 3.13, lines 05-06). In each iteration, i, the progress tree with N_i nodes and $(N_i + 1)/2$ leaves has $2 \log N$ memory cells associated with each leaf. At the conclusion of the iteration, (at least) $N_i \log N$ new memory cells are clear.

Theorem 3.3.8 Algorithm Z is a $WA(N, P, 0)$ algorithm that for any pattern of fail-stop errors has $S = O(N + P \log^3 N/(\log \log N)^2)$ for $1 \le P \le N$.

Proof: We first evaluate and then total the work of the algorithm during each of the stages of its execution. In each use of algorithm W, we will have $G = 2 \log N$ memory locations associated with each leaf of the progress tree, and we will use Lemma 3.3.6 with different instantiations of H to evaluate the upper bound of work.

Stage 0: Sequentially clear $\log N$ memory using all surviving processors. The work using the initial $P_0 \le P$ processors is: $W_0 = O(P_0 \cdot \log N)$.

Stage 1: $P_1 \le P_0 \le P$. Using an instance of Theorem 3.3.6 with $H = \frac{1}{2} \log N$, the work is:

$$W_1 = O((\log N + P_1 \log \log N / \log \log \log N) \cdot (\log P_1 + \log \log N + \log N)).$$

Stage i: $P_i \le P_{i-1} \le N$. Using an instance with $H = \frac{1}{2} \log^i N$:

$$W_i = O((\log^i N + P_i \cdot i \log \log N/(\log i + \log \log \log N))$$
$$\cdot (\log P_i + i \log \log N + \log N))$$

The *Final Stage* τ is when $\log^\tau N = N/\log N$, i.e., $\tau = \frac{\log N}{\log \log N} - 1$. Summing the work yields: $S = \sum_{i=0}^{\tau} W_i$

$$= W_0 + O(\sum_{i=1}^{\tau} (\log^i N + P_i \frac{i \log \log N}{\log i + \log \log \log N})(\log P_i + i \log \log N + \log N)).$$

For our purposes it suffices to obtain a big-O result. Simplifying the sum (the sum above looks more formidable than it actually is) results in $S = O(N + P \log^3 N/(\log \log N)^2)$. ∎

This approach has the following range of optimality:

Corollary 3.3.9 Algorithm Z is a $WA(N, N(\log \log N)^2/\log^3 N, 0)$ algorithm with $S = O(N)$ for any pattern of fail-stop errors.

Memory clean-up and algorithm Z^{-1}

In some settings it may be required that, prior to the algorithm termination, any auxiliary memory used by the algorithm is cleared, so that the memory contains only the results of the intended computation. An algorithm similar to algorithm Z can be constructed so that it *inverts* the bootstrap procedure and clears the contaminated shared memory.

When algorithm W is used in each iteration of the memory clean-up procedure, we call the resulting procedure algorithm Z^{-1}, The complexity of algorithm Z^{-1} is identical to the complexity of algorithm Z. We leave the details as an exercise for the reader.

For algorithm simulation and for transformed algorithms we examine in Chapter 5, the additional complexity cost is *additive* both for algorithm Z and for algorithm Z^{-1}.

3.4   DETECTABLE RESTART WRITE-ALL

Algorithm W in the previous section is an efficient fail-stop (no restart) *Write-All* solution. If we assume that after a failure processors can be restarted synchronously at the beginning of the processor enumeration phase W1, then the algorithm is still correct. However, it cannot directly handle less restricted processor restarts. This is because the processor enumeration and allocation phases become inefficient and possibly incorrect, since no accurate estimates of active and synchronized processors can be obtained when the adversary can revive any of the failed processors at any time.

In this section we present two algorithms that can handle detectable processor restarts: algorithm V and algorithm X.

Algortihm V is based on algorithm W and it has efficient fail-stop (no-restart) work and failure overhead ratio σ of $O(\log^2 N)$. However, this algorithm may not terminate if the adversary does not allow any of the processors that were alive at the beginning of an iteration to complete that iteration. Even if the extended algorithm were to terminate, its work might not be bounded by a function of N and P.

Algorithm X uses the local allocation paradigm to achieve bounded work for any pattern of failures with at least one processor active at any point in the computation. Algorithms V and X can be interleaved to achieve both the bounded overhead ratio and bounded work for any failure pattern.

3.4.1 Bounded Overhead: Algorithm V

We first observe that even in the presence of restarts, the second phase of algorithm W can implement processor allocation in $O(\log N)$ time by using the permanent processor PID in the top-down divide-and-conquer allocation. This also suggests that the processor enumeration phase of algorithm W does not improve its efficiency when processors can be restarted.

Therefore we present a modified version of algorithm W, that we call V. To avoid a complete restatement of the details of algorithm W, the reader is encouraged to refer to Section 3.3.1.

Definition of algorithm V

We formulate algorithm V using the data structures of the optimized algorithm W, i.e., by positioning $\log N$ work elements at each leaf of progress tree data structure.

Input: Shared array $x[1..N]$; $x[i] = 0$ for $1 \le i \le N$.

Output: Shared array $x[1..N]$; $x[i] = 1$ for $1 \le i \le N$.

Data structures: The algorithm uses full binary trees with $\frac{N}{\log N}$ leaves for progress estimation and processor allocation. There are $\log N$ array elements associated with each leaf of the progress tree. Each processor, instead of using its PID during the computation, uses the PID modulo $\frac{N}{\log N}$. When the number of processors P is such that $P > \frac{N}{\log N}$, this assures that there is a uniform initial assignment of at least $\lfloor P/\frac{N}{\log N} \rfloor$ and no more than $\lceil P/\frac{N}{\log N} \rceil$ processors to the work elements at each leaf.

Control flow: Algorithm V is an iterative algorithm using the following three phases (the top-level parallel loop pseudocode is in Figure 3.14).

Phase V1 – *processor allocation:* The processors are allocated using permanent PIDs in a dynamic top-down traversal of the progress tree to assure load balancing ($O(\log N)$ time).

Phase V2 – *work:* The processors perform work at the leaves they reached in phase V1 (there are $\log N$ array elements per leaf).

Phase V3 – *progress measurement:* The processors begin at the leaves of the progress tree where they ended phase V2 and update the progress tree dynamically, using bottom-up traversal ($O(\log N)$ time).

Processor re-synchronization after a failure and a restart is an important implementation detail. One way of realizing processor synchronization is through

```
01    forall processors PID=1..N parbegin
02        Phase V2: Visit leaves based on PID to work on the input data
03        Phase V3: Traverse the d tree bottom up to measure progress.
04        while the root of the d tree is not N do
05            Phase V1: Traverse the d, a, c trees top down to allocate processors
06            Phase V2: Perform work on the input data
07            Phase V3: Traverse the d tree bottom up to measure progress
08        od
09    parend.
```

Figure 3.14 A high level view of algorithm V

the utilization of an iteration wrap-around counter that is based on the synchronous PRAM clock. If a processor fails, and then is restarted, it waits for the counter wrap-around to rejoin the computation. The point at which the counter wraps around depends on the length of the program code, but it is fixed at "compile time".

Analysis of algorithm V

We now analyze the performance of this algorithm first showing its performance in the fail-stop setting, and then with both fail-stops and restarts. In the following lemma we produce an upper bound for the block-steps executed by algorithm V using the progress tree with N leaves, i.e., not yet using the optimized data structures.

Lemma 3.4.1 The number of block-steps of algorithm V using P processors, on input of size N using progress tree with N leaves, is $B_{N,P} = N + O(P \log P)$, for $P \leq N$.

Proof: In each iteration i of the algorithm, the active processors allocate themselves to the unvisited leaves using their PIDs. Lemma 3.3.2 from the analysis of algorithm W applies, with P replacing the estimated number of live processors R_i. If U of the array elements are still not visited according to the progress treem then this allocation achieves load balancing with no more than $\lceil \frac{P}{U} \rceil$ processors assigned to each unvisited element. Such allocation takes one block-step for each active processor.

For the purpose of the analysis, we list the elements of the *Write-All* array in ascending order according to the time at which the elements are visited (ties are broken arbitrarily). We divide this list into adjacent segments numbered sequentially starting with 0, such that the segment 0 contains $K_0 = N - P$

elements, and segment $j \geq 1$ contains $K_j = \lfloor \frac{P}{j(j+1)} \rfloor$ elements, for $j = 1, ..., m$ and for some $m \leq \sqrt{P}$.

Let U_j be the least possible number of unvisited elements when processors were being assigned to the elements of the jth segment. U_j can be computed as $U_j = N - \sum_{i=0}^{j-1} K_i$. U_0 is of course N, and for $j \geq 1$, $U_j = P - \sum_{i=1}^{j-1} K_i \geq P - (P - \frac{P}{j}) = \frac{P}{j}$. Therefore no more than $\lceil \frac{P}{U_j} \rceil$ processors were assigned to each element.

The number of block-steps performed by the algorithm is:

$$
\begin{aligned}
B_{N,P} &\leq \sum_{j=0}^{m} K_j \left\lceil \frac{P}{U_j} \right\rceil && \leq K_0 + \sum_{j=1}^{m} \left\lfloor \frac{P}{j(j+1)} \right\rfloor \left\lceil \frac{P}{P/j} \right\rceil \\
&= K_0 + O\left(P \sum_{j=1}^{m} \frac{1}{j+1} \right) && = N + O(P \log P) && \text{(Equation 79)}
\end{aligned}
$$

∎

In the next lemma we show that algorithm V is a polylogarithmically robust algorithm for the fail-stop model without restarts.

Lemma 3.4.2 The work of algorithm V using $P \leq N$ processors that are subject to fail-stop errors without restarts is $S = O(N + P \log^2 N)$.

Proof: We factor out any work that is wasted due to failures by charging this work to the failures. Since the failures are fail-stop, there can be at most P failures, and each processor that fails can waste at most $O(\log N)$ steps corresponding to a single iteration of the algorithm. Therefore the work charged to the failures is $O(P \log N)$, and it will be amortized in the rest of the work.

We next evaluate the work that directly contributes to the progress of the algorithm by distinguishing two cases below. In each of the cases, it takes $O(\log \frac{N}{\log N}) = O(\log N)$ time to perform processor allocation, and $O(\log N)$ time to perform the work at the leaves. Thus each block-step (and each iteration) of the algorithm takes $O(\log N)$ time.

Case 1: $1 \leq P < \frac{N}{\log N}$. In this case, at most 1 processor is initially allocated to each leaf of the progress tree. We use Lemma 3.4.1 to establish an upper bound on the blocks-step of the algorithm, except that instead of N leaves, the progress tree has $N/\log N$ leaves. Each block-step and leaf visit takes $O(\log N)$ time; therefore the work is:

$$
\begin{aligned}
S &= B_{\frac{N}{\log N}, P} \cdot O(\log N) &&= O\left(\left(\frac{N}{\log N} + P \log P \right) \cdot \log N \right) \\
&= O(N + P \log P \log N) &&= O(N + P \log^2 N).
\end{aligned}
$$

Case 2: $\frac{N}{\log N} \leq P \leq N$. In this case, no more than $\lceil P / \frac{N}{\log N} \rceil$ processors are initially allocated to each leaf. Any two processors that are initially allocated to the same leaf, should they both survive, will behave identically throughout the computation. Therefore we can estimate the number of block steps assuming $N/\log N$ processors and then use $\lceil P/\frac{N}{\log N} \rceil$ processor allocation as a multiplicative factor in estimate the work.

By Lemma 3.4.1, we establish the number of block-steps as:

$$B_{\frac{N}{\log N},P} = O\left(\frac{N}{\log N} + P\log P\right) = O\left(\frac{N}{\log N}\log\frac{N}{\log N}\right)$$

From this, and the cost of a block-step of $O(\log N)$, the work is:

$$S = \left\lceil P/\frac{N}{\log N}\right\rceil \cdot O\left(\frac{N}{\log N}\log\frac{N}{\log N}\right) \cdot O(\log N) = O(P\log^2 N).$$

The results of the two cases combine to yield $S = O(N + P\log^2 N)$. ∎

The following corollary extracts the slightly better bound analyzed in the case (1) above, and it also covers the processor range for which the work of the algorithm is optimal.

Corollary 3.4.3 The work of algorithm V using $P \leq N/\log N$ processors that are subject to fail-stop errors without restarts is $S = O(N + P\log N\log P)$.

The upper bound analysis is tight:

Theorem 3.4.4 There is a fail-stop adversary that causes the work of algorithm V to be $S = \Omega(P\log^2 N)$ for the number of processors $N/\log N \leq P \leq N$, and $S = \Omega(N + P\log N\log P)$ for the number of processors $1 \leq P \leq N/\log N$.

Proof: Consider the following adversary for $P = N/\log N$. At the outset the adversary fail-stops all processors that are initially assigned to the, say, left subtree of the progress tree. Let the number of unvisited array elements be U. By the balanced allocation of Lemma 3.3.2, the N processors (dead or alive) will be assigned in a balanced fashion to the left and right segments of the contiguous U unvisited elements. Initially, U_0 is $N/\log N$, and so the algorithm will terminate in $\log U_0 = \Theta(\log N)$ block-steps when such an adversary is encountered. Each block-step takes $\Theta(\log N)$ time using the remaining $P/2$ processors. Thus the work is $S \leq \frac{P}{2}\Theta(\log N)\Theta(\log N) = \Theta(P\log^2 N) = \Omega(N\log N)$.

When P is larger than $N/\log N$, then each leaf is allocated at least $\lfloor P/\frac{N}{\log N}\rfloor$ and no more than $\lceil P/\frac{N}{\log N}\rceil$ processors. All processors allocated to the same leaf have their PIDs equal modulo $N/\log N$. Therefore the work is increased by at least a factor of $\lfloor P/\frac{N}{\log N} \rfloor$ as compared to the case $P = N/\log N$. I.e., $S = \lfloor P/\frac{N}{\log N} \rfloor \Omega(N \log N) = \Omega(P \log^2 N)$.

Finally, when $P < N/\log N$, the result follows similarly using the strategy of the case (1) of Lemma 3.4.2. ∎

Note that algorithm V is simpler than algorithm W, but its work performance is only $\log \log N$ times worse than that of algorithm W.

The next theorem expresses the work of the algorithm for arbitrary failures and detectable restarts:

Theorem 3.4.5 Algorithm V in the presence of an arbitrary failure and detectable restart pattern F of size M has work $S = O(N + P \log^2 N + M \log N)$, using the initial number of processors $P \leq N$.

Proof: The proof of Lemma 3.4.2 does not rely on the fact that in the absence of restarts, the number of active processors is non-increasing. However, the lemma does not account for the work that might be performed by processors that are active during a part of an iteration but do not contribute to the progress of the algorithm due to failures. To account for all work, we are going to charge to the array being processed the work that contributes to progress, and any work that was wasted due to failures will be charged to the failures and restarts. Lemma 3.4.2 accounts for the work charged to the array. Otherwise, we observe that a processor can waste no more than $O(\log N)$ time steps without contributing to the progress due to a failure and/or a restart. Therefore this amount of wasted work is bounded by $O(M \log N)$. This proves the theorem. (Note that S of V is small for small $|F|$, but not bounded by a function of P and N for large $|F|$). ∎

3.4.2 Bounded Work: Algorithm X

We present algorithm X for the *Write-All* problem whose important property is that it has bounded sub-quadratic work for any pattern of failures and restarts. Algorithm X has $S = O(N \cdot P^{\log \frac{3}{2}})$ using $P \leq N$ processors. If a very large number of failures does occur, say $|F| = \Omega(N \cdot P^{0.59})$, then the algorithm's overhead ratio σ becomes optimal: it takes a fixed number of computing steps per failure/recovery.

Like algorithm V, algorithm X utilizes a progress tree of size N, but it is traversed by the processors independently, not in synchronized phases. This reflects the local nature of the processor allocation in algorithm X as opposed to the global allocation used in algorithms V and W. Each processor, acting independently, searches for work in the smallest immediate subtree that has

```
01    forall processors PID=0..P − 1 parbegin
02        Perform initial processor assignment to the leaves of the progress tree
03        while there is still work left in the tree do
04            if subtree rooted at current node u is done then move one level up
05            elseif u is a leaf then perform the work at the leaf
06            elseif u is an interior tree node then
07                Let u_L and u_R be the left and right children of u respectively
08                if the subtrees rooted at u_L and u_R are done then update u
09                elseif only one is done then go to the one that is not done
10                else move to u_L or u_R according to PID bit values
11            fi fi
12        od
13    parend.
```

Figure 3.15   A high level view of the algorithm X.

work that needs to be done. It then performs the necessary work, and moves out of that subtree when all work within it is completed.

Definition of algorithm X

Input: Shared array $x[1..N]$; $x[i] = 0$ for $1 \leq i \leq N$.

Output: Shared array $x[1..N]$; $x[i] = 1$ for $1 \leq i \leq N$.

Data structures: The algorithm uses a full binary tree of size $2N − 1$, stored as a linear array in $d[1 \ldots 2N − 1]$ in shared memory. An internal tree node $d[i]$ $(i = 1, \ldots, N − 1)$ has the left child $d[2i]$ and the right child $d[2i + 1]$. The tree is used for progress evaluation and processor allocation. The values stored in $[d]$ are initially 0.

The N elements of the input array $x[1 \ldots N]$ are associated with the leaves of the tree. Element $x[i]$ is associated with $d[i + N − 1]$, where $1 \leq i \leq N$.

Each processor uses some constant amount of private memory to perform simple arithmetic computations. An important private constant is PID, containing the initial processor identifier.

The total memory used is $O(N + P)$.

Control flow: The algorithm consists of a single initialization and of the parallel *loop*. A high level view of the algorithm is in Figure 3.15; all line numbers refer to this figure. (The detailed code for the algorithm is also given in Figure 3.17 that is discussed later).

The initialization (line 01) assigns the P processors to the leaves of the progress tree so that the processors are assigned to the first P leaves. The *loop* (lines

02-13) consists of a multi-way decision (lines 03-12). If the current node u is marked done, the processor moves up the tree (line 04). If the processor is at a leaf, it performs work (line 05). If the current node is an unmarked interior node and both of its subtrees are done, the interior node is marked by changing its value from 0 to 1 (line 08). If a single subtree is not done, the processor moves down appropriately (line 09).

For the final case (line 10), the processors move down when neither child is done. This last case is where a non-trivial decision is made. The PID of the processor is used at depth h of the tree node based on the value of the hth most significant bit of the binary representation of the PID: bit 0 will send the processor to the left, and bit 1 to the right.

If each processor was traversing the tree alone, it would traverse it in a post-order fashion using the bits of its PID to re-interpret the meaning of "left" and "right". Bit value 0 leads to the "standard" interpretation of "left" and "right", while value 1 reverses them. This results in each processor "intending" to traverse the leaves of the tree according to a permutation determined by its PID, except that the progress by other processors effectively prunes the progress tree when sub-trees are finished. In effect, each processor traverses a sub-tree with the same root.

Regardless of the decision made by a processor within the *loop* body, each iteration of the body consists of no more than four shared memory reads, a fixed time computation using private memory, and one shared memory write (the detailed code is given in Figure 3.17).

Example 3.6 *Algorithm X example:* Consider algorithm X for $N = P = 8$. The progress tree d of size $2N - 1 = 15$ is used to represent the full binary progress tree with eight leaves. The 8 processors have PIDs in the range 0 through 7. Their initial positions are indicated in Figure 3.16 under the leaves of the tree. The diagram illustrates the state of a computation where the processors were subject to some failures and restarts. Heavy dots indicate nodes whose subtrees are finished. The paths being traversed by the processors are indicated by the arrows. Active processor locations (at the time when the snapshot was taken) are indicated by their PIDs in brackets. In this configuration, should the active processors complete the next iteration, they will move in the directions indicated by the arrows: processors 0 and 1 will descend to the left and right respectively, processor 4 will move to the unvisited leaf to its right, and processors 6 and 7 will move up. □

We now comment on the detailed algorithm X code in Figure 3.17. One of the advantages of this algorithm is that it can be used in the settings with detectable failures and restarts such that the recovered processors lose their private memory but restart is specially designated states.

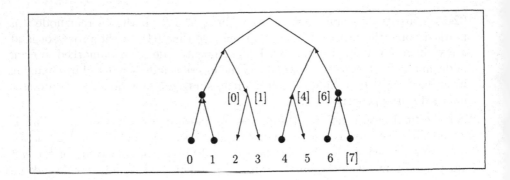

Figure 3.16   Processor traversal of the progress tree.

In the code, the **action-recovery-end** construct is used to denote the actions and the recovery procedures for the processors. Although it is possible to specify different actions and recoveries, in the algorithm we specify that the action and the recovery is the same. In other words, the action is also its own recovery action, should a processor fail at any point within the action block. The **action-recovery** construct can be implemented by appropriately checkpointing the instruction counter in stable storage as the first instruction of an action, and reading the instruction counter upon a restart. This is amenable to automatic implementation by a compiler. This approach also makes the algorithm usable in the settings where a failure may cause the loss of processors' local memory.

The notation "PID[log(k)]" is used to denote the binary true/false value of the $\lfloor \log(k) \rfloor$-th bit of the $\log(N)$-bit representation of PID, where the most significant bit is the bit number 0, and the least significant bit is bit number $\log N$.

The algorithm can also solve the *Write-All* problem "in place", by using the array $x[1..N]$ as a tree of height $\log(N/2)$ with the leaves $x[N/2..N-1]$, and doubling up the processors at the leaves, and using $x[N]$ as the final element to be initialized and used as the algorithm termination sentinel. With this modification, the array $d[1..2N-1]$ is not needed. The asymptotic efficiency of the algorithm is not affected.

Analysis of algorithm X

The correctness and termination of algorithm X is shown in the following lemma.

Lemma 3.4.6 Algorithm X with P processors is a correct, terminating and fault-tolerant solution for the *Write-All* problem of size N in the fail-stop

```
forall processors PID = 0..P−1 parbegin
  shared x[1..N];          -- the Write-All array
  shared d[1..2N − 1];     -- "done", the progress tree
  shared w[0..P − 1];      -- non-volatile "where" array of processor locations
  private where, done;     -- current node index and its "done" value
  private left, right;     -- left/right child values in progress tree

  action, recovery
    w[PID] := 1+PID; -- the initial positions
  end;

  action, recovery
    while w[PID] ≠ 0 do -- while haven't exited the tree
      where := w[PID]; -- current progress tree location
      done := d[where]; -- doneness of this subtree
      if done then w[PID] := where div 2; -- move up one level
      elseif not done ∧ where ≥ N − 1 then -- at a leaf
        if x[where − N] = 0 then x[where − N] := 1; -- initialize leaf
        elseif x[where − N] = 1 then d[where] := 1; -- indicate "done"
        fi
      elseif not done ∧ where < N − 1 then -- interior tree node
        left:= d[2 * where]; right := d[2 * where + 1]; -- left/right child values
        if left ∧ right then d[where] := 1; -- both children done
        elseif not left ∧ right then w[PID] := 2 * where; -- go left
        elseif left ∧ not right then w[PID] := 2 * where + 1; -- go right
        elseif not left ∧ not right then -- both subtrees are not done
          -- move down according to the PID bit
          if not PID[log(where)] then w[PID] := 2 * where; -- move left
          elseif PID[log(where)] then w[PID] := 2 * where + 1; -- move right
      fi fi fi
    od
  end
parend.
```

Figure 3.17 Algorithm X detailed pseudo-code.

restartable model. The algorithm terminates in $\Omega(\log N)$ and $O(P \cdot N)$ time steps.

Proof: We first observe that the processor loads are localized in the sense that a processor exhausts all work in the vicinity of its original position in the tree, before moving to other areas of the tree. If a processor moves up out of a subtree then all the leaves in that subtree were visited. We also observe that it takes exactly one iteration to: (i) change the value of a progress tree node from 0 to 1, (ii) to move up from a (non root) node, or (iii) to move down left, or (iv) down right from a (non leaf) node. Therefore, given any node of the progress tree and any processor, the processor will visit and spend exactly one loop iteration at the node no more than four times.

Since there are $2N - 1$ nodes in the progress tree, any processor will be able to execute no more than $O(N)$ loop iterations. If there are P processors, then all processors will be able to complete no more than $O(P \cdot N)$ loop iterations. Furthermore, at any point in time at least one processor is active. Therefore it will take no more than $O(P \cdot N)$ sequential loop iterations of constant size for the algorithm to terminate.

Finally, we also observe that all paths from a leaf to the root are at least $\log N$ long, therefore at least $\log N$ loop iterations per processor will be required for the algorithm to terminate.   ∎

In the above lemma the focus is on termination and correctness — the exact time analysis is revisited in Remark 3.8.

Now we prove the main work lemma. Recall that the expression "$S_{N,P}$" denotes the maximum work on inputs of size N using P initial processors and for *any* failure pattern. In other words, $S_{N,P}$ is S, as in Definition 2.2.2, but maximized over failure patterns of any size: $S_{N,P} = \max_M S_{N,M,P}$. Note that in this lemma we assume $P \geq N$.

Lemma 3.4.7 Algorithm X for the *Write-All* problem of size N with $P \geq N$ initial processors and for any pattern of failures and restarts has $S_{N,P} = O(P \cdot N^{\log \frac{3}{2}})$.

Proof: We show by induction on the height of the progress tree that there are positive constants c_1, c_2, c_3 such that $S_{N,P} \leq c_1 P \cdot N^{\log \frac{3}{2}} - c_2 P \log N - c_3 P$.

For the base case: we have a tree of height 0 that corresponds to an input array of size 1 and at least as many initial processors P. Since at least one processor, and at most P processors will be active, this single leaf will be visited in a constant number of steps. Let the work expended be $c'P$ for some constant c' that depends only on the lexical structure of the algorithm. Therefore $S_{1,P} = c'P \leq c_1 P \cdot 1^{\log \frac{3}{2}} - c_2 P \cdot 0 - c_3 P$ when c_1 is chosen to be larger than or equal to $c_3 + c'$ (for any constant c_3).

Now consider a tree of height $\log N$ (≥ 1). The root has two subtrees (left and right) of height $\log N - 1$. By the definition of algorithm X, no processor will leave a subtree until the subtree is *marked*, i.e., the value of the root of the subtree is changed from 0 to 1. We consider the following sub-cases: (1) both subtrees are marked simultaneously, and (2) one of the subtrees is marked before the other.

Case 1: If both subtrees are marked simultaneously, then the algorithm will terminate after the two independent subtrees terminate plus some small constant number of steps c' (when a processor moves to the root and determines that both of the subtrees are marked). Both the work S_L expended in the left subtree of, and the work S_R in the right subtree are bounded by $S_{N/2,P/2}$. The added work needed for the algorithm to terminate is at most $c'P$, and so the total work is:

$$
\begin{aligned}
S &\leq S_L + S_R + c'P \leq 2S_{N/2,P/2} + c'P \\
&\leq 2\left(c_1 \frac{P}{2}\left(\frac{N}{2}\right)^{\log\frac{3}{2}} - c_2 \frac{P}{2} \log \frac{N}{2} - c_3 \frac{P}{2}\right) + c'P \\
&= c_1 \frac{2}{3} PN^{\log\frac{3}{2}} - c_2 P \log \frac{N}{2} - c_3 P + c'P \\
&\leq c_1 P \cdot N^{\log\frac{3}{2}} - c_2 P \log N - c_3 P
\end{aligned}
$$

for sufficiently large c_1 and any c_2 depending on c', e.g., $c_1 \geq 3(c_2 + c')$.

Case 2: Assume without loss of generality that the left subtree is marked-one first with $S_L = S_{N/2,P/2}$ work being expended in this subtree. Any active processors from the left subtree will start moving via the root to the right subtree. The length of the path traversed by any processor as it moves to the right subtree after the left subtree is finished is bounded by the maximum path length from a leaf to another leaf $c' \log N$ for a predefined constant c'. No more than the original $P/2$ processors of the left subtree will move, and so the work of moving the processors is bounded by $c'(P/2) \log N$.

We observe that the cost of an execution in which P processors begin at the leaves of a tree (with $N/2$ leaves) differs from the cost of an execution where $P/2$ processors start at the leaves, and $P/2$ arrive at a later time via the root, by no more than the cost $c'(P/2) \log N$ accounted for above.

This is so because a simulating scenario can be constructed in which the second set of $P/2$ processors, instead of arriving through the root, start their execution with a failure, and then traverse along a path through the marked nodes (if any) in the progress tree, until they reach an unmarked node that is either a leaf, or whose descendants are marked.

Having accounted for this difference, we see that the work S_R to complete the right subtree using up to P processors is bounded by $S_{N/2,P}$ (by the definition of S, if $P_1 \leq P_2$, then $S_{N,P_1} \leq S_{N,P_2}$). After this, each processor will spend some constant number of steps moving to the root and terminating the algorithm. This work is bounded by $c''P$ for some small constant c''.

The total work S is:

$$
\begin{aligned}
S &\leq S_L + c'\frac{P}{2}\log N + S_R + c''P \\
&\leq S_{N/2,P/2} + c'\frac{P}{2}\log N + S_{N/2,P} + c''P
\end{aligned}
$$

$$
\begin{aligned}
S &\leq c_1\frac{P}{2}\left(\frac{N}{2}\right)^{\log\frac{3}{2}} - c_2\frac{P}{2}\log\frac{N}{2} - c_3\frac{P}{2} + c'\frac{P}{2}\log N \\
&\quad + c_1 P\left(\frac{N}{2}\right)^{\log\frac{3}{2}} - c_2 P\log\frac{N}{2} - c_3 P + c''P \\
&= c_1 P N^{\log\frac{3}{2}} - c_2 P\log N\left(\frac{3}{2} - \frac{c'}{2c_2}\right) - c_3 P\left(\frac{3}{2} - \frac{c''}{c_3} - \frac{3c_2}{2c_3}\right) \\
&\leq c_1 P \cdot N^{\log\frac{3}{2}} - c_2 P\log N - c_3 P
\end{aligned}
$$

for sufficiently large c_2 and c_3 depending on fixed c' and c'', e.g., $c_2 \geq c'$ and $c_3 \geq 3c_2 + 2c''$.

Since the constants c', c'' depend only on the lexical structure of the algorithm, the constants c_1, c_2, c_3 can always be chosen sufficiently large to satisfy the base case and both the cases (1) and (2) of the inductive step. This completes the proof of the lemma. ∎

The quantity $P \cdot N^{\log\frac{3}{2}}$ is about $P \cdot N^{0.59}$. We next show a particular pattern of failures for which the completed work of algorithm X matches this upper bound.

Lemma 3.4.8 There exists a pattern of fail-stop/restart errors that cause the algorithm X to perform $S = \Omega(N^{\log 3})$ work on the input of size N using $P = N$ processors.

Proof: We can compute the exact work performed by the algorithm when the adversary adheres to the following strategy:

(a) All processors, except for the processor with PID 0 are initially stopped.

(b) The processor with PID 0 will be allowed to sequentially traverse the progress tree starting at the leftmost leaf and finishing at the rightmost leaf. The traversal will be essentially a post-order traversal, except that the processor will not begin at the root of the binary tree, but at the leftmost leaf.

(c) Any processors with PID $\neq$ 0 that find themselves at the same leaf as processor 0 are restarted in synchrony with processor 0 and are allowed to traverse the progress tree at the same pace as processor 0 until they reach a leaf, where they are fail-stopped by the adversary.

The computation terminates when all leaves are visited.

Thus the leaves of the progress tree are visited left to right, from the leaf number 1 to the leaf number N. At any time, if i is the number of the rightmost visited leaf, then only the processors with PIDs 0 to $i - 1$ have performed at least one loop iteration thus far.

The cost of such strategy can be expressed inductively as follows:

The cost C_0 of traversing a tree of size 1 using a single processor is 1 (unit of work).

The cost C_{i+1} of traversing a tree of size 2^{i+1} is computed as follows: first, there is the cost C_i of traversing the left subtree of size 2^i. Then, all processors move to the right subtree and participate (subject to failures) in the traversal of the right subtree at the cost of $2C_i$ — the cost is doubled, because the two processors whose PIDs are equal modulo i behave identically. Thus $C_{i+1} = 3C_i$, and $C_{\log N} = 3^{\log N} = N^{\log 3}$. ∎

Algorithm X'

Now we show how to use algorithm X with P processors to solve *Write-All* problems of size N such that $P \leq N$. Given an array of size N, we break the N elements of the input into $\frac{N}{P}$ groups of P elements each (the last group may have fewer than P elements). The P processors are then used to solve $\frac{N}{P}$ *Write-All* problems of size P one at a time. We call this construction *algorithm X'*.

Remark 3.7 *Algorithm X with $P \leq N$ processors*: Strictly speaking, it is not necessary to modify algorithm X for $P \leq N$ processors. Algorithm X can be used with $P \leq N$ processors by initially assigning the P processors to the first P elements of the array to be visited. It can also be shown that X and X' have the same asymptotic complexity; however, the analysis of X' is very simple, as we show below. ☐

Theorem 3.4.9 Algorithm X' with P processors solves the *Write-All* problem of size N ($P \leq N$) in the fail-stop restartable model using completed work $S = O(N \cdot P^{\log \frac{3}{2}})$. In addition, there is an adversary that forces algorithm X' to perform $S = \Omega(N \cdot P^{\log \frac{3}{2}})$ work.

Proof: By Lemma 3.4.7, $S_{P,P} = O(P \cdot P^{\log \frac{3}{2}}) = O(P^{\log 3})$. Thus the overall work will be $S = O(\frac{N}{P} S_{P,P}) = O(\frac{N}{P} P^{\log 3}) = O(N \cdot P^{\log \frac{3}{2}})$.

Using the strategy of Lemma 3.4.8, an adversary causes the algorithm to perform work $S_{P,P} = \Omega(P^{\log 3})$ on each of the $\frac{N}{P}$ segments of the input array. This results in the overall work of: $S = \Omega(\frac{N}{P} P^{\log 3}) = \Omega(N \cdot P^{\log \frac{3}{2}})$. ∎

Remark 3.8 *On the worst-case time of algorithm X*: Lemma 3.4.6 gives only a loose upper bound for the worst time performance of algorithm X — there we are primarily concerned with termination. The actual worst case time for algorithm X can be no more than the upper bound on the completed work. This is because at any point in time there is at least one processor that is active. Therefore, for algorithm X' with $P \leq N$, the time is bounded by $O(N \cdot P^{\log \frac{3}{2}})$. In particular, for $P = N$, the time is bounded by $O(N^{\log 3})$. In fact, using the worst case strategy of Lemma 3.4.8, an adversary can "time share" the cycles of the processors so that only one processor is active at any given time, with the processor with PID 0 being one step ahead of other processors. The resulting time is then $\Omega(N^{\log 3})$.   □

3.5 UNDETECTABLE RESTARTS AND ASYNCHRONY

In algorithms X and X', processors work for the most part independently of other processors; they attempt to avoid duplicating already-completed work but do not co-ordinate their actions with other processors. This property allows the algorithm to run with the same work and time bounds in the asynchronous model or the model where restarts are undetectable.

The result for the for the model with undetectable restarts (or asynchronous processors) is similar to Theorem 3.4.9:

Theorem 3.5.1 Algorithm X' with P processors solves the *Write-All* problem of size N $(P \leq N)$ in the asynchronous model with $S = O(N \cdot P^{\log \frac{3}{2}})$.

Proof: We first note that algorithm X with P processors solves the *Write-All* problem of size N $(P \geq N)$ in the asynchronous model with work $S = O(P \cdot N^{\log \frac{3}{2}})$. If we let $S_{N,P}$ be the total work done by algorithm X on a problem of size N with P processors, then $S_{N,P}$ satisfies the same recurrence as given in the proof of Lemma 3.4.7. The proof, which never uses synchrony, goes through exactly as in that lemma, except that case 1 (where left and right subtrees have their roots marked simultaneously) does not occur. The proof for algorithm X' follows the proof of Theorem 3.4.9.   ■

Processors in algorithm X use the local allocation paradigm in selecting what *Write-All* array elements to work on. We now present the randomized algorithm AW where processors use a hashed allocation paradigm, and a family of algorithms AW^T that use hybrid allocation paradigm that has attributes of the local allocation as in algorithm X and hashed allocation as in algorithm AW.

```
01 forall processors PID= 1..P ≤ N parbegin
02     N array elements are divided into P work groups B[1..P] of N/P elements
03     Each processor PID obtains:
04     private permutation π of {1, 2, ..., P}
05     for i = 1..P do
06        if group B[πᵢ] is not marked "done"
07        then perform sequential work on the N/P elements
08             of the group B[πᵢ] and mark the group "done"
09        fi
10     od
11 parend.
```

Figure 3.18   A high level view of algorithm *AW*.

3.5.1   The Randomized Algorithm AW

Several algorithms for the *Write-All* problem use the hashed allocation paradigm in which processors are randomly assigned to work elements. One such approach uses, for N work elements, random permutations over $\{1,\ldots,N\}$ as schedules for the P processors that determine in what order are the work elements visited by the processors. An algorithm directly using such technique cannot achieve a better work bound than $\Omega(N \cdot P)$, since each element is redundantly visited by each of the P processors, and this results in linear overhead. However, by introducing parallel slackness and dividing the *Write-All* array elements into work groups, it is possible to configure algorithms that are fault-tolerant and efficient.

The basic technique of this approach is abstracted as algorithm AW and is given as the high level code in Figure 3.18. Algorithm AW uses randomization only in the very beginning of the computation where processors randomly choose private permutations π in lines 03-04. Each processor then uses its π to visit the work groups in the order of $\pi = (\pi_1 \ldots \pi_P)$. (For a permutation π, we use the notation π_j to denote the j-th element of the permutation.)

For a particular execution of algorithm AW, let S_k be the work performed by processor k in that execution. We break S_k two parts:

(i) S_k^π, the work spent, for each group $B[\pi_i]$, on checking the completion status of each group in line 06, and

(ii) S_k^ω, the work spent in visiting the array elements that are the members of each group that it finds not to be "done".

It is easy to see that $S_k^\pi = O(P)$, since each π has P elements. Let G_k be the number of workgroups that the processor k finds not to be "done" (in line 06). Then $S_k^\omega = O(G_k \cdot N/P)$, and so the work for a *particular execution* of the

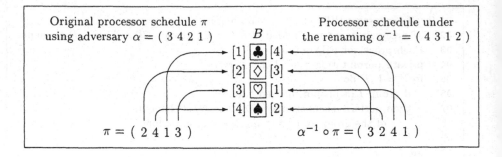

Original processor schedule π
using adversary $\alpha = (\ 3\ 4\ 2\ 1\ )$

B

Processor schedule under
the renaming $\alpha^{-1} = (\ 4\ 3\ 1\ 2\ )$

[1] ♣ [4]
[2] ◇ [3]
[3] ♡ [1]
[4] ♠ [2]

$\pi = (\ 2\ 4\ 1\ 3\ )$

$\alpha^{-1} \circ \pi = (\ 3\ 2\ 4\ 1\ )$

Figure 3.19 Processor schedule relabeling in algorithm AW.

algorithm is:

$$S = \sum_{k=1}^{P}(S_k^{\pi} + S_k^{\omega}) = P^2 + \frac{N}{P}\sum_{k=1}^{P}G_k \qquad \text{(Equation 92)}$$

Let the permutation α of $\{1,\ldots,P\}$ be the order (determined by an adversary) in which the groups are completed (marked done) in a particular execution. In algorithm AW, the indexing of the groups in the array $B[1..P]$ plays no role (i.e., the indices are symbolic), since the groups are visited according to the permutations π. Then we can relabel the groups in B and in each permutation π according to α^{-1} without changing the particular execution associated with α. With such a normalizing relabeling, the permutations π are replaced by permutations $\nu = a^{-1} \circ \pi$, and the groups are visited in the order of $\alpha^{-1} \circ \alpha = e$, the identity permutation (here $\circ$ stands for permutation composition). We will use ν for normalized permutation schedules where α and π are clear from the context.

Example 3.9 *Relabeling permutation schedules*: Consider algorithm AW with $P = 4$. Let $\pi = (2\ 4\ 1\ 3)$ be some processor's permutation. Suppose the adversary causes the groups to be completed in the order defined by $\alpha = (3\ 4\ 2\ 1)$. If we rename the groups according to $\alpha^{-1} = (4\ 3\ 1\ 2)$, then the adversary causes the groups to completed in the order $e = (1\ 2\ 3\ 4)$, and the processor's permutation becomes $\alpha^{-1} \circ \pi = (3\ 2\ 4\ 1)$, and, of course, the groups are visited by this processor in the same order as before the renaming (see Figure 3.19, the order is ◇♠♣♡). □

We will be taking advantage of such normalizing relabeling of the executions of algorithm AW by observing that for the normalized adversary schedule, the work groups are completed strictly in the increasing order of the group index in the normalized schedule. Each step of a given processor k, according to its schedule π, contributes a unit of work towards S_k^π, but not all steps necessarily contribute to G_k, since some groups may be completed by other processors.

Consider the step $\nu_s = (\alpha^{-1} \circ \pi)_s$ (for some $1 \le s \le P$) in the normalized schedule. If the processor k finds the group with index ν_s to be not done, it means that no groups with the indices larger than ν_s have been completed by the definition of the normalized completion schedule e. On the other hand, if there is t such that $t < s$ and $\nu_t > \nu_s$, than by the time the processor checks the completion status of ν_s, it most certainly finds it to be completed, since it visited ν_t in the past, and by the completion schedule the groups 1 to ν_t have been completed. Thus, the only steps ν_s that can contribute to G_k are such that ν_s is a *left-to-right maximum* in ν:

Lemma 3.5.2 In algorithm AW with the group completion schedule determined by α, the number of work groups G_k, completed by a processor k using the permutation schedule π^k, is bounded by the number of left-to-right maxima in $\alpha^{-1} \circ \pi$.

We denote the number of left-to-right maxima in a permutation π by $LR(\pi)$. For a set of permutations Ψ, we define $LR(\Psi) \equiv \sum_{\pi \in \Psi} LR(\pi)$, and we define $\alpha \circ \Psi \equiv \{\alpha \circ \pi : \pi \in \Psi\}$. Using Lemma 3.5.2 and Equation 92, we obtain the bound on work S_α for a particular α:

$$S_\alpha \le P^2 + \frac{N}{P} \sum_{k=1}^{P} G_k \le P^2 + \frac{N}{P} \sum_{k=1}^{P} LR(\alpha^{-1} \circ \pi) \quad \text{(Equation 93)}$$

It is well known that for a random permutation of q elements, the expected number of left-to-right maxima is H_q, the harmonic number, that is very close to the natural logarithm of q. For intuition, observe that for a random permutation α, the probability of α_i being $\max_{1 \le j \le i}\{\alpha_j\}$ is $1/i$. If a processor chooses its permutation schedule π at random, then the permutation $\alpha^{-1} \circ \pi$, for a given α is also a random permutation, only relabeled. It can be shown that the work of algorithm AW for randomly chosen permutations is, with high probability:

$$S \le P^2 + \frac{N}{P} \sum_{k-1}^{P} H_P = P^2 + \frac{N}{P} O(P \log P) = P^2 + O(N \log P)$$

In particular, we achieve robustness (with high probability) for $P = \sqrt{N}$, in which case $S = O(N \log N)$. Our goal, however is determinism, and as we will see, it is also possible to achieve this bound without randomization.

The term "contention" was chosen to represent the potential overlap in processors completing the same work groups as measured by the number of left-to-right maxima. We define $Cont(\pi, \alpha)$, the "contention of π with respect to α" to be $LR(\alpha^{-1} \circ \pi)$, and similarly $Cont(\Psi, \alpha) \equiv \sum_{\pi \in \Psi} Cont(\pi, \alpha) = LR(\alpha^{-1} \circ \Psi)$.

We can now evaluate the performance of algorithm AW in terms of the maximum contention for a set of permutations Ψ that is defined as $Cont(\Psi) = \max_{\alpha}\{Cont(\Psi, \alpha)\}$.

Lemma 3.5.3 Algorithm AW with P processors using permutation schedules $\Psi = \{\pi^1, \ldots, \pi^P\}$ solves the *Write-All* problem of size N ($P \leq N$) in the asynchronous model with work $S = O(P^2 + \frac{N}{P}Cont(\Psi))$.

Proof: We obtain S by maximizing the work of a particular execution in Equation 93 over all possible completion schedules α using Lemma 3.5.2:

$$
\begin{aligned}
S &\leq \max_{\alpha}\{S_{\alpha}\} &&= \max_{\alpha}\{P^2 + \frac{N}{P}\sum_{\pi^k \in \Psi} LR(\alpha^{-1} \circ \pi^k)\} \\
&= P^2 + \frac{N}{P}\max_{\alpha}\{LR(\alpha^{-1} \circ \Psi)\} &&= P^2 + \frac{N}{P}\max_{\alpha^{-1}}\{Cont(\Psi, \alpha)\} \\
&= P^2 + \frac{N}{P}Cont(\Psi). &&
\end{aligned}
$$
∎

It can be shown that for any P, there exists a set of P permutations $\Psi = \{\pi^1, \ldots, \pi^P\}$ over $[P]$ such that $Cont(\Psi) \leq 2P \cdot H_P = O(P \log P)$. Moreover, such set can be deterministically constructed. When so equipped, the work of algorithm AW is characterized in the following result:

Theorem 3.5.4 Algorithm AW with P processors using a set of permutation Ψ with $Cont(\Psi) = O(P \log P)$ solves the *Write-All* problem of size N ($P \leq N$) in the asynchronous model with work $S = O(P^2 + N \log P)$; when $P = \sqrt{N}$, the algorithm is robust.

Unfortunately, the algorithm is not very efficient for the full range of processors. In the next section we describe a deterministic algorithm that uses the basic strategy of algorithm AW as a subroutine, and that is polynomially robust for $P = N$.

3.5.2 Algorithm AW^T and Generalized Progress Trees

We present an algorithm that uses *generalized progress trees* for detection of unfinished work in the style of the local paradigm, and that uses permutation schedules to select potential work in the style of the hashed paradigm. The data structures of the algorithm can be parameterized, so that its work is $S = N^{1+\varepsilon}$ for $P = N$, and for any $\varepsilon > 0$.

In algorithm X, processors traverse the work elements in the order determined by the processors' PIDs and the structure of the progress tree. At each internal node of the tree, a processor chooses between the two children based on whether any of the children are not "done", and based on the bit in that processor's PID corresponding to the depth of the node. This bit can be interpreted as a permutation of the two children. When a processor arrives at a node, it uses one of the two permutations to choose the order of the progress tree traversal. The choice of the permutation is based on the bit in the binary expansion of the processor's PID in position corresponding to the depth of the node.

We now generalize this approach using a hybrid allocation paradigm that combines the progress tree of algorithm X with the permutation processor schedules of algorithm AW. We call the resulting generalization *algorithm AW^T*:

Definition of algorithm AW^T

Input: Shared array $x[1..N]$; $x[i] = 0$ for $1 \leq i \leq N$.

Output: Shared array $x[1..N]$; $x[i] = 1$ for $1 \leq i \leq N$.

Data structures: For the *Write-All* array of size N, the progress tree is a q-ary ordered tree of height h, thus $N = q^h$. Each interior node of the tree has a data bit, indicating whether the sub-tree rooted at the node is done (value 1) or not (value 0).

The progress tree is stored in a linear array $d[0..(qN-1)/(q-1) - 1]$ using the same technique as used to store a binary tree, with $d[0]$ being the root and the q children of the interior node $d[n]$ being the nodes $d[qn+1], d[qn+2], \ldots, d[qn+q]$. We define N_T, the size of the progress tree, to be $(qN-1)/(q-1)$. The space occupied by the tree is $O(N)$ The *Write-All* array elements are attached to the leaves of the progress tree, such that the leaf $d[n]$ is mapped to the *Write-All* array element $x[N - N_T + n + 1]$.

We use $P = N$ processors and we represent their PIDs in terms of their q-ary expansion. Such expansion requires $h = \log_q N$ of q-ary digits, and for the processor whose PID is p, we denote such expansion by $p_0 p_1 \ldots, p_{h-1}$. The q-ary expansions of PID is stored in the array $p[0..h - 1]$.

The order of traversals within the progress tree is determined by the set $\Psi = \{\pi^0, \pi^1 \ldots, \pi^{q-1}\}$ of permutations over $[q]$, i.e., over $\{1, 2 \ldots, q\}$.

Control flow: Each processor uses, at the node of depth i, the ith q-ary digit of its PID p to select the permutation π^{p_i}. The processor traverses the q subtrees in the order determined by π^{p_i}, but it visits a subtree only if the corresponding done bit is not set. The pseudocode for algorithm AW^T is given

```
00    forall processors PID=0..P − 1 parbegin
01       shared π₁,...,π_q  -- readonly set of permutations Ψ
02       shared d[0..(qN−1)/(q−1) − 1]  -- progress tree of size N_T
03       private n init = 0  -- current node index, begin at the root
04       private i init = 0  -- current depth in the tree
05       AWT(n, i)
06    parend.

10    procedure AWT(  -- Recursive progress tree traversal
11                    n,  -- current node index
12                    i)  -- depth of the current node
13       private p[0..d − 1] const = PID_(q)  -- d digits of q-ary expansion of PID
14       if d[n] = 0  -- any work to be done here?
15       then  -- current node is NOT done – still work left
16         if i = h       -- is n a leaf?
17         then d[n] := 1; x[N − N_T + n + 1] := 1  -- Perform work on the leaf
18         else  -- not a leaf – visit subtrees
19           for j = 1 . . q do  -- visit subtrees in the order of π^{p[i]}
20               AWT(d[qn + π_j^{p[i]}], i + 1)  -- visit subtree in the j-th position of π^{p[i]}
21           od
22       fi fi
23    end.
```

Figure 3.20   A high level view of the algorithm AW^T.

in Figure 3.20 in terms of the recursive procedure AWT (lines 10-23) that is executed in parallel by all processors.

Analysis of algorithm AW^T

It is not difficult to see that this algorithm solves the *Write-All* problem since, as in algorithm X (see Lemma 3.4.6), a processor leaves a subtree only when there is no work left to be done. In particular, if only a single processor is active, it will traverse the entire tree in search of work. We now sketch the analysis of work S for algorithm AW^T.

Let S_P be the work of algorithm AW^T with P processors using the progress tree with P leaves. We are going to calculate S_P using a recurrence, similarly to the analysis of algorithm X. At each level of the progress tree, the work of algorithm AW^T is also accounted for in the same way as in the analysis leading to Equation 92. More specifically, at depth 1 of the progress tree all processors will traverse the q nodes in search of work. This contributes the quantity $P \cdot q$ to S_P. At depth 1 and below the processors use only their q-ary digits $p[1..d−1]$ (line 20 of Figure 3.20). There are q groups of P/q processors such that their

PIDs differ only in the first q-ary digit. The work of such a group of processors in traversing any of the subtrees with roots at depth 1 of the progress tree is at most $S_{P/q}$. Whether or not at least one processor in such a group traverses and completes a subtree and marks it done is determined by the contention of the set of permutations Ψ used by the algorithm.

Thus we have the following recurrence: $S_P \leq P \cdot q + S_{P/q} \cdot Cont(\Psi)$. The solution to the recurrence is (the sum is a geometric series):

$$S_P \leq q \cdot P \sum_{k=0}^{\log_q P} \left(\frac{Cont(\Psi)}{q}\right)^k \leq 2q \cdot P \left(\frac{Cont(\Psi)}{q}\right)^{\log_q P}$$
$$= O\left(q \cdot P^{\log_q Cont(\Psi)}\right)$$

To solve the *Write-All* problem for $N > P$, we use the algorithm $\lceil N/P \rceil$ times and get the following work bound:

Lemma 3.5.5 Algorithm AW^T with P processors solves the *Write-All* problem of size N $(P \leq N)$ using a q-ary progress tree and a set Ψ of q permutations on $[q]$ in the asynchronous model with work $S = O(q N \cdot P^{\log_q Cont(\Psi)-1})$.

We can obtain algorithm X with $P = N$ from algorithm AW^T by choosing $q = 2$ and $\Psi = \{(1\ 2), (2\ 1)\}$. It is easy to calculate that $Cont(\Psi) = 3$, and so for algorithm X we have $S = O(2N \cdot P^{\log_2 3 - 1}) = O(N \cdot P^{\log \frac{3}{2}})$, as expected.

It turns out that algorithm AW^T can be parameterized so that it is not only polynomially robust, but it can be made more efficient (asymptotically) than any other polynomial algorithm:

Theorem 3.5.6 For any $\varepsilon < 1$, there exist q and Ψ such that algorithm AW^T with P processors using q-ary trees and permutations in Ψ is a polynomially robust algorithm that solves the *Write-All* problem of size N $(P = N)$ in the asynchronous model with work $S \leq O(N \cdot P^\varepsilon)$.

Proof: We begin by choosing Ψ such that $Cont(\Psi) \leq cq \log_2 q)$ where c is a small constant. As we have indicated, such Ψ exist and can be constructed (see bibliographic notes). Since q is a parameter that does not depend on P, even a brute force approach that computes contention for all possible Ψ is acceptable (but not practical for larger q). By substituting $cq \log q$ for $Cont(\Psi)$ in Lemma 3.5.5 we get:

$$S = O(q N \cdot P^{\log_q Cont(\Psi)-1}) \qquad = O(q N \cdot P^{\log_q(cq \log_2 q)-1})$$
$$= O(q N \cdot P^{\log_q q-1} \cdot P^{\log_q(\log_2 q^c)}) \qquad = O(q N \cdot P^{\log_q(\log_2 q^c)}).$$

Since $\lim_{q \to \infty} \log_q(\log_2 q^c) = 0$ one can find q such that $\log_q(\log_2 q^c) < \varepsilon$ for any $\varepsilon > 0$. Of course, for large q the algorithm is not very practical. ∎

PID	Schedule Ψ				Coset α ∘ Ψ for α = (4 3 1 2)				Number of left-to-right maxima
	1	2	3	4					
1	1	2	3	4	4	3	1	2	1
2	2	4	1	3	3	2	4	1	2
3	3	1	4	2	1	4	2	3	2
4	4	3	2	1	2	1	3	4	3
									Total: 8

Table 3.1 Processor schedules for algorithm Y with $m = 5$.

3.5.3 The Heuristic Algorithm Y

One of the disadvantages of deterministic hashed allocation paradigm algorithms is that the processor schedules may be difficult to compute on-line. In this section we propose a heuristic, called *algorithm Y*, for derandomizing algorithm AW such that the processor schedules are trivial to compute. The analysis of the algorithm is stated in terms of a conjecture which contains an interesting connection between multiprocessor scheduling, combinatorics and group theory.

Algorithm Y uses $P = \sqrt{N}$ processors for inputs of size N. We chose the smallest prime m such that $P < m$. Primes are sufficiently dense, so that there is at least one prime between P and $2P$, and the complexity of the algorithm will not be distorted when P is padded so that $P + 1 = m$ is a prime. We construct the multiplication table for the numbers $1, 2, \ldots m - 1$ modulo m. It is not difficult to show that each row of this table is a permutation of $\{1, 2, \ldots m - 1\}$. Furthermore, such set of permutations together with permutation composition is itself a group.

In algorithm Y, a processor with PID i uses the i-th permutation as its schedule (see an example of such schedule in Table 3.1).

Note that the table need not be pre-computed, as any item can be computed directly by any processor with the knowledge of its PID, and the number of work elements w it has processed thus far as $(PID \cdot w) \bmod m$. A detailed pseudo-code for the deterministic algorithm Y is given in Figure 3.21.

We conjecture that the worst case work of this deterministic algorithm is no worse than the expected work of the randomized algorithm AW. We have performed exhaustive experimental analysis for moderate values of m and all cases it resulted in the work being is $O(N \log N)$. This is the same as the expected work using random permutations.

```
01 forall processors PID = 1..P = √N parbegin
02     -- The x[1..N] array is viewed as divided into √N work groups
03     -- of N/P = √N elements in each: x[1..√N], x[1 + √N..2√N], etc.
04     shared x[1..N];          -- shared memory
05     shared done[1..P];       -- group done markers
06     private w init = 0;      -- groups done by each processor
07     private k;               -- next work group number to examine

08     while w ≠ P do -- While not all P = √N groups done
09         k := (PID · w) mod m -- current workgroup number
10         if not done[k] -- group is not marked finished
11         then for i = 1..√N = N/P do -- perform sequential work on the group
12             x[(w − 1)√N + i] := 1;
13             od
14             done[k] := true -- mark workgroup as finished
15         fi
16         w := w + 1; -- advance processor's groups done counter
17     od
18 parend.
```

Figure 3.21   A detailed view of the deterministic algorithm Y.

The P permutations that are computed by the processors constitute a group. We call the set of the permutations and the corresponding group Ψ. From Lemma 3.5.3, $S_Y = O(P^2 + \frac{N}{P} Cont(\Psi)) = O(N + \sqrt{N} \cdot Cont(\Psi))$. From the definition of contention in terms of left-to-right maxima in Section 3.5.1, $Cont(\Psi, \alpha)$ for any α is the same as $Cont(\alpha^{-1} \circ \Psi, e)$, where e is the identity permutation. Of course $\alpha^{-1} \circ \Psi$ is a left coset of Ψ, and $Cont(\alpha^{-1} \circ \Psi, e) = LR(\alpha^{-1} \circ \Psi)$ (see an example in Table 3.1).

Thus, to show that the worst case work of algorithm Y is $O(N \log N)$, it is sufficient to show that $Cont(\Psi) = O(P \log P) = O(\sqrt{N} \cdot \log N)$. This problem is restated in group-theoretic terms:

Given a prime m, consider the group $G = \langle \{1, 2, \ldots, m - 1\}, \bullet \pmod{m} \rangle$. The multiplication table for G, when the rows of the table are interpreted as permutations of $\{1, \ldots, m - 1\}$, is a group K of order $m - 1$, a subset of the symmetric group S_{m-1}.

Conjecture 3.5.7 For each $\alpha \in S_{m-1}$, the sum of the number of left-to-right maxima for all elements of the coset $\alpha \circ K$, is $O(m \log m)$.

We now can state the following for algorithm Y:

Theorem 3.5.8 If Conjecture 3.5.7 holds then algorithm Y solves the *Write-All* problem of size N using $P = \sqrt{N}$ processors and work $S = O(N \log N)$.

3.6   CONTROLLING CONCURRENCY

Among the key lower bound results for the *Write-All* problem is the fact that no efficient fault-tolerant CREW PRAM *Write-All* algorithms exist — if the adversary is dynamic then any P-processor solution for the *Write-All* problem of size N will have (deterministic) work $\Omega(N \cdot P)$. Thus memory access concurrency is necessary to combine efficiency and fault-tolerance. However, while most solutions for the *Write-All* problem indeed make heavy use of concurrency, the goal of minimizing concurrent access to shared memory is attainable for the models with stop failures (and naturally extended to synchronous restarts).

3.6.1   Minimizing Concurrency: Processor Priority Trees

We now present a *Write-All* algorithm in which we bound the *total amount of concurrency* used in terms of the *number of dynamic processor faults* of the actual algorithm run. The algorithm is an extension of algorithm W and its key new ingredient is the organization of all processors that need to access a common memory location into a *processor priority tree* (PPT).

In the rest of our discussion we assume that T is a memory location that needs to be accessed by $p \leq P$ processors simultaneously. We first concentrate on concurrent writes and treat concurrent reads in the next section.

A *PPT* is a binary tree whose nodes are associated with processors based on a processor numbering. All levels of the tree but the last are full and the leaves of the last level are packed to the left. PPT nodes are numbered from 1 to p in a breadth-first left-to-right fashion where the parent of the ith node has index $\lfloor i/2 \rfloor$ and its left/right children have indices $2i$ and $2i + 1$, respectively. Processors are also numbered from 1 to p and the i-th processor is associated with the i-th node.

Priorities are assigned to the processors based on the level they are at. The root has the highest priority and priorities decrease according to the distance from the root. Processors at the same level of the tree have the same priority, which is lower than that of their parents. See Figure 3.22 for an example of a PPT with $p = 12$ (dashed boxes represent "missing" processors).

Processor priorities are used to determine when a processor can write to the common memory location T. All the processors with the same priority attempt to write to T concurrently but *only if higher priority processors have failed to do so*. To accomplish this the processors of a PPT concurrently execute algorithm CW, shown in Figure 3.23. Starting at the root (highest priority) and going down the tree one level at a time, the processors at each level first read T and

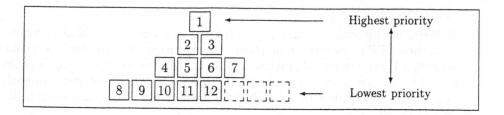

Figure 3.22 PPT (processor priority tree) for $p = 12$.

then concurrently update it iff it contains an old value. This implies that if level i processors effect the write, *all* processors at higher levels must have failed.

Whereas unrestricted concurrent writes by $p \leq P$ processors take only one step to update T, a PPT requires as many steps as there are levels in the tree, i.e., $O(\log p)$. The following lemma is instrumental in bounding the write concurrency:

Lemma 3.6.1 If algorithm CW is executed in the presence of a failure pattern F, then its write concurrency ω is no more than the number of failures $|F|$.

Proof: From the description of algorithm CW it is clear that location T is updated by the processors of at most one level, say i. In this case all processors on levels $0, \ldots, i - 1$ must have failed. Since level j has 2^j processors the total number of processors on these levels is $\sum_{j=0}^{i-1} 2^j = 2^i - 1$ and hence $|F| \geq 2^i - 1$. On the other hand, level i has at most 2^i live processors and hence $\omega \leq 2^i - 1$. The lemma follows by combining the two inequalities. ∎

```
01 forall processors ID = 1..p parbegin
02     -- Processors write a new value to location T as follows
03     for i = 0 .. ⌊log p⌋ do  -- For each level i of processor priority tree
04         if 2^i ≤ ID < 2^{i+1} then  -- The processors at level i
05             READ location T
06             if T does not contain new value then
07                 WRITE new value to T
08         fi fi
09     od
10 parend.
```

Figure 3.23 Pseudocode for the controlled write algorithm CW.

Algorithm W_{CW}

A *Write-All* algorithm with controlled write concurrency is obtained by incorporating PPTs into the four phases of algorithm W. We call the result *algorithm W_{CW}*. In this algorithm, each concurrent write is replaced in these phases by an execution of algorithm CW. We allow $\lfloor \log P \rfloor + 1$ steps for each execution of algorithm CW, thus slowing down each iteration of algorithm W by a $O(\log P)$ factor.

PPTs are organized and maintained as follows. At the outset of the algorithm and at the beginning of each execution of phase W1 each processor forms a PPT by itself. As processors traverse bottom-up the trees used by algorithm W they may encounter processors coming from the sibling node. In this case the two PPTs are *merged* to produce a larger PPT at the common parent of the two nodes. To use Lemma 3.6.1 to bound the overall write concurrency of the algorithm, we must guarantee that a newly constructed PPT has no processors that have already been accounted for as dead in the above lemma. The dead processors are above the level that effected the write in each of the two PPTs being merged. The PPTs are *compacted* before merging to eliminate these processors.

To compact and merge two PPTs, the processors of each PPT store, in the memory location they are to update, three extra values: (1) the size of the PPT, (2) the index of the level that effected the write and (3) a time-stamp, along with the new value to be stored in this location. A time-stamp in this context is just a sequence number that need not exceed N (as in Section 3.3). Since there can be at most P processors, $O(\log N) + O(\log N) + O(\log P) + O(\log \log P) = O(\log N)$ bits of information need to be stored for the new value, the time-stamp, the size of the tree and the level index.

After the $\log P$ steps of algorithm CW, the processors of the two PPTs about to be merged, read concurrently the information stored in the two memory locations the PPTs updated previously and compute the size of the resulting merged PPT. This size is the sum of the sizes of the two PPTs, less the number of the certifiably dead processors above the levels that effected the writes. By convention, when two PPTs are merged the processors of the left PPT are added to the bottom of the right PPT. This process is illustrated in Figure 3.24.

The time-stamp is needed so that processors can check whether the values they read are current (i.e., there is some PPT at the sibling node and merging has to take place) or stale. If i and j are the levels that effected the write in the left and right PPTs respectively, then the numbers of remaining live processors are no more than $P'_L = P_L - 2^i + 1$ and $P'_R = P_R - 2^j + 1$ respectively.

In Phase W2, the PPTs need to be *split* according to the divide-and-conquer strategy of the phase. This phase can be implemented without concurrent

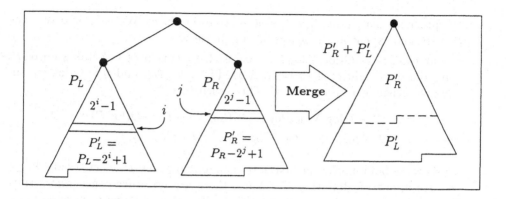

Figure 3.24　Compacting and merging two processor priority trees (PPTs).

writes (cf. Remark 3.4) and the only modification is that processors need to keep track of the size of the PPT they belong to and their position within this PPT. As processors traverse the progress tree top-down they move to the left or right child of the current node in proportion to the number of unvisited leaves in the left and right subtrees, as in the original algorithm W. This causes each PPT to be split in two at each step. If a PPT has k processors of which k' need to go left and the remaining $k - k'$ need to go right, then by convention the first k' processors of the PPT are allocated to the PPT that moves to the left child and the remaining $k - k'$ processors form the PPT that moves to the right child.

It is not difficult to see how algorithm W_{CW} is produced by systematic replacement of concurrent writes of algorithm W with algorithm CW, and by maintaining the necessary PPTs during the traversals. The following theorem describes its performance.

Theorem 3.6.2 Algorithm W_{CW} is a robust *Write-All* algorithm with $\omega \leq |F|$ and $S = O(N \log N \log P + P \log P \log^2 N / \log \log N)$, where $1 \leq P \leq N$.

Proof: The fault-tolerance and termination properties of the algorithm follow from the respective properties of algorithms W and CW, and from the construction we just replace each write step in algorithm W by a call to algorithm CW.

To show the bound on S we invoke Lemma 3.3.4 according to which the total number of block steps of algorithm W is at most $U + P \log U / \log \log U$, where U is the initial number of unvisited leaves. The number of available processor steps is $(U + P \log U / \log \log U)(t_t + t_l)$, where t_t is the time needed to traverse the processor enumeration and progress trees in phases W1, W2, and W4, and t_l is the time spent at the leaves during phase W3.

In our case, $t_t = O(\log N \log P)$ since each execution of CW takes $O(\log P)$ time and the height of the trees traversed is $O(\log N)$, and $t_l = O(\log P)$, the time of a single execution of CW. Thus, with $U = N$

$$
\begin{aligned}
S &= (N + P \log N / \log \log N)(O(\log N \log P) + O(\log P)) \\
&= O(N \log N \log P + P \log P \log^2 N / \log \log N).
\end{aligned}
$$

To show the bound on ω, we first note that contributions to ω occur only during the executions of algorithm CW since there are no other concurrent writes. If there were m executions of algorithm CW, then for any such execution i ($1 \leq i \leq m$), let ω_i denote its contribution to ω. Let $F_i \subseteq F$ be the failure pattern that consists of the failures of the processors above the PPT level that effected the write or of all the processors of the PPT if all failed during the execution.

From the proof of Lemma 3.6.1, $\omega_i \leq |F_i|$. Due to compaction of PPTs all processors named in F_i are eliminated at the end of execution of algorithm CW and hence can cause at most one concurrent write (contribute at most once to ω). By summing the contributions from all invocations of algorithm CW we conclude that the overall write concurrency is $\omega = \sum_{i=1}^{m} \omega_i \leq \sum_{i=1}^{m} |F_i| \leq |F|$. Note that failed processors that are below the level that completed the write in algorithm CW are not removed by compaction but they do not cause any concurrent writes. ∎

3.6.2 Controlling Read/Write Concurrency

Algorithm CW can be extended to control concurrent reads. The basic idea here is to replace concurrent reads in algorithm CW by simulated *broadcasts* through each PPT. The broadcasts are performed in an elaborate way that allows us to control read concurrency without degrading the performance of algorithm CW. It relies on the observation that each level of a PPT contains one more processor than all the levels above it. This allows us to use levels $0, \ldots, i - 1$ to broadcast to level i in constant time.

Algorithm CR/W

A high level view of this algorithm, that we call algorithm CR/W, is given in Figure 3.25. The broadcast takes place through a shared memory array B (see the figure). Such an array is used by each PPT so that processors can communicate with each other based on their positions in the PPT; $B[k]$ stores values read by the kth processor of the PPT. This allows processors

```
01 -- Code executed by each of the p processors in the PPT
02 Initialize B[ID] -- broadcast location for processor ID
03 for i = 0 ... ⌊log p⌋ do -- for each level i of the PPT
04     if 2^i ≤ ID < 2^{i+1} then -- if the processor is at level i
05        READ B[ID]
06        if B[ID] has not been updated then
07           READ (value, level) from T
08           if T contains some old value then
09              level := i -- level i effects the write
10              WRITE (newvalue, level) to T
11           else if 2^{level} ≤ ID − 2^i + 1 < 2^i then
12              ID := ID − 2^i + 1 -- replace the processor that was to update B[ID]
13     fi fi fi fi
14     if ID < 2^{i+1} and ID + 2^{i+1} ≤ p then -- if the processor's level is ≤ i
15        WRITE newvalue to B[ID + 2^{i+1}] -- broadcast to level i + 1
16     fi
17 od
```

Figure 3.25 High level view of algorithm CR/W for the controlled read/write. ID is the position of the processor in the PPT and *newvalue* is the value to be written.

to communicate without requiring them to know each other's identity. These arrays can be stored in a segment of memory of size P for all the PPTs (we leave this as an exercise for the reader).

Each processor on levels $0, \ldots, i-1$ is associated with exactly one processor on each of levels $i, i+1, \ldots$. Specifically, the jth processor of the PPT is responsible for broadcasting to the jth (in a left-to-right numbering) processor of each level below its own. The algorithm proceeds in $\lfloor \log p \rfloor + 1$ iterations that correspond to the PPT levels. At iteration i, each processor of level i reads its B location (line 5). If this location has not been updated, then the processor reads T directly (lines 6–7).

Since a PPT level has potentially more live processors than all the levels above it combined, there is in general at least one processor on each level that reads T since no processor at a higher level is assigned to it. If a level is full, this processor is the rightmost one (the root of the PPT for level 0). As long as there are no failures this is the only direct access to T. Concurrent accesses can occur only in the presence of failures. In such a case several processors on the same level may fail to receive values from processors at higher levels, in which case they will access T directly incurring concurrent reads.

A processor that needs to read T directly first checks whether it contains the value to be written (line 8) and then writes to it (line 10) if it does not. As can be seen from the figure, whenever processors update T they write not only the new value for T but also the index of the level that effected the write.

If a processor P_k that accesses T directly verifies that T has the correct value and the failed processor that should have broadcast to P_k is at or below the level that effected the write, then P_k assumes the position of the failed processor in the PPT (lines 11–12). This effectively moves failed processors towards the leaves of the PPT and plays an important role in establishing the bound on the read concurrency. Failed processors are moved towards the leaves only if they are not above the level that effects the write since processors above this level will be eliminated by compaction as was done in the previous section.

Algorithms CR1 and CR2

In addition to algorithm CR/W we use two simpler algorithms when all the processors of a PPT need to read a common memory location but no write is involved.

The first algorithm, referred to as algorithm $CR1$, is similar to algorithm CR/W but without the write step (lines 8–10). It is also simpler than algorithm CR/W in that processors that are found to have failed are pushed towards the bottom of the PPT irrespective of the level they are at. This algorithm is used for bottom-up traversals in algorithm W.

The second algorithm, referred to as algorithm $CR2$, uses a simple top-down broadcast through the PPT. Starting with the root each processor broadcasts to its two children; if a processor fails then its two children read T directly. Thus the processors of level i are responsible to broadcast only to processors of level $i + 1$. No processor movement takes place. This algorithm is used for top-down traversals in algorithm W.

It is not difficult to see that each of the algorithms CR/W, $CR1$, and $CR2$ require $O(\log P)$ time for PPTs of at most P processors.

Algorithm $W_{CR/W}$

Incorporating algorithms CR/W, $CR1$,and $CR2$ along with the techniques of PPT compaction and merging into algorithm W results in a *Write-All* algorithm that controls both read and write concurrency. We call this *algorithm $W_{CR/W}$*.

The description of the four phases of the algorithm follow.

In **phase W1** processors begin by forming single-processor PPTs. The objective is for processors to write to each internal node of the enumeration tree the sum of the values stored at its two children. For this they use algorithm

CR/W to store the new value, the size of the PPT, the index of the level that completed the write, and a time-stamp.

Upon completion of CR/W all PPTs are compacted. In order to merge PPTs the processors of each need to read the data stored at the enumeration tree node that is the sibling of the node they just updated. For this, algorithm $CR1$ is used and after it finishes PPTs are merged. At this point the processors of the merged PPTs know the value they need to write at the next level of the enumeration tree. This value is just the sum of the value written in CR/W and the value read in $CR1$. Therefore one invocation of algorithms CR/W and $CR1$ is needed for each level of the enumeration tree.

Phase W2 involves no concurrent writes and can be implemented using mostly local computations. Surviving processors traverse top-down the progress tree to allocate themselves to the unvisited leaves. The only global information needed at each level is the values stored at the two children of the current node of the progress tree. These values are read using two calls to algorithm $CR2$, one for each child. Using this information the processors of a PPT compute locally whether they need to go left or right. No compaction or merging is done in this phase. As PPTs move downwards they are split (as in phase W2 of algorithm W_{CW}).

In **phase W3** processors organize themselves into PPTs based on the information they gathered during the previous phase and proceed to write 1 to the locations that correspond to the leaf they reached. Each of these writes uses algorithm CR/W and is followed by compaction. No merging is involved.

Phase W4 initially uses the PPTs that resulted at the end of phase W3. The task to be performed is similar to that of phase W1. As before CR/W is used for writing followed by compaction and then one call to $CR1$, after which PPTs are merged.

The analysis of algorithm $W_{CR/W}$ is involved and we point the reader to references in bibliographic notes. Here we state the theorem that provides bounds on the performance of algorithm $W_{CR/W}$.

Theorem 3.6.3 Algorithm $W_{CR/W}$ is a robust *Write-All* algorithm with $S = O(N \log N \log P + P \log P \log^2 N / \log \log N)$, read concurrency $\rho \leq 7|F| \log N$, and write concurrency $\omega \leq |F|$, where $1 \leq P \leq N$.

Optimal algorithm $W_{CR/W}^{opt}$

By parameterizing the data structures of algorithm $W_{CR/W}$, we can make its work to be optimally $O(N)$. We call the result of the parameterization *algorithm* $W_{CR/W}^{opt}$. The main idea is to cluster the input data into groups of size $\log N \log P$ and using the progress tree with $N/\log N \log P$ leaves.

To show optimality we use the load balancing property of algorithm W shown in Lemma 3.3.2. This property guarantees that available processors are allocated evenly to the unvisited leaves in phase W2. Let U_i and P_i be the numbers of unvisited leaves and available processors, respectively, at the beginning of the ith iteration of the while loop of algorithm $W_{CR/W}$. By the balanced allocation property, if $U_i \geq P_i$, then at most one processor is allocated to each unvisited leaf.

In each iteration of the main loop, processors examine the overestimate of remaining processors P_i and the overestimate of the number of unvisited leaves U_i at the beginning of each iteration. If $U_i \geq P_i$ we are guaranteed that there will be at most one processor per leaf at the beginning of phase W3 so that there is no need to use algorithm CR/W and compaction. Instead processors go sequentially through the $\log N \log P$ elements of the leaf they reached spending $O(1)$ time for each element. If, on the other hand, $U_i < P_i$ several processors may be allocated to the same leaf and algorithm CR/W is used. The latter situation occurs infrequently enough that the algorithm becomes optimal for a certain range of processors, as we show below.

Theorem 3.6.4 Algorithm $W_{CR/W}^{opt}$ is a robust *Write-All* algorithm with $S = O(N + P\frac{\log^2 N \log^2 P}{\log \log N})$, write concurrency $\omega \leq |F|$, and read concurrency $\rho \leq 7|F|\log N$, where $1 \leq P \leq N$.

Proof: Let P_i be the (overestimate of the) number of live processors and U_i be the (overestimate of the) number of unvisited leaves at the beginning of the ith iteration. We divide the iterations into two cases:

Case 1: $U_i \geq P_i$. In this case phase W3 requires $O(\log N \log P)$ time, the same as the time to traverse the enumeration and progress trees. By *case 1* in the proof of Lemma 3.3.4 the number of block steps for all such iterations is at most U_0, where U_0 is the initial number of leaves. In this case $U_0 = N/\log N \log P$ and the total work for all such iterations is

$$S_1 = \frac{N}{\log N \log P} O(\log N \log P) = O(N).$$

Case 2: $U_i < P_i$. In this case all the processors could be allocated to the same leaf. Thus, in the worst case, $\log P$ time must be spent at each element of the leaf and since there are $\log N \log P$ elements per leaf the worst case time to update a leaf is $O(\log N \log^2 P)$. By *case 2* in the proof of Lemma 3.3.4 the number of block steps for all such iterations is at most $O(P\frac{\log N}{\log \log N})$. Hence the total work of all these iterations is

$$S_2 = O(P\tfrac{\log N}{\log \log N}) \, (O(\log N \log P) + O(\log N \log^2 P)) = O(P\tfrac{\log^2 N \log^2 P}{\log \log N}).$$

We must also account for any work performed by processors that fail in the middle of an iteration. There are at most $O(P)$ such block steps each costing $O(\log N \log^2 P)$ so that the total work in this case is $S_0 = O(P \log N \log^2 P)$. Combining this with the two cases, we have

$$S = S_0 + S_1 + S_2 = O\left(N + P\frac{\log^2 N \log^2 P}{\log \log N}\right).$$

The algorithm is optimal when we choose P so that the second term is $O(N)$. The bound on ω is obtained as before by noticing that whenever a PPT has more than one processor, the tree is compacted after the write to eliminate any processors that have caused concurrent writes. The bound on ρ is obtained as in Theorem 3.6.3. ∎

Remark 3.10 *A limit on reductions of memory access concurrency*: Our ability to further reduce memory access concurrency is eventually limited by the lower bound showing that no robust *Write-All* algorithm exists with write concurrency $\omega \leq |F|^\varepsilon$ for $0 \leq \varepsilon < 1$ (see Theorem 4.1.8). □

3.6.3 Controlling Concurrency with Uninitialized Memory

The algorithms controlling memory concurrency that we considered so far require that memory be initially clear. Here we incorporate algorithm CR/W into algorithm Z to obtain a *Write-All* algorithm with limited concurrency that dispenses with the requirement that memory be clear.

A problem that arises if we try to combine the two algorithms directly is that we can no longer guarantee good read and write concurrency. This stems from the fact that to achieve these bounds the PPTs that are built at the beginning of phase W1 must contain no processors that are known to have failed. This is easy to do in the algorithms considered so far since each PPT starts out with at most one processor. In algorithm Z, however, there can be several processors that are assigned to the same leaf of the enumeration tree and thus belong to the same PPT at the beginning of W1; this happens whenever $P > N_i$ (see Figure 3.13). The assignment of processors to such leaves is made based on the processor PIDs and since this does not take into account failed processors, the resulting PPTs may have dead processors that have already been accounted for in ω.

Algorithm $Z_{CR/W}$

We now describe algorithm $Z_{CR/W}$ that is able to control memory access concurrency even when the memory is not initially clear. The algorithm uses an enumeration tree with P leaves for all its iterations, so that each PPT will have at most one processor at the beginning of W1. To initialize this tree we note that phase W1 is a static phase in the sense that a given processor traverses the same path through the enumeration tree every time W1 is executed. In particular, since processors can not restart once they have failed, if a node of the enumeration tree is accessed at all, it must be accessed the first time W1 is executed. The consequence of this is that we do not need to clear the entire enumeration tree but only that portion that can be accessed during the first execution of W1. To achieve this, processors make an initial bottom-up traversal of the enumeration tree similar to the traversal of W1 (i.e., each processor traverses the same path it would traverse in W1) and clear the locations that they would access in W1. This process is carried out as follows.

Processors start at the leaves of the enumeration tree, with the ith processor at the ith leaf, so that each processor forms a PPT by itself. PPTs then traverse the tree bottom-up taking the same paths as in phase W1. The operation performed by the PPTs at each node they reach consists of clearing the node they are at using CR/W, PPT compaction, clearing the sibling node using CR/W, PPT compaction, reading the contents of the node they are at using CR1, and finally PPT merging. The reason for clearing the sibling node is that during phase W1 processors need to access the node they are at and its sibling and we need to make certain that this sibling will not contain garbage data. The reason for the remaining operations is to assist with merging. Essentially, this initialization phase is like W1 but processors clear the sibling nodes instead of summing. The cost of this initialization is $O(\log N \log P)$ since the enumeration tree is of height $O(\log N)$ and the time spent at each level is $O(\log P)$.

This algorithm that uses the P-leaf enumeration tree and that uses algorithm $W^{opt}_{CR/W}$ to clear progressively larger areas of memory has the performance bounds as follows:

Theorem 3.6.5 Algorithm $Z_{CR/W}$ with contaminated memory of size $O(P)$ is a robust *Write-All* algorithm with $S = O(N + P \log^2 P \log^3 N/(\log \log N)^2)$, read concurrency $\rho \leq 7|F| \log N$, and write concurrency $\omega \leq |F|$, where $1 \leq P \leq N$.

Proof: Algorithm $W^{opt}_{CR/W}$ uses clusters of size $\log N \log P$ and we choose $K_i = \log N \log P, i \geq 0$ as the parameters for algorithm Z (see Figure 3.13). Initially processors clear a memory area of size $K_0 = \log N \log P$ using algorithm CR/W; this costs $P \log N \log^2 P$.

Following this there are $\log N/(\log(\log N \log P)) - 1 = O(\log N/\log \log N)$ applications of algorithm $W^{opt}_{CR/W}$ where the ith application clears a memory area of size $N_i = (\log N \log P)^{i+1}$. This analysis is very similar to the analysis in

Theorem 3.3.8 and the work bound follows by the same method; the only difference is the different value for the K_i's and that the work of each iteration is given by Theorem 3.6.4. The bounds on ρ and ω are obtained as in the previous theorems in this section. ∎

3.6.4 Bounded Maximum Access

For the algorithms developed in the previous section, the cumulative read and write concurrencies are bounded, but during *some* time steps the read and write concurrency might still be as high as $\Theta(P)$ for large $|F|$. In this section, we describe algorithm W_{ave} that employs a general pipelining technique to limit the maximum *per step* concurrency in algorithm W.

Algorithm W_{ave} is constructed as a variant of algorithm W. As a first approach to limiting concurrency we note that phases W1, W2, and W4 of algorithm W involve traversal of trees of logarithmic depth with only one level of the trees being used at any given time. A solution that naturally suggests itself is to divide the processors into waves and have them move through the trees separately by introducing a time delay between the waves. If we choose the number of waves carefully it is possible to reduce the number of concurrent accesses without degrading the asymptotic work of the algorithm. In particular, since the trees are of height $\log N$ we can divide the processors into $\log N$ waves each of $P/\log N$ processors. During each of the phases W1, W2, and W4 we send the processors through the appropriate trees one wave at a time thus reducing the number of concurrent accesses to at most $P/\log N$ for any memory location. Since the values computed at the nodes of the trees during each phase will be correct only after the last wave of processors finishes, waves that finish earlier must wait for the last wave to arrive before beginning the next phase. This introduces a $O(\log N)$ *additive* overhead per phase, doubling the running time of each phase but not affecting the asymptotic efficiency of the algorithm.

For phases W2 and W4, it is not significant how we divide the processors into waves. However, phase W1 requires that processors be assigned to waves in a left to right fashion, i.e., the leftmost $\log N$ processors form the first wave, the next $\log N$ processors are in the second wave and so on. This is because phase W1 computes prefix sums and a processor must not reach a node of the processor enumeration tree before any processor with smaller PID.

This pipelining idea can be generalized by allowing a greater number of processor waves. In particular, for any $k \geq 1$ we can partition the processors into $\log^k N$ waves each of $P/\log^k N$ processors. Since there can only be $\log N$ active waves during any traversal, each phase will be slowed down by a factor of $\log^{k-1} N$. This yields the following result for algorithm W_{ave}:

Theorem 3.6.6 Algorithm W_{ave} parameterized with $\log N$ work elements at the leaves and with $\log^k N$ waves is a robust algorithm for the *Write-All* problem with $S = O(N \log^{k-1} N + P \log^{k+1} N / \log \log N)$ for any $k \geq 1$ and with at most $P / \log^k N$ concurrent accesses at any time for any memory location.

Remark 3.11 *Performance of algorithm W_{ave} with $\log N$ waves:* For $k = 1$ there is no asymptotic degradation in the efficiency of the algorithm as compared wth algorithm W. $\Box$

Even though the pipelining of processor waves reduces the number of concurrent accesses for each memory location, the algorithm still makes a lot of concurrent accesses overall. For example, for $k = 1$ and $P = N$ the algorithm makes $\Omega(\log N (\frac{N}{\log N} - 1)) = \Omega(N)$ concurrent writes when no processors fail since each wave makes $\frac{N}{\log N} - 1$ concurrent writes at the root and there are $\log N$ such waves.

The use of processor waves can be combined with the PPTs previous sections to yield an algorithm that uses *waves of priority trees* to control both the per step and the overall concurrency:

Theorem 3.6.7 Algorithm $W_{CR/W}^{opt}$ with pipelined PPTs is a robust *Write-All* algorithm with $S = O(N \log^{k-1} N + P \log^2 P \log^{k+1} N / \log \log N)$ for any $k \geq 1$, read concurrency $\rho \leq 7|F| \log N$, write concurrency $\omega \leq |F|$ and with at most $P / \log^k N$ concurrent accesses at any time for any memory location.

3.7   OPEN PROBLEMS

Algorithm W is the most efficient as of this writing algorithm for the model with stop-failures (and with synchronous restarts), but it is not known whether it is the best possible algorithm. If a better algorithm exists, finding one will be very challenging.

Algorithm X can be used in the fail-stop no-restart model, but its upper bound is known to be no better than $\Theta(N \log^2 N / \log \log N)$, i.e., it is is no better than the upper bound for algorithm W for the fail-stop no-restart model. However, since algorithm X is implemented using local allocation strategy and can be used in all models considered, it is important to understand its efficiency. In particular, what is the overhead ratio σ of algorithm X? Is it better than that of algorithm V that has $\sigma = O(\log^2 N)$?

The analysis of algorithm Y is still a matter of conjecture with only experimental results supporting it. We conjecture that it uses $O(N \log N)$ work (Section 3.5.3).

We have shown that it is possible to control memory access concurrency for failures without restarts using algorithm $W_{CR/W}$. Controlling memory access concurrency in the presence of restarts (which are detectable but not synchronous) or asynchrony is an open problem.

The major open problem for the case of undetectable restarts is whether there is a *polylogarithmically* robust *Write-All* solution, i.e., one with work $N \cdot \text{polylog}(N)$. Here the only known lower bound is $\Omega(N \log N)$ – we turn to lower bounds in the next chapter.

3.8   BIBLIOGRAPHIC NOTES

Algorithm W for *Write-All* problem in the fail-stop no-restart setting with omniscient on-line adversary is due to Kanellakis and Shvartsman [56]. Martel proved the tightest upper bound (Lemma 3.3.4) for algorithm W [83]. Kedem, Palem, Raghunathan and Spirakis developed a variation of algorithm W that has the same upper bound and that uses additional data structures to enable local optimizations [62]. Algorithms V for the fail-stop model with detectable restarts is due to Kanellakis and Shvartsman [57].

Algorithm Z solving the *Write-All* problem with contaminated (uninitialized) memory is due to Shvartsman [111]. The *Write-All* algorithms and simulations (e.g., [56, 62, 63, 110]) or the algorithms that can serve as *Write-All* solutions (e.g., the algorithms in [26, 87]) assume that a linear portion of shared memory is either cleared or initialized to some known values.

Algorithm E for static initial faults is due to Kanellakis, Michailidis and Shvartsman [54]. It can be shown, using the results of Beame, Kik and Kutylowski [16], that this algorithm is optimal.

Buss, Kanellakis, Ragde and Shvartsman [20] present algorithm X in the fail-stop model with restarts and asynchronous settings. The **action-recovery** notation and approach to structuring algorithms is discussed in depth by Schlichting and Schneider [108]. Buss and Ragde [20] also developed an optimal three-processor asynchronous algorithm for the *Write-All* problem. Although the idea of the algorithm is simple – two of the processors work on the array from its ends while the third from the middle – the details are non-trivial. It is not known whether optimal algorithms exist in the asynchronous model for larger numbers of processors. López-Ortiz [78] showed the best known lower bound of $S = \Omega(N \log^2 N / \log \log N)$ for algorithm X in the fail-stop no-restart model. In the asynchronous setting, several works discuss algorithmic primitives that can be adapted to serve as *Write-All* solutions. These can be found in the works of Cole and Zajicek [26] and Martel, Subramonian and Park [87]. These can have very efficient expected work solutions for off-line adversaries.

Algorithms AW and AW^T are really named after Anderson and Woll [9], who developed several efficient algorithms for the asynchronous parallel model. Anderson and Woll formulated the permutation-based approach to solving the *Write-All* problem, they developed the algorithms and showed the existence of the appropriate permutations that make the work of algorithm AW^T to be $O(N^{1+\varepsilon})$ for any $\varepsilon > 0$. Naor and Roth [91] also showed how to construct such suitable permutations. Left-to-right (or right-to-left) maxima of permutations play an important role in algorithms based on the approach developed by Anderson and Woll. The basic facts dealing with such maxima are covered by Knuth [64]. Kanellakis and Shvartsman [59] proposed algorithm Y as a determinization of algorithm AW. The algorithm depends on primes being sufficiently dense – see the discussion by Cormen, Leiserson and Rivest in [30, Sec. 33.8], and the statement of the open problem involves basic facts from group facts, e.g., see a standard text by Birkhoff and MacLane [18].

Algorithms controlling concurrent memory access, including $W_{CR/W}$, the related optimality results and the pipelining techniques are due to Kanellakis, Michailidis and Shvartsman [54]. The reader is encouraged to consult this reference for a more detailed presentation of the results.

4

LOWER BOUNDS, SNAPSHOTS AND APPROXIMATION

I N SEARCH of efficient fault-tolerant algorithms, it is important to also consider the lower bounds for relevant problems. The efficiency achieved by a fault-tolerant *Write-All* algorithm in a particular parallel model needs to be contrasted with the lower bound results for the model. If there is a gap between the upper and lower bounds results, then there is a possibility of developing better algorithms.

In Chapter 3 we presented several fault-tolerant and efficient solutions for the *Write-All* problem. Some algorithms can be parameterized so that their work becomes optimal (linear in N), when the initial number of processors is P is smaller than N. To achieve maximum speed-up, it is also important to consider the full range of processors, that is the case of $N = P$. Can optimal *Write-All* solutions be developed for $P = N$? In this chapter this question is answered in the negative — no optimal N-processor solutions exist for the *Write-All* problem of size N. For any algorithm that implements an N-processor solution for the *Write-All* problem, an omniscient adversary can construct a failure pattern that will cause the algorithm to perform a *superlinear* in N number of processing steps.

Even if we endow the processors with the ability to take *instant memory snapshots*, i.e., the ability to read and locally process the entire shared memory at unit cost, then optimality is still not achievable. The best possible work in this case is $\Theta(N \log N / \log \log N)$, and this work is indeed achievable in the model.

We also show that concurrent writes are necessary for the existence of efficient synchronous algorithms – concurrent writes are an important source of redundancy in our approach. When concurrent writes are not allowed, e.g., as in the CREW model, the lower bound on work is quadratic.

The lower bound results in this chapter apply to the worst case work of the deterministic algorithms, and the expected work of deterministic and randomized algorithms that are subject to omniscient on-line adversaries.

CHAPTER 4

4.1 LOWER BOUNDS FOR SHARED MEMORY MODELS

In this section we present the lower bound results for CRCW and CREW shared memory models. These are the "standard" PRAM models in which any processor can read from or write to a single memory location in unit time.

It is not difficult to see that any solution for the *Write-All* problem requires $\Omega(N)$ time in the worst case. This linear lower bound is due to a very simple adversary that causes failures of all but one processor at the beginning of the computation. The sole surviving processor will need to take at least N steps in initializing the *Write-All* array.

Of course when the initial number of processors $P = N$ and when large numbers of processors are active during the computation the *Write-All* algorithm will terminate much faster, but optimal performance cannot be achieved even when there are no failures.

4.1.1 A Logarithmic Time Lower Bound

We now show that given any N-processor CRCW PRAM algorithm for the *Write-All* problem of size N, the adversary can force fail-stop (no restart) errors that result in $\Omega(N \log N)$ steps being performed. Moreover, at least a logarithmic number of parallel steps will be taken in any execution of any *Write-All* algorithm in the CRCW model.

We start with several definitions. Let A be any N-processor *Write-All* algorithm. Let $M_1, M_2, \ldots$ be the shared memory locations accessible to the processors. Without loss of generality, let the first N shared memory locations store the *Write-All* array $x[1..N]$.

We define E_0 to be the failure-free execution of A. We next define several executions of algorithm A that are determined by specific adversary strategies in which the processors are stopped following the read cycles and prior to the write cycles.

We define N different executions E_i of A for $1 \leq i \leq N$ as follows. At step $t = 1$ the adversary stops all processors that would have written into *Write-All* array location $x[i]$ during the write cycle of this step. At step $t > 1$ the adversary stops any processor with PID p if this is the first step in which the state of processor p in E_i becomes different from its state in E_0 at the same step. (It is possible that the adversary fails all processors.)

We say that execution index i $(1 \leq i \leq N)$ *affects* processor p by step t if processor p fails at or before the step t in E_i.

We define $\alpha(i, p, t) = \begin{cases} 1 & \text{if } i \text{ affects } p \text{ by step } t \\ 0 & \text{otherwise} \end{cases}$

We define $\alpha_t = \max_p \sum_{i=1}^{N} \alpha(i, p, t)$ to denote the maximum number of indices that can affect a processor at or before step t. From the construction of E_i, $\alpha_1 = 1$.

Lemma 4.1.1 $\alpha_t \leq 2^{t-1}$ for $t \geq 1$.

Proof: We will say that the execution index i *affects* a shared memory location M_m at step $t \geq 2$ if the contents of M_m at the end of step t are different in E_0 and E_i. For $t = 1$ we declare that in E_i the memory location M_i (i.e., $x[i]$) is affected.

Let $\beta(i, m, t) = \begin{cases} 1 & \text{if } t = 1 \text{ and } 1 \leq m \leq N, \text{i.e., } M_m \text{ stores } x[m] \\ 1 & \text{if } t \geq 2 \text{ and } i \text{ affects } M_m \text{ by step } t \\ 0 & \text{otherwise} \end{cases}$

Let $\beta_t = \max_m \sum_{i=1}^{N} \beta(i, m, t)$. Thus $\beta_1 = 1$.

We first show that $\alpha_t \leq \beta_{t-1} + \alpha_{t-1}$ for $t \geq 2$. (Recurrence 117.1)

Processors are affected by reading. Let PID p read memory location M_m at step t. If PID p is dead at step $t \geq 2$, then it is affected by all indices that affect it by step $t - 1$.

If PID p is alive at the start of step t, it has not yet been affected and therefore it will read the same location that it reads in E_0, say M_m.

Thus $\sum_{i=1}^{N} \alpha(i, p, t) \leq \sum_{i=1}^{N} \alpha(i, p, t - 1) + \sum_{i=1}^{N} \beta(i, m, t - 1)$.

Therefore, $\alpha_t \leq \alpha_{t-1} + \beta_{t-1}$. This proves Recurrence 117.1.

Memory locations are affected by processors not writing. At $t \geq 2$, if the location M_m is written into by some processor in E_i, then the location is not affected by the index i. This is because the writing processor has not yet been affected and therefore will write the same value as in E_0.

We next show that $\beta_t \leq \alpha_{t-1} + \beta_{t-1}$ for $t \geq 2$. (Recurrence 117.2)

If some M_m is *not* written into in E_0, then the adversary will allow for it to be written into in any E_i. In this case $\sum_{i=1}^{N} \beta(i, m, t) = \sum_{i=1}^{N} \beta(i, m, t-1) \leq \beta_{t-1}$.

If M_m *is* written into in E_0, then for M_m to be affected at t, every processor that writes into it at t in E_0 must have failed. Therefore, M_m is affected by the *intersection* of the sets of indices affecting each of these processors.

Thus, $\sum_{i=1}^{N} \beta(i, m, t) \leq \alpha_t$, and by using Recurrence 117.1, $\sum_{i=1}^{N} \beta(i, m, t) \leq \alpha_{t-1} + \beta_{t-1}$. Therefore, $\beta_t \leq \alpha_{t-1} + \beta_{t-1}$, proving Recurrence 117.2.

The theorem follows from the solution to Recurrences 117.1 and 117.2 given the base cases $\alpha_1 = 1$ and $\beta_1 = 1$ ∎

Lemma 4.1.2 The execution E_0 takes $\Omega(\log N)$ steps.

Proof: Given a specific PID p, consider the step $t = \log N$ in all executions E_e ($1 \leq e \leq N$). From Lemma 4.1.1, $\sum_{e=1}^{N} \alpha(e, p, t) \leq \alpha_t \leq 2^{t-1} = N/2$. Therefore, for some E_e we have that $\alpha(e, p, t) = 0$. In other words, at the beginning of step $t = \log N$ the processor with PID p is alive and for all steps prior to t its state in E_e is the same as its state in E_0. Note that E_e could not have possibly terminated since termination requires that at least one processor writes to location $x[e]$, but all such processors are prevented from doing so by the adversary. Therefore execution E_0 takes at least as long as E_e, i.e., at least $\log N$ steps.   ∎

Theorem 4.1.3 Any N-processor *Write-All* algorithm on inputs of size N and in the absence of failures takes time $\Omega(\log N)$ and has $S = \Omega(N \log N)$.

Proof: The result follows as a consequence of Lemma 4.1.2.   ∎

These failure-free bounds have matching upper bounds. Any *Write-All* algorithm can be prefixed by a stage in which the processors, after initializing the *Write-All* array to 1, perform a standard logarithmic time summation. If the sum of the array elements is N, the algorithm terminates having performed $\Theta(N \log N)$ work.

Corollary 4.1.4 Any N-processor *Write-All* algorithm on inputs of size N takes time $\Omega(\log N)$.

4.1.2 Concurrency vs. Redundancy

The choice of CRCW (concurrent read, concurrent write) model that is used as the basis for much of this work is not accidental. In the next section we show that the use of CRCW is justified because of a lower bound that shows that the CREW (concurrent read, exclusive write) model does not admit synchronous fault-tolerant efficient algorithms. Thus both the redundancy provided by the presence of multiple processors and the concurrency due to multiple processors writing to the same memory location are necessary to combine fault-tolerance and efficiency.

A lower bound for CREW PRAM

In the absence of failures, it is possible to simulate a P-processor CRCW PRAM on a P-processor CREW or EREW PRAM with only a factor of $O(\log P)$ more parallel work. We now show that a more pronounced distinction exists between CRCW and CREW PRAMs (and thus also EREW PRAMs) when the processors are subject to failures.

Theorem 4.1.5 Given any (deterministic or randomized) N-processor CREW PRAM algorithm that solves the *Write-All* problem of size N, an adversary can force fail-stop errors that result in $\Omega(N^2)$ work steps being performed by the algorithm.

Proof: To prove this, we first define an auxiliary *Write-One* problem as follows: *Given a scalar variable s whose value is initially 0, set this variable to 1.*

Let B be the most efficient asymptotically CREW algorithm that solves the *Write-One*. Such an algorithm is no more efficient asymptotically than the algorithm given below that utilizes an *oracle* to predict the best selection of a processor that is chosen to write the value 1 exclusively:

```
forall processors PID=1..N parbegin
    shared integer s;
    while s = 0 do
            if PID = Oracle() then s := 1 fi
    od
parend.
```

To exhibit the worst case behavior the adversary fails the processor that was selected by the *Oracle*() to perform the exclusive write until a single processor remains. The last remaining processor is then allowed to write 1 by the adversary. The loop body is executed N times. The first iteration is completed by $N - 1$ processors. In general, the i-th iteration for $1 \le i < N$ is completed by $N - i$ processors. The final iteration is completed by the single remaining processor. Therefore $S \ge 1 + \sum_{i=1}^{N-1}(N - i) = \Omega(N^2)$.

Finally, it can be shown by a simple reduction to the *Write-One* problem that any N-processor CREW solution to the *Write-All* problem has the worst case of $S = \Omega(N^2)$. ∎

Remark 4.1 *Lower bound for* CREW *with restarts:* The lower bound above applies also to models with restarts. It is not difficult to see that here the situation is even worse – the adversary can cause any algorithm not to terminate by repeatedly stopping and then restarting the designated writers. □

A lower bound for write concurrency

The lower bound for the CREW and EREW models presented in the previous section shows that having redundant computing resources is not sufficient to combine fault-tolerance and efficiency. Both redundancy and memory access concurrency are necessary.

Even though CREW and EREW models do not admit efficient solutions for the *Write-All* problem, we still would like control memory access concurrency in the CRCW model.

In Section 2.3.2 we defined measures ρ and ω that gauge the concurrent memory accesses of a computation. In Section 3.6.2 we presented a *Write-All* algorithm with $\omega \leq |F|$. It is interesting to consider whether there is a polylogarithmically robust algorithm with even smaller ω. Here we show that this is not the case for a large class of functions of $|F|$.

Specifically, we show that there is no robust algorithm for the *Write-All* problem with concurrency $\omega \leq |F|^\varepsilon$ for $0 \leq \varepsilon < 1$.

For this we again consider a simpler *Write-One* problem which involves P processors and a single memory location. The objective is to write 1 into the memory location subject to faults determined by an on-line adversary. The adversary will try to maximize the work while the algorithm will try to minimize it by appropriately scheduling the available processors, subject to the constraint that only up to $|F|^\varepsilon$ concurrent writes are permitted.

We allow algorithms that can sense when the location has been written by employing an *oracle*, thus having no need to certify the write. Algorithms without such power can not perform better than oracle algorithms and hence the lower bound applies to them as well. This is because given a non-oracle algorithm A there is an oracle algorithm B that mimics A up to the point where A writes to memory. At this point B stops while A has to continue in order to certify the write thus incurring additional work.

Since not all processors can write concurrently the algorithm will need to form "waves" of processors. The adversary will fail each wave (but the last) right before the processors in the wave write to the memory. In this way the adversary prolongs the conclusion of the process until the very last step while charging each processor for as many steps as possible. As the following lemma shows, the algorithm's best answer to this strategy is to use a greedy approach, that is, assign to each wave as many processors as possible within the constraints.

Lemma 4.1.6 The work of *Write-One* algorithms that are subject to a write concurrency constraint is minimized when processors are allocated greedily.

Proof: Let $\mathcal{W}_1, \mathcal{W}_2, \ldots, \mathcal{W}_k$ be the processor waves and let S be the total work of the algorithm. Assuming that the original schedule is not greedy, let $\mathcal{W}_i$, $1 \leq i < k$ be the first wave that contains fewer processors than are allowed by the write concurrency constraint, e.g., $|F|^\varepsilon$. By reassigning a processor from $\mathcal{W}_j$ to $\mathcal{W}_i$ for some $i < j \leq k$ we obtain a schedule with work $S' = S - (j - i) < S$ and hence the original non-greedy schedule is not optimal. ∎

We can now show the following:

Lemma 4.1.7 There is no polylogarithmically robust algorithm for the *Write-One* problem with write concurrency $\omega \leq |F|^\varepsilon$, for $0 \leq \varepsilon < 1$.

Proof: Since $|F| \leq P$, where P is the number of initial processors, it suffices to show that the bound holds for the broader class of *Write-One* algorithms that allow up to P^ε concurrent writes per step. As follows from Lemma 4.1.6, P^ε processors should be allocated to each wave and hence there will be $P/P^\varepsilon = P^{1-\varepsilon}$ steps (for simplicity we assume that P is a multiple of P^ε). Then the work of the algorithm is $\sum_{i=1}^{P^{1-\varepsilon}} (P - iP^\varepsilon) + P^\varepsilon > \frac{P^{2-\varepsilon}}{2} - \frac{P}{2} = \Omega(P^{2-\varepsilon})$. ∎

A similar result for the *Write-All* problem follows from the lemma:

Theorem 4.1.8 There is no polylogarithmically robust algorithm for the *Write-All* problem with write concurrency $\omega \leq |F|^\varepsilon$, for $0 \leq \varepsilon < 1$.

Proof: Consider a *Write-All* algorithm for instances of size N with P processors. The adversary picks an array location and fails only processors that attempt to write to it according to the strategy outlined earlier in this section. According to Lemma 4.1.7, the work of the algorithm will be $\Omega(P^{2-\varepsilon})$. ∎

4.2 LOWER BOUNDS WITH MEMORY SNAPSHOTS

We now consider lower bounds for stronger parallel models where the processors can take unit time *memory snapshots*, i.e., each processor can read and locally process the entire shared memory at unit cost. It turns out that optimality is not achievable for $P = N$ even for such models. However, with and without restarts, these models have upper bounds that match the lower bounds. The lower bounds of course also hold for fault-prone PRAMs with conventional memory access with the single shared memory access per processor per unit time.

Investigating computational bounds for the snapshot model is interesting for several reasons. For the failure model without restarts, the snapshot lower bound leads to the lower bound for algorithm W that shows that our analysis of the algorithm is tight. The approach we take can be used to derive lower bounds for any algorithm that allocates work to processors in synchronized phases.

For the snapshot model with undetectable restarts, the lower bound on work matches the bound in Section 4.1.1 that does not use the snapshot assumption. This suggests that to derive stronger lower bounds for shared memory models with undetectable restarts (or asynchrony), we need to use explicitly the fact that in unit time only a fixed number of memory cells can be read or written by any processor.

Finally, we constructively show tight upper bound for the snapshot model with and without restarts. This additional algorithmic insight may contribute to better algorithms if new error detection and load balancing techniques become available.

In this section, we say that an algorithm is *optimal* if its upper bound matches that of the corresponding lower bound.

4.2.1   No Restarts and Optimality of Snapshot Write-All

We now prove a lower bound for the model without restarts that, in the snapshot model has a matching upper bound.

The following mathematical facts are used in the lower bounds proof. The first fact is based on the properties of averages and sums.

Fact 4.2.1 Given a sorted list of m nonnegative integers $a_1, a_2, \ldots, a_m$ $(m > 1)$ then we have for all j $(1 \leq j < m)$ that $\left(1 - \frac{j}{m}\right) \sum_{i=1}^{m} a_i \leq \sum_{i=j+1}^{m} a_i$.

The next fact estimates the number of times a positive quantity can be divided by another positive quantity when floors are taken after each division.

Fact 4.2.2 Given $G > 1, N > G$, and integer σ such that $\sigma < \frac{\log N}{\log G} - 1$, then the following inequality holds: $\underbrace{\lfloor \ldots \lfloor \lfloor N / G \rfloor / G \rfloor \ldots / G \rfloor}_{\sigma \ times} > 0$.

In the above fact, σ is the number of divisions by G. We will be using this fact with $G = \log N$. The last fact is used to produce a big-O estimate of an expression used in the proof.

Fact 4.2.3 $\left(1 - \frac{1}{\log N}\right)^{\frac{\log N}{\log \log N}} = 1 - \frac{1}{\log \log N} + O\left(\frac{1}{(\log \log N)^2}\right).$

Now the theorem:

Theorem 4.2.4 Given any (deterministic or randomized) N-processor CRCW PRAM *Write-All* algorithm problem, an adversary can force failures that result in $\Omega(N \frac{\log N}{\log \log N})$ steps being performed by the algorithm, even if the processors can read and locally process all shared memory at unit cost.

Proof: We are going to present a strategy for the adversary that results in this worst case behavior. Let A be the best possible algorithm that implements a robust solution for the *Write-All* problem. Each processor participating in the algorithm is allowed to read the entire shared memory, and locally perform arbitrary computation on it in unit time.

Let $P_0 = N$ be the initial number of processors, and $U_0 = N$ be the initial number of unvisited array elements. The strategy of the adversary is outlined below. Step numbers refer to the PRAM steps. For each step, the adversary will be determining which processors will be allowed to write and which will be stopped.

Step 1: The adversary chooses $U_1 = \lfloor U_0 / \log U_0 \rfloor$ array elements with the least number of processors assigned to them. This can be done since the adversary knows all the actions to be performed by A. The adversary then fail-stops the processors assigned to these array elements, if any.

To estimate the number of surviving processors and to express this mathematically, we will be using Fact 4.2.1 with the following definitions:

Let $m = U_0$, and let $a_1, \ldots, a_m$ be the sorted in ascending order quantities of processors assigned to each array element, moreover, let a_m also include the quantity of any un-assigned processors (i.e., a_1 is the least number of processors assigned to an array element, a_2 is the next least quantity of processors, etc.). Let $j = U_1$. Thus the adversary failed exactly $\sum_{i=1}^{j} a_i$ processors.

The initial number of processors is: $\sum_{i=1}^{m} a_i = P_0$, therefore, the number of surviving processors P_1 is: $\sum_{i=j+1}^{m} a_i = P_1$. Using Fact 4.2.1, we get:

$$P_1 \geq (1 - U_1/U_0)P_0$$

or, after substituting for U_1 and using the properties of *floor*:

$$P_1 \geq \left(1 - \frac{\lfloor U_0 / \log U_0 \rfloor}{U_0}\right) P_0 \geq \left(1 - \frac{1}{\log U_0}\right) P_0$$

Step 2: The adversary again chooses among the U_1 remaining unvisited array elements $U_2 = \lfloor U_1 / \log U_0 \rfloor$ elements with the least number of processors assigned to them. Using Fact 4.2.1 again in a similar way:

$$P_2 \geq \left(1 - \frac{\lfloor U_1 / \log U_0 \rfloor}{U_1}\right) P_1 = \left(1 - \frac{\lfloor \lfloor U_0 / \log U_0 \rfloor / \log U_0 \rfloor}{\lfloor U_0 / \log U_0 \rfloor}\right) P_1$$

$$\geq \left(1 - \frac{\lfloor U_0 / \log U_0 \rfloor / \log U_0}{\lfloor U_0 / \log U_0 \rfloor}\right) P_1 = \left(1 - \frac{1}{\log U_0}\right) P_1$$

$$\geq \left(1 - \frac{1}{\log U_0}\right)^2 P_0$$

Step i: The adversary chooses among U_{i-1} unvisited array elements $U_i = \lfloor U_{i-1}/\log U_0 \rfloor$ elements with least number of processors assigned to them. Again, applying Fact 4.2.1:

$$P_i \geq \left(1 - \frac{\lfloor U_{i-1}/\log U_0 \rfloor}{U_{i-1}}\right) P_{i-1} \geq \left(1 - \frac{1}{\log U_0}\right) P_{i-1}$$

$$\geq \left(1 - \frac{1}{\log U_0}\right)^i P_0$$

This process is repeated for as long as there are any unvisited array elements, at which point the surviving processors will successfully terminate the algorithm.

Let ρ be the step at which the last unvisited element is finally visited. Let us use Fact 4.2.2 with $G = \log N$ and σ the largest integer such that $\sigma < \log N/\log\log N - 1$. Then $U_\sigma = \lfloor \ldots \lfloor \lfloor N \underbrace{/G\rfloor/G\rfloor \ldots /G\rfloor}_{\sigma\ times} > 0$, and so ρ must be greater than σ because $U_\rho = 0$.

Thus we have $\rho \geq \frac{\log U_0}{\log\log U_0} - 1 = \frac{\log N}{\log\log N} - 1 > \sigma$.

We want to estimate $S = \sum_{i=0}^{\rho} P_i$.

By the adversary strategy given above, for all PRAM steps i: $P_i \geq (1-\frac{1}{\log U_0})^i P_0$. Therefore:

$$S = \sum_{i=0}^{\rho} P_i \geq \sum_{i=0}^{\rho} \left(1 - \frac{1}{\log N}\right)^i P_0$$

Using the summation of a geometric progression we obtain:

$$S \geq P_0 \frac{1 - (1 - \frac{1}{\log N})^{\rho+1}}{1 - (1 - \frac{1}{\log N})} = P_0 \log N \left(1 - \left(1 - \frac{1}{\log N}\right)^{\rho+1}\right)$$

$$\geq P_0 \log N \left(1 - \left(1 - \frac{1}{\log N}\right)^{\frac{\log N}{\log\log N}}\right)$$

Using Fact 4.2.3 result, $(1 - \frac{1}{\log N})^{\frac{\log N}{\log\log N}} = 1 - \frac{1}{\log\log N} + O(\frac{1}{(\log\log N)^2})$, we obtain the following lower bound on the number of PRAM processor steps:

$$S \geq P_0 \log N \left(1 - 1 + \frac{1}{\log\log N} + O\left(\frac{1}{(\log\log N)^2}\right)\right)$$

$$= P_0 \frac{\log N}{\log\log N} + O\left(P_0 \frac{\log N}{(\log\log N)^2}\right)$$

Therefore $S = \Omega\left(N \frac{\log N}{\log\log N}\right)$.   ∎

Worst case adversary for algorithm W

The lower bound in Theorem 4.2.4 is for the snapshot model, but it leads directly to a strategy that an adversary can deploy against algorithm W of Section 3.3 which does not use snapshots.

Theorem 4.2.5 There is a processor failure pattern for algorithm W that results in $S = \Theta(N \log^2 N / \log \log N)$, for $P = N$.

Proof: This is accomplished by using the adversary that fail-stops processors as in the proof of the Theorem 4.2.4, except that instead of PRAM steps, the adversary uses *block-steps*, and the processors are stopped only during phase W3 where the operations on the actual data take place. ∎

This theorem shows that our upper bound analysis of algorithm W given in Theorem 3.3.5 is tight.

Optimality of no-restart snapshot allocation

Here we show that the lower bound of $\Omega(N \frac{\log N}{\log \log N})$ is the strongest possible bound for the fail-stop model without restarts under the memory snapshot assumption. We show this by presenting a snapshot *Write-All* solution, called *algorithm* W_{snap}, whose work matches the lower bound above.

Algorithm W_{snap}, with $P = N$, is similar to algorithm W, except that instead of using logarithmic time block-steps, algorithm W_{snap} uses unit-time memory snapshots for processor enumeration, balanced processor allocation and progress estimation. Thus each block-step consists of a constant number of snapshots, and is performed in constant time.

Theorem 4.2.6 If processors can use unit time memory snapshots, then *Write-All* problem can be solved with $S = O(N \log N / \log \log N)$ using N processors.

Proof: When using constant time block-steps of algorithm W_{snap}, the block-step analysis performed for W in Lemma 3.3.4 applies in-full to block-steps of algorithm W_{snap}. For $P = N$, the lemma shows that the number of block-steps is $O(N + P \frac{\log N}{\log \log N}) = O(N \log N / \log \log N)$. Since each block-step consists of a constant number of memory snapshots, the work of the algorithm is $O(N \log N / \log \log N)$. ∎

The snapshot *Write-All* solution, algorithm W_{snap}, given in the proof above performs work equal to the lower bound work in Theorem 4.2.4. Algorithm W_{snap} is therefore *optimal* with respect to the lower bound for no restarts.

Corollary 4.2.7 The work complexity of algorithm W_{snap} is the best achievable for the fail-stop model with memory snapshots.

4.2.2   Restarts and Optimal Snapshot Allocation

Here we show that up to a logarithmic overhead in work will be required by any *Write-All* algorithm in the models with undetectable restarts, and thus also for the models with asynchrony. This is the strongest lower bound possible under the memory snapshot assumption.

Specifically, we show $N + \Omega(P \log P)$ work lower bounds (when $P \leq N$) for models with detectable and undetectable restart models, even when the processors can take unit time memory snapshots.

Theorem 4.2.8 Given any P-processor CRCW PRAM *Write-All* algorithm for a problem of size N ($P \leq N$), an adversary (that can cause arbitrary processor failures and restarts) can force the algorithm to perform $N + \Omega(P \log P)$ work steps.

Proof: Let A be any algorithm for the *Write-All* problem subject to arbitrary failure/restarts. Consider each PRAM cycle. The adversary uses the following strategy:

Let $U > 1$ be the number of unvisited array elements, i.e., the elements that no processor succeeded in writing to. For as long as $U > P$, the adversary induces no failures. The work needed to visit $N - P$ array elements when there were no failures is at least $N - P$.

As soon as a processor is about to visit the element $N - P + 1$ making $U \leq P$, the adversary fails and then restarts all P processors. For the upcoming cycle, the adversary examines the algorithm to determine how the processors are assigned to write to array elements. The adversary then lists the first $\lfloor \frac{U}{2} \rfloor$ unvisited elements with the least processors assigned to them. The total number of processors assigned to these elements does not exceed $\lceil \frac{P}{2} \rceil$. The adversary fails these processors, allowing all others to proceed. Therefore at least $\lfloor \frac{P}{2} \rfloor$ processors will complete this step having visited no more than half of the remaining unvisited array locations.

This strategy can be continued for at least $\log P$ iterations. The work performed by the algorithm will be $S \geq N - P + \lfloor \frac{P}{2} \rfloor \log P = N + \Omega(P \log P)$. ∎

Note that the bound holds even if processors are only charged for writes into the array of size N. The simplicity of this strategy ensures that the results hold for the undetectable restarts and for any model with asynchronous processor behavior.

Optimality of snapshot allocation with restarts

The above lower bound is the tightest possible bound under the assumption that the processors can read and locally process the entire shared memory at unit cost. Although such an assumption is very strong, we present the matching upper bound for two reasons. First, it uses a processor allocation strategy based on algorithm V in Section 3.4.1. Second, it demonstrates that any improvement to the lower bound must take account of the fact that processors can read only a constant number of cells per update cycle.

Theorem 4.2.9 If processors can read and locally process the entire shared memory at unit cost, then a solution for the *Write-All* problem in the restartable fail-stop model can be constructed such that its work using P processors on an input of size N is $S = N - P + O(P \log P)$, when $P \leq N$.

Proof: The processors use a strategy similar to that used in algorithm V, except that instead of logarithmic block-steps, they use memory snapshots. At each step that a processor PID is active, it reads the N elements of the array $x[1..N]$ to be visited. Say U of these elements are still not visited. The processor numbers these U elements from 1 to U based on their position in the array, and assigns itself to the ith unvisited element such that $i = \lceil PID \cdot \frac{U}{P} \rceil$. This achieves load balancing with no more than $\lceil \frac{P}{U} \rceil$ processors assigned to each unvisited element. The reading and local processing is done as a snapshot at unit cost.

We list the elements of the *Write-All* array in ascending order according to the time at which the elements are visited (ties are broken arbitrarily). We divide this list into adjacent segments numbered sequentially starting with 0, such that the segment 0 contains $V_0 = N - P$ elements, and segment $j \geq 1$ contains $V_j = \lfloor \frac{P}{j(j+1)} \rfloor$ elements, for $j = 1, ..., m$ and for some $m \leq \sqrt{P}$.

Let U_j be the least possible number of unvisited elements when processors were being assigned to the elements of the jth segment. U_j can be computed as $U_j = N - \sum_{i=0}^{j-1} V_i$. U_0 is of course N, and for $j \geq 1$, $U_j = P - \sum_{i=1}^{j-1} V_i \geq P - (P - \frac{P}{j}) = \frac{P}{j}$. Therefore no more than $\lceil \frac{P}{U_j} \rceil$ processors were assigned to each element.

The work performed by the algorithm is given below (this is identical to the computation of the number of block-steps in Lemma 3.4.1, see Equation 79):

$$S \leq \sum_{j=0}^{m} V_j \left\lceil \frac{P}{U_j} \right\rceil = N + O(P \log P) . \qquad \blacksquare$$

The snapshot *Write-All* solution given in the proof above has work equal to the lower bound work in Theorem 4.2.8. It is therefore *optimal* with respect to the lower bound for *Write-All* with restarts.

A similar result holds in the asynchronous model using the same proof.

Theorem 4.2.10 If processors can read and locally process the entire shared memory at unit cost, then a solution for the *Write-All* problem in the asynchronous model can be constructed with total work $N - P + O(P \log P)$ using P processors on input of size N, for $P \leq N$.

4.3   APPROXIMATE WRITE-ALL

So far we have required that *all* array locations be set to 1; this is the *exact Write-All* problem. In this section we relax the requirement that all locations be set to 1 and instead require that only a fraction of them be written into. For any $0 < \varepsilon < \frac{1}{2}$ we define the *approximate Write-All* problem, denoted AWA(ε), as the problem of initializing at least $(1 - \varepsilon)N$ array locations to 1.

We can interpret the exact *Write-All* as a computation of a function from inputs to outputs, where the result of an exact *Write-All* algorithm is a single vector value (with all locations set to 1), whereas the approximate *Write-All* would correspond to the computation of a relation, where the output could be one of several different vectors (with any $(1 - \varepsilon)N$ locations set to 1).

We now show that computing some relations robustly is easier than computing functions robustly in the fail-stop model without restarts.

Consider the majority relation $\mathcal{M}$: Given a binary array $x[1..N]$, $x \in \mathcal{M}$ when $|\{x[i] : x[i] = 1\}| > \frac{1}{2}N$. It turns out that $O(N \log N)$ work is sufficient to compute a member of the majority relation.

Let us parameterize the majority problem in terms of the approximate *Write-All* problem by using the quantity ε such that $0 < \varepsilon < \frac{1}{2}$. As discussed above we would like to initialize at least $(1 - \varepsilon)N$ array locations to 1. Surprisingly, algorithm W has the desired property:

Theorem 4.3.1 Given any constant ε such that $0 < \varepsilon < \frac{1}{2}$, algorithm W solves the AWA(ε) problem with $S = O(N \log N)$ using N processors.

Proof: Algorithm W converges monotonically since at least one new array element is visited during each block step of the algorithm (see Lemma 3.3.3). Let U be the number of unvisited elements at the beginning of an iteration. The expression controlling the mail loop of algorithm W can be changed so that if $U < \varepsilon N$, then the algorithm terminates.

Consider a particular block-step of algorithm W prior to its termination. Since $U \geq \varepsilon N$ and since the number of active processors $P \leq N$, the number of processors assigned to each unvisited element is constant by the balanced allocation Lemma 3.3.2.

No visited array element is visited again, and so the $(1 - \varepsilon)N$ elements are visited by a constant number of processors resulting in linear in N number of block steps. Each block step takes $O(\log N)$ time and the work of the algorithm is $S = O(N \log N)$. ∎

It is possible to get even closer to solving the exact *Write-All* at the modest expense of a multiplicative $\log \log N$ factor in work:

Theorem 4.3.2 For each constant k, there is a robust $\text{AWA}(\frac{1}{\log^k N})$ algorithm that has work $S = O(N \log N \log \log N)$.

Proof: We choose $\varepsilon = 1/2^k$ (for some constant k) and use the approximate *Write-All* algorithm W. If we iterate the algorithm $\log \log N$ times, the number of unvisited leaves will be $N\varepsilon^{\log \log N} = N(\log N)^{\log \varepsilon} = N(\log N)^{-k} = N/\log^k N$. ∎

4.4 OPEN PROBLEMS

For the stop failures model without restarts, a gap of $\log N / \log \log N$ remains between the upper bound of algorithm W of $O(N \log^2 / \log \log N)$ and the lower bound of $\Omega(N \log N)$ Is there an optimal (with respect to the lower bound) algorithm for *Write-All* in the fail-stop no-restart model, e.g., with $O(N + P \log N)$ work? Narrowing this gap appears to be a challenging problem.

An even larger gap exists for the fail-stop model with any kind of unlimited restarts. The known lower bound is $\Omega(N \log N)$ and the known upper bound is $O(N^{1+\varepsilon})$.

Although much is known about handling static faults, an interesting open problem remains: Prove the $\Omega(N + P \log N)$ lower bound on *Write-All* on a CRCW PRAM with initial faults only and without the snapshot assumption. Note that the lower bounds of Section 4.1.1 makes use of on-line faults.

4.5 BIBLIOGRAPHIC NOTES

The logarithmic lower bound on time of any execution for deterministic *Write-All* in Section 4.1.1 was derived by Kedem, Palem, Raghunathan and Spirakis in [62]. The proof uses techniques introduced by Cook, Dwork and Reischuk [29] for proving lower bounds in the CREW PRAM model. For this and other important lower bounds, see Karp and Ramachandran in [60]. Martel and Subramonian [86] have extended this logarithmic lower bound to randomized algorithms against oblivious adversaries.

In the absence of failures, it is possible to simulate a P-processor CRCW PRAM on a P-processor CREW or EREW PRAM with only a factor of $O(\log P)$ more parallel work, see the survey of Karp and Ramachandran [60]. When dynamic failures are introduced, efficient simulations on CREW or EREW PRAMs become impossible because of the quadratic CREW lower bound. This was shown by Kanellakis and Shvartsman [56].

Fail-stop no-restart CRCW lower bound with memory snapshots in Section 4.2.1 are due to Kanellakis and Shvartsman [56]. The proofs of the three mathematical facts from that section is also found there. Lower bound in Section 4.2.2 for the fail-stop restartable and asynchronous model, and the matching upper bound with memory snapshots are by Buss, Kanellakis, Ragde and Shvartsman [20]. Approximate *Write-All* is introduced and discussed by Kanellakis and Shvartsman in [59].

5

FAULT-TOLERANT SIMULATIONS

IN THIS chapter we discuss the simulation of fault-free PRAMs on fault-prone PRAMs. The simulation is based on a technique for executing arbitrary PRAM steps on a PRAM whose processors are subject to fail-stop failures. In each of the specific simulations, the execution of a single N-processor PRAM step on a fail-stop P-processor PRAM has the same asymptotic complexity as that of solving a N-size instance of the *Write-All* problem using P fail-stop processors. We also show that in some cases it is possible to develop fault-tolerant algorithms that improve on the efficiency of the oblivious simulations. Finally, we discuss parallel efficiency classes and *closures* with respect to fault tolerant simulations.

5.1 ROBUST SIMULATIONS

To recall, we say that a PRAM is *fault-tolerant* if it completes its task in the presence of an arbitrary failure pattern, in the failure model $\mathcal{F}$ for which it was designed. We say that a fault-free PRAM $\mathcal{A}$ is simulated by the PRAM $\mathcal{B}$ tolerant of failures in model $\mathcal{F}$ when any sequence of instructions of $\mathcal{A}$ can be executed on $\mathcal{B}$ in the presence of any failure pattern $F \in \mathcal{F}$. We are interested in simulations that are robust, that is, that combine fault-tolerance and efficiency:

Definition 5.1.1 Let $\mathcal{A}$ be an N-processor PRAM, whose parallel-time on inputs of size n is less than or equal to τ, that is simulated by a fault-tolerant P-processor PRAM $\mathcal{B}$ with work S in failure model $\mathcal{F}$. We say the fault-tolerant simulation is:

- *Optimal* for $\mathcal{F}$, if $S = O(N \cdot \tau)$,

- *Robust* for $\mathcal{F}$, if $S = O(N \cdot \tau \cdot \log^c N)$ for a constant c,

- *Polynomial* for $\mathcal{F}$, if $S = O(N \cdot \tau \cdot N^\varepsilon)$ for a constant ε, $0 < \varepsilon < 1$.   □

In the next section we show how to execute general parallel assignments, introduced in Section 1.4, in the presence of failures. We then generalize the basic technique to robust executions of arbitrary PRAM steps.

5.2 FROM PARALLEL ASSIGNMENT TO A FAULT-TOLERANT INTERPRETER

We use the *general parallel assignment* (GPA) problem of Definition 5.2.1 as a means for demonstrating the basic simulation technique we develop in this chapter. The technique is then formalized in the construction of a fault-tolerant PRAM interpreter. Any solution for the *Write-All* problem can be used as a building block in approach to simulating parallel algorithms or in transforming parallel algorithms into robust algorithms.

5.2.1 General Parallel Assignment

In the failure-free setting, the *general parallel assignment* problem, of computing and storing in an array $y[1..N]$ the values of the function f, that depend on the initial values of the array y, is easily solved by the optimal algorithm below. For simplicity, we assume that f can be computed in $O(1)$ sequential time[1]. Y_i denotes the initial value of $y[i]$. In the code fragments below, the declarations of variables simply announce the types of the variables that are created and initialized elsewhere.

```
shared integer array y[1..N];
{ y[i] = Yᵢ for 1 ≤ i ≤ N }
forall processors PID = 1..N parbegin
    y[PID] := f(PID, y[1..N])
parend
{ y[i] = f(i, ⟨Y₁, ..., Y_N⟩) for 1 ≤ i ≤ N }
```

In developing a fault-tolerant solution, we assume (for the moment) there are means for reassigning surviving processors that have completed their initial tasks of computing the function value to any of the remaining such tasks. We next convert the assignment to an idempotent form, where the individual assignments to array elements can be correctly executed when processors fail and when multiple attempts – at different times and by different processors – are made to execute the assignments.

---

[1] Such functions include all computations necessary to model the cycles of conventional machine instructions. The assumption may be unnecessary when the goal is to transform a specific fault-free algorithm that contains such computation into a robust one.

The assignments are made idempotent by introducing two *generations* of the array y and using binary generation version numbers:

```
shared integer array y[0..1][1..N];
private bit integer v (init 0);
{ y[v][i] = Y_i for 1 ≤ i ≤ N }
forall processors PID = 1..N parbegin
    y[v + 1][PID] := f(PID, y[v][1..N]);
    v := v + 1 (mod 2)
parend
{ y[v][i] = f(i, ⟨Y_1, ..., Y_N⟩) for 1 ≤ i ≤ N }
```

Here, the bit v is the current version number tag (**mod** 2), so that $y[v][1..N]$ is the array of current values. In computing function f only these values of x are used as input. The computed values of f are stored in $y[v + 1][1..N]$ creating the next generation of array y. After all the assignments are performed, the binary version number is incremented (**mod** 2).

Now assume we have a robust algorithm for the *Write-All* problem at our disposal. Let R be the code that implements the algorithm. Without loss of generality we assume that the names y and f do not occur in R. Consider all places in the code R where the assignments "$x[e] := 1$" appear, for some variable or expression e. Let R' be the code obtained from R as follows. We insert the code "$y[v + 1][e] := f(e, y[v][1..N])$" before each occurrence of "$x[e] := 1$" in R. We insert the statement to increment the private binary version number v before the HALT statement of each processor's code.

This simple transformation of the code R yields a robust N-processor GPA algorithm R'. The correctness of R' follows from the correctness of R. Assignments to y do not affect the *Write-All* computation, and when R terminates, so does R'. Since all elements of x change value from 0 to 1 during any execution of R, it follows that in any execution of R', the "next" generation of the array y stores the required values of f which are computed using the "current" generation of y. Such robust GPA construction leads to the following result:

Proposition 5.2.1 The work complexities of solving the *general parallel assignment* problem is asymptotically equal to the work of solving the *Write-All* problem. □

Similarly to the GPA, by using any *Write-All* solution and by appropriately choosing the function f, we can perform any single parallel computations step in the presence of processor failures, e.g., initializing an array of size N, or copying N computed values from one array to another. To simulate an arbitrary parallel step, we need to use an iterative parameterized approach so that the targets of the assignment correspond to the memory locations written by the simulated processors, and that the function f represents the machine instructions executed by the simulated processors.

5.2.2   A Fault-Tolerant PRAM Interpreter

We define a universal PRAM interpreter that specifies the abstract PRAM model in terms of a program. The PRAM algorithms developed for any of the "standard" models, i.e., CRCW, CREW or EREW models, can be automatically compiled to be executed by our interpreter using the RAM program compilation techniques, but taking additional steps to preserve the semantics defined for the alternative and iterative high-level commands as described in Section 2.1.3.

If we are able to simulate the PRAM interpreter in another model of parallel or distributed computation, then any program for one of the standard PRAMs becomes also the program for the other model. If we understand the efficiency of a PRAM program and the complexity of simulating the PRAM interpreter in another model, then we are able to evaluate the efficiency of this program in the context of the other model. Of course our goal is develop simulations that preserve the efficiency of the original algorithm. This is exactly what we pursue in this chapter as we use the interpreter as the basis for simulating fault-free PRAMs in the settings when processor failures are introduced.

The PRAM interpreter Π

To formalize the execution of compiled PRAM programs that are specified as code in the PRAM "machine language", we formulate a definition in conjunction with the pseudocode of the PRAM interpreter Π given in Figure 5.1. The interpreter we defined below implements the synchronous computation performed by any PRAM.

Definition 5.2.1 A universal PRAM interpreter Π is a P-processor PRAM defined as follows:

- The P processors have unique identifiers PID in the range 1 to P.

- Each processor has an instruction buffer IB, and a set of internal registers collectively referred to as the record r. The number of registers per processor, $|r|$, is l. The registers in r include an instruction counter IC, a read register RR and a write register WR used for reads/writes from/to shared memory.

- Shared array PROG[$1..P,1..size$], stores the instructions of a compiled PRAM program (where $size$ does not depend on P). The program for processor i is in PROG[$i,1..size$]), with one instruction per array element.

```
01 forall processors PID=1..P parbegin
02       shared SM[1..m]; -- shared memory
03       shared PROG[1..P,1..size]; -- P programs of length size
04       private IB -- instruction buffer
05       private r record -- private registers
06             IC, -- instruction counter
07             RR, -- read register (a buffer)
08             WR, -- write register (an address)
09             ... end -- up to polylog of general-purpose registers
10       r.IC := 1; -- start at the first instruction
11       while r.IC ≠ 0 do -- while not HALT
12             IB          := PROG[PID,r.IC]; -- fetch ⟨ R, C, W, J ⟩ into IB
13             r.RR        := SM[R(r)]; -- read cycle
14             r           := C(r);       -- compute cycle
15             SM[W(r)] := r.WR;          -- write cycle
16             r.IC        := J(r);       -- next instruction
17       od
18 parend
```

Figure 5.1 Universal PRAM Interpreter Π.

- Π uses shared memory cells SM[1..m] for some m, with the first N cells containing the input for the compiled program stored in the PROG array. Shared memory cells and registers are capable of storing $O(\log \max\{N, P\})$ bits each.

- The instructions consist of four encoded operations $\langle R, C, W, J \rangle$. After reading an instruction into IB, a processor interprets this code as follows (line numbers refer to Figure 5.1):

  Read cycle (line 09): processor reads into RR the contents of shared memory location SM[$R(r)$],

  Compute cycle (line 10): processor assigns to registers in r the results of the computation $C(r)$,

  Write cycle (line 11): processor writes the contents of register WR to the shared memory location SM[$W(r)$],

  Update instruction counter (line 12): processor computes the next instruction address; IC = 0 is a halt. □

As is the case with sequential processors, the instructions are stored in memory, the address of an instruction to be executed next is stored in an *instruction counter* register, and in order to execute an instruction, it is fetched into an

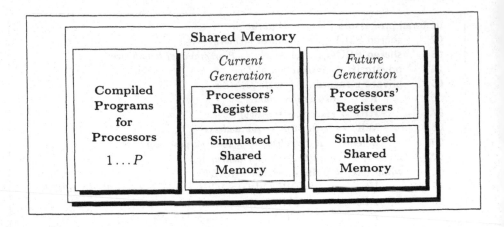

Figure 5.2   The structure of shared memory for simulations.

instruction buffer. When control structures such as **while-do** and **if-then-else** are used, then the branching of control is compiled as assignments to instruction counters. The processor private memory cells are stored in general purpose *registers*, collectively represented as the record $\mathbf{r}$. The number of registers per processor, $l = |\mathbf{r}|$, is typically constant for uniprocessors, however in parallel processing it is important to provide each processor with larger private memories in order to allow them to perform as much local computation as possible without having to access the shared memory. We will consider private memories of sizes up to $O(\log^k N)$ for some constant k. This does not diminish the computational power of the model, since if an algorithm assumes a larger than available private memory, a dedicated portion of shared memory can be allocated to each processor.

In Definition 5.2.1 above, $R()$, $W()$ and $J()$ are expressions involving private registers, and $C()$ is the code for the individual processor's compute cycles. PRAM programs are executed by the interpreter Π that accepts a compiled PRAM program and its input as data.

The fault-tolerant PRAM interpreter Π^{FT}

We now transform the interpreter Π into the fault-tolerant interpreter Π^{FT}. The result of this is that s fault-free PRAM program can now be executed in the presence of failures – the program is compiled and presented as the input to Π^{FT}.

We start with Π as given in Figure 5.1 and construct Π^{FT} in a series of steps. The shared memory in Π^{FT} is managed as follows (see Figure 5.2):

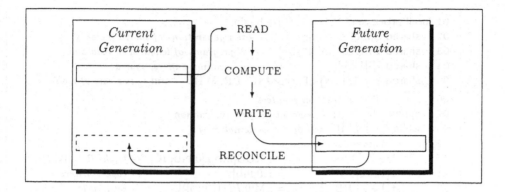

Figure 5.3 Processing within a simulation step.

1. The compiled PRAM program is stored in a segment of shared memory.

2. The rest of shared memory is used to simulate the shared memory of the simulated PRAM; it is divided into two *generations* that we call *current* and *future*.

3. Private memories (registers) of the simulated processors are stored in each generation of the simulated shared memory.

Each machine instruction of the compiled PRAM program uses *current* memory generation for reading memory cells and *future* memory generation for writing. The simulation proceeds iteratively for each parallel step until the simulated PRAM halts as follows (see Figure 5.3):

1. Each simulated PRAM step is executed by reading *current* memory as necessary, performing the local computation corresponding to the simulated instruction, and writing to *future* memory as necessary.

2. *Current* and *future* memories are reconciled, by copying the changed cells and new register values from the *future* generation to the *current*, to produce new *current* memory,

3. Simulated instruction counters are examined to detect termination (instruction counter value 0 is defined to be the HALT instruction).

Each group of actions above will be placed in the work phase of a *Write-All* algorithm. Now we describe the construction in more detail.

```
01 forall processors PID= 1..P parbegin
02    shared SM[0..1, 1..m];        -- two generations of shared memory
03    shared PROG[1..N, 1..size];   -- N programs of length size, read-only
04    shared IB[1..N];              -- instruction buffers, shared
05    shared r[0..1, 1..N] of record IC, RB, WB, ... end -- two sets of registers
06       -- Initialize instruction counters
07    r[0,PID].IC := 1;  -- start at the first instruction
08    while r[0,PID].IC ≠ 0 do  -- while not HALT
09         -- Tentative computation
10          IB[PID]              := PROG[PID,r[0,PID].IC];  -- fetch ⟨R, C, W, J⟩
11          r[1,PID]             := r[0,PID];               -- copy registers
12          r[1,PID].RB          := SM[0,R(r[1,PID])];      -- read cycle
13          r[1,PID]             := C(r[1,PID]);            -- compute cycle
14          SM[1,[W(r[1,PID])]   := r[1,PID].WB;            -- write cycle
15          r[1,PID].IC          := J(r[1,PID]);            -- next instruction
16       -- Reconcile shared memory
17          SM[0,W(r[1,PID])]    := SM[1,W(r[1,PID])];
18       -- Reconcile registers
19          r[0,PID]             := r[1,PID]
20    od
21 parend
```

Figure 5.4   Interpreter Π that uses two generations of shared memory.

Construction details

Figure 5.4 illustrates an intermediate step of the construction, and Figure 5.5 is the final pseudo-code for Π^{FT}.

Observe that the semantics of the simulated programs are not changed when their processors' registers are stored in shared memory, since they are accessed only for the purposes of simulating the actions of the processor to whom the registers belong. The registers r use $l = O(|r| \cdot N)$ memory cells. The registers of individual processors are distinguished by being indexed by PIDs (lines 04-05; all lines refer to Figure 5.4). All shared memory and registers are stored into two generations: *current* (using subscript 0) and *future* (subscript 1) (lines 02 and 05). All memory references are now made using the generation subscript 0 or 1 (lines 10-19). Doing so does not affect the asymptotic memory requirement of size $O(m + l)$. The result of this transformation is that the memory that can be read by processors that have not yet completed a particular action (due to failures or asynchrony) is not changed until it is safe to do so. This creates idempotent PRAM instructions that can be executed multiple times when more than one active processor is allocated to them or when multiple attempts to execute an instruction are made.

The statements of the interpreter are grouped into four actions to compute future memory values and to reconcile current and future memories. The initialization of ICs takes place in line 07. The contents of the **while** loop of Figure 5.4 are grouped into 3 actions: the action on lines 09-15 performs the tentative PRAM step computation using *current* memory as input, and *future* memory as output and as a scratchpad used for tentative computation; the action on lines 16-17 reconciles shared memory; and the action on lines 18-19 reconciles processor registers.

Now a *Write-All* algorithm is used to execute each of the four actions in its work phases. See Figure 5.5, steps **a**, **b**, **c** and **d**. This assures that all actions of a given phase are performed before any of the actions of the next phase are attempted. Note that there is no assumption that $P = N$, since *Write-All* solutions automate the assignment of processors to tasks.

Write-All algorithms normally utilize workspace memory of size $\Theta(N)$ on inputs of size N using P processors ($P \leq N$). This memory initially is assumed to contain zeroes (or is initialized to zeroes using a memory-contamination tolerant algorithm). Consecutive use of a *Write-All* solution in a single algorithm requires that this workspace is zeroed. This is accomplished by utilizing two interchangeable workspaces of size $\Theta(N)$, call them *H1* and *H2*. When one of the workspaces is used in the algorithm to simulate $\Theta(N)$ actions of the simulated PRAM, the $\Theta(N)$ memory locations of the other workspace are simultaneously cleared. This simple, but modular clean-up technique affects neither the overall asymptotic memory usage, nor the asymptotic efficiency of robust algorithms when the cleanup steps are interleaved with the computation steps (as shown in Figure 5.5).

Lastly, we need to check for the algorithm termination by verifying that all processors halted. This is done by computing shared sc halt to be *true*, iff for all PIDs, IC=0. This can be accomplished in unit time on a CRCW PRAM in the absence of failures. Here we compute HALT as follows: it is initialized to *true*, then using the *Write-All* technique, processors examine the simulated ICs and execute "HALT := *false*" for each IC $\neq 0$ (Figure 5.5, step **e**).

Remark 5.1 *Use of* CRCW *variants in simulations*: In this simulation, due to failures, the synchronous tentative PRAM step simulations may occur asynchronously – in the sense that the synchronous PRAM steps of the simulated processors can be performed at different times by the simulating processors. However since no simulated processor reads or writes registers of other processors, it does not matter in what order the shared memory is written by the simulated processors. While, during the simulation of a single PRAM step, the

```
forall processors PID=1..P parbegin
      shared PROG[...], SM[...], IB[...], r[...]
      shared H1, H2;  -- two auxiliary workspaces of size Θ(N)
      shared HALT initial false;  -- termination flag
      a: Initialize ICs to 1 and clear H2 using H1;
      while not HALT do  -- while not all processors halted
            b: Perform a tentative PRAM step and clear H1 using H2;
            c: Reconcile shared memory and clear H2 using H1;
            d: Reconcile registers and clear H1 using H2;
            e: Compute: HALT=false iff ∃ PID : IC[PID] ≠ 0
                  and clear H2 using H1;
      od
parend.
```

Figure 5.5 Pseudo-code for Π^{FT}.

future shared memory locations are written at different times or by multiple processors as the result of the simulation, the values written to the same memory locations during the step are always the same. Therefore the simulation of PRAM steps can be executed on a PRAM with the COMMON, ARBITRARY or PRIORITY concurrent write disciplines.   □

Remark 5.2 *Lowering memory overhead of simulations*: The simulation uses two generations of memory. Although simplifying the presentation, this doubling of memory is not strictly necessary. Since each simulated processor can only write a constant number of shared memory locations plus all of its registers per instruction, it is sufficient to provide the future generation of memory for (i) $\Theta(N)$ cells to store the information about the writes of the N simulated processors, and for (ii) $l = \Theta(N \cdot |r|)$ cells to store the registers of these processors. The reconciliation step then copies these values to the current memory. □

Analysis of the simulation

Let us define $S_{N,P}$ to be the work of solving the *Write-All* problem of size N, using P ($P \leq N$) processors.

The complexity of applying the technique employed by Π^{FT} to a single PRAM step is bounded by the complexity of solving the *Write-All* problem in steps **a**, **c** and **e** of Figure 5.5, plus the complexity of robustly writing and copying $l = O(N \cdot |r|) = O(N \log^k n)$ shared memory (assuming the number of registers $|r|$ per processor to be up to a polylog in n, the size of the input to the simulated

PRAM) in steps b and d. To copy l memory, we apply the *Write-All* technique l/N times at the cost of $S_{N,P}$ per application. Therefore, the total cost per single PRAM step is

$$
\begin{aligned}
S &= O(S_{N,P} + (l/N)S_{N,P}) &&= O(S_{N,P} + |r|S_{N,P}) \\
&= O(S_{N,P} + \log^k n \cdot S_{N,P}) &&= O(S_{N,P} \cdot \log^k n).
\end{aligned}
$$

Leading to the following result:

Theorem 5.2.2 The cost of simulating a single parallel step of N fault-free processors, each using L private registers, on P fail-stop processors in failure model $\mathcal{F}$, is $O(S_{N,P} \cdot L)$, where $S_{N,P}$ is the work complexity of solving the *Write-All* problem of size N in $\mathcal{F}$ using P processors.

When the simulated PRAM does not need the additional private memory, the cost of a single PRAM step simulation is $O(S_{N,P})$, i.e., it is asymptotically equal to the cost of solving a *Write-All* problem of size N using P processors.

Corollary 5.2.3 The cost of simulating a single parallel step of N fault-free processors (that uses fixed amount or no private memory), on P fail-stop processors in failure model $\mathcal{F}$, is the same as the work complexity of solving the *Write-All* problem of size N in $\mathcal{F}$ using P processors.

5.3 GENERAL SIMULATIONS

We now use the results from the previous section to analyze PRAM simulations in different failure models. For the case of initial failures, the algorithms are simulated on fault-prone EREW PRAMS. For other failure models, the algorithms are simulated on fault-prone CRCW PRAMS – as we have seen in Chapter 4, the lower bounds on the CREW model do not allow efficient *Write-All* solutions in synchronous settings with omniscient adversaries. Additionally, for undetectable restarts or full asynchrony, the simulations can be done on asynchronous PRAMS using interleaving concurrency semantics.

5.3.1 Initial Static Failures

Simulating PRAMS subject to initial processor failures is simpler than for the on-line failure models and such simulations can be done bypassing most of the mechanisms used in the fault-tolerant PRAM interpreter. Instead, algorithm E of Section 3.2 can be used to set up simulations of PRAM algorithms on fail-stop PRAMS that are subject to static initial processor and initial memory faults.

The simulation starts by using the enumeration phase E1 of algorithm E. The enumeration algorithm determines the number P of active processors. The rest of the simulation consists of a loop, in which the P processors use the two generations of memory to perform the work of N simulated processors, with each of the P processors simulating N/P processors. Thus no further application of *Write-All* algorithm is necessary. If we assume that the N processors halt in synchrony on the simulated PRAM, then the time overhead of the simulation is just $O(\log N)$ for the enumeration phase, and the work overhead is $O(P \log N)$. Both overheads are *additive*. Since algorithm E does not require concurrency in memory access, and it does not require any clear shared memory, we have the following:

Theorem 5.3.1 Any N-processor, τ-parallel-time EREW PRAM algorithm can be robustly simulated on a fail-stop EREW PRAM that is subject to static initial processor and initial memory faults. The work of the simulation is $N \cdot \tau + O(P \log N)$, where P is the number of live processors.

Of course it is possible to simulate other than EREW PRAMs, e.g., CRCW or CRCW. In such cases the simulating PRAM uses the same memory access discipline as the PRAM for which the original algorithm is written and the read (ρ) and write (ω) concurrencies of the simulation are no more than those of the simulated algorithm. This is because $\rho = \omega = 0$ for algorithm E and no more than N processors are active in the rest of the simulation thus incurring no additional concurrency overhead.

Remark 5.3 *Optimality of simulations with initial failures*: The simulations are optimal when $N \cdot \tau = \Omega(P \log N)$.   □

5.3.2   Failures and Synchronous Restarts

We now use Π^{FT} and show that robust and optimal simulations are possible when the simulating processors are subject to failures without restarts. The results also apply when restarts are allowed in synchrony at certain points reached by the simulation, e.g., at the start of the simulation of a new PRAM step, or at the start of a new *Write-All*-based step within the simulation of the PRAM step.

Theorem 5.3.2 Any N-processor EREW, CREW, or COMMON CRCW PRAM algorithm that uses arbitrary shared memory and polylogarithmic in the input size private memories can be robustly simulated on a fail-stop P-processor COMMON or ARBITRARY CRCW PRAM, when $P \le N$.

Proof: We use algorithm W as the robust *Write-All* solution in the simulation of Section 5.2.2. For COMMON or ARBITRARY CRCW PRAMs, Theorem 3.3.5 establishes $S_{N,P} = O(N \log^2 N / \log \log N)$. Then the proof follows from Π^{FT} construction, Theorem 5.2.2 and Definition 5.1.1(2).

Correct EREW and CREW PRAMs programs can of course be executed on CRCW PRAMs without changing the program semantics. Thus the result holds for EREW and CREW models. ∎

To achieve optimal simulation, we use an optimal *Write-All* solution.

Theorem 5.3.3 Any N-processor EREW, CREW, or COMMON CRCW PRAM algorithm can be optimally simulated (with constant overhead) on a fail-stop N-processor CRCW PRAM, when $P \leq N \log \log N / \log^2 N$.

Proof: Here we use algorithm W within its range of optimality with Π^{FT} that uses no (or constant) private memory per processor. We use algorithm W as the robust *Write-All* solution in the simulation of Section 5.2.2. For COMMON or ARBITRARY CRCW PRAMs, Theorem 3.3.7 establishes $S_{N,P} = O(N)$ for the required range of processors. Then the proof follows from Corollary 5.2.3 and Definition 5.1.1(1). ∎

Remark 5.4 *Simulations with synchronous restarts*: It is not difficult to see that the above results also hold for synchronous restarts when the simulating processors are restarted during the simulation in synchrony at the start of the discrete *Write-All*-based steps of Π^{FT}. □

In the next section we establish simulation results for restarts that are detectable but not synchronous.

5.3.3 Processor Failures with Detectable Restarts

We now consider restartable fail-stop model with unrestricted, but detectable processor restarts. We begin by formally stating the main result for a deterministic simulation of any N-processor synchronous PRAM on P fail-stop processors with detectable restarts ($P \leq N$), and then discuss its proof.

Theorem 5.3.4 Any N-processor PRAM algorithm can be executed on a restartable fail-stop P-processor CRCW PRAM, with $P \leq N$. Each N-processor PRAM step i is executed in the presence of any pattern F_i of *failures* and *detectable restarts* of size M_i with:
(1) work $S = O(\min\{N + P \log^2 N + M_i \log N, \ N \cdot P^{\log \frac{3}{2}}\})$,
(2) overhead ratio $\sigma = O(\log^2 N)$.
EREW, CREW, and COMMON CRCW PRAM algorithms are simulated on fail-stop COMMON CRCW PRAMs; ARBITRARY CRCW PRAMs are simulated on fail-stop CRCW PRAMs of the same type.

We first describe how algorithms V of Section 3.4.1 and X' of Section 3.4.2 are combined with the framework we have established to yield efficient executions of PRAM programs on PRAMs that are subject to stop-failures and detectable restarts.

Lemma 5.3.5 There exists a *Write-All* solution using $P \leq N$ processors on instances of size N such that for any pattern F of failures and detectable restarts with $|F| \leq M$, has $S = O(\min\{N + P \log^2 N + M \log N, \ N \cdot P^{\log \frac{3}{2}}\})$, and the overhead ratio $\sigma = O(\log^2 N)$.

Proof: The executions of algorithms V and X' can be interleaved to yield an algorithm that achieves the performance as stated. The work complexity is asymptotically equal to the minimum of the work performed by V and X'. The overhead ratio is directly "inherited" from algorithm V by the same reasoning because of the Definition 2.2.4 of σ and S. The restarts need to be detectable to enable the restarted processors to synchronize in algorithm V.   ∎

Application of the simulation techniques from the Section 5.2.2 in conjunction with algorithms V and X' yields polynomially efficient, per Definition 5.1.1(3), simulations of any non-fault-tolerant PRAM programs in the presence of arbitrary failure and detectable restart patterns. Theorem 5.3.4 follows from Lemma 5.3.5, the construction of Π^{FT}, and Corollary 5.2.3. The following corollaries are also interesting:

Corollary 5.3.6 Under the hypothesis of Theorem 5.3.4, and if $|F| \leq P \leq N$, then: $S = O(N + P \log^2 N)$ and $\sigma = O(\log^2 N)$.

The fail-stop (without restarts) behavior of the combined algorithm is subsumed by this corollary. The next result gives additional insight into the efficiency of our solution:

Corollary 5.3.7 Under the hypothesis of Theorem 5.3.4:
(1) when $|F|$ is $\Omega(N \log N)$, then σ is $O(\log N)$,
(2) when $|F|$ is $\Omega(N^{1.59})$, then σ is $O(1)$.

Thus the overhead ratio σ of our algorithm actually improves for large failure patterns. These results also suggest that it is harder to deal efficiently with a few worst case failures than with a large number of failures.

Our next corollary demonstrates a non-trivial range of parameters for which the completed work is optimal according to Definition 5.1.1, i.e., the work performed in executing a parallel algorithm on a faulty PRAM is asymptotically equal to the *Parallel-time* $\times$ *Processors* product for that algorithm.

Corollary 5.3.8 Any N-processor, τ-time PRAM algorithm can be simulated on a $P \leq N/\log^2 N$ processor fail-stop CRCW PRAM with detectable restarts, such that when during the simulation of *each* N-processor step i of that algorithm, $|F_i| = O(P \log N)$, then $S = O(\tau \cdot N)$.

Of course it is also true that optimality is preserved in the absence of failures or when during the execution of each N processor step there are $O(\log N)$ failures and restarts per each simulating processor.

Remark 5.5 *Algorithm AW^T in simulations with detectable restarts*: Algorithm AW^T can also be used in simulations. When it is used, the upper bound on work per each simulated PRAM step is $O(N^{1+\varepsilon})$, for any $\varepsilon > 0$, and using $P = N$ processors. $\square$

We next discuss undetectable restarts and asynchrony.

5.3.4 Undetectable Restarts and Asynchrony

Whether the model allows concurrent memory access or imposes an interleaving on memory accesses, the model with fail-stop failures and undetectable restarts is essentially identical to the PRAM model with asynchronous processor behavior and atomic memory read/write access. We choose to view the disparity in processor speeds as failures. This is because the very reason for massively parallel shared memory computation, the close cooperation among many processors in solving a common computational task, is undermined when processors are able to proceed at widely varying speeds. In the presence of arbitrary asynchrony or when the restarts are undetectable, deterministic simulations become difficult due to the possibility of processors that are delayed by failures writing stale values to shared memory.

For these reasons, simulation approaches using information dispersal techniques and randomization have been pursued for asynchronous settings.

Here we briefly consider a deterministic polynomially efficient simulation, for fast, polylogarithmic time parallel algorithms. The simulations are simplified when we solve the problem of dealing with delayed processors by using poly-logarithmically more memory. We use the techniques from Section 5.2.2, and we allocate as many *future* generations of memory as there are PRAM steps to simulate. Each generation is indexed by the simulation step number t. The simulation step numbers are stored in well-known place in shared memory as a sequence – because of unbounded time delays due to failures, simply incre-menting the step number t is not sufficient, since this does not prevent a slow processor from writing a stale value. The registers of the processors are stored in shared memory, along with each generation of shared memory.

After completing the simulation of the step t, and before starting the simula-tion of a new parallel step, a processor uses binary search of the step number sequence to find the newest simulated step number. When reading from a cer-tain location in shared memory, a processor linearly searches past generations of this location to find the latest written value, i.e., a non-zero value. If the simulated location was never written (or if zero was the only value ever writ-ten), the processor will detect it by not finding a non-zero value in previous generations of memory.

In the result below we use algorithm AW^T of Section 3.5.1 as the *Write-All* so-lution. Because algorithm is polynomially robust, the polylogarithmic searches during the simulation do not affect the polynomial efficiency of the simulation.

Theorem 5.3.9 Any N-processor, $\log^{O(1)} N$-time, m-memory PRAM algorithm can be (deterministically) simulated on a fail-stop P-processor CRCW PRAM $(P \leq N)$ with undetectable restarts, and using shared memory $m \cdot \log^{O(1)} N$. Each N-processor PRAM step is executed in the presence of any pattern F of *failures* and *undetected restarts* with $S = O(N^\varepsilon)$, for $\varepsilon > 0$.

5.4   CONTROLLING CONCURRENCY AND MEMORY INITIALIZATION

So far we have not considered the memory access concurrency of simulations in the presence of dynamic faults. Here we use the results of Section 3.6.2 in simulations that control memory access concurrency with the help of algo-rithm $W^{opt}_{CR/W}$ of Section 3.6.2. In particular, we obtain the following:

Theorem 5.4.1 Any N processor, τ parallel time EREW PRAM algorithm can be simulated on a fail-stop no-restart (or synchronous restart) P-processor

CRCW PRAM with work $O(\tau \cdot (N + P \log^2 P \log^2 N / \log \log N))$ so that the write concurrency of the simulation is $\omega \leq |F|$ and the read concurrency is $\rho \leq 7|F| \log N$, for any failure pattern F and $1 \leq P \leq N$.

The work bound of this theorem also holds for simulations of non-EREW algorithms but the concurrency bounds depend on the concurrency of the simulated algorithm. If ω_0 and ρ_0 are the write and read concurrencies of the simulated algorithm, respectively, then for the simulation we have $\omega \leq |F| + \omega_0$ and $\rho \leq 7|F| \log N + \rho_0 O(\log N)$. Alternatively, we can maintain the same concurrency bounds at the expense of increasing the work by a logarithmic factor by first converting the original algorithm into an equivalent EREW algorithm (as discussed in Chapter 2).

Similar results can be derived for contaminated initial memory using algorithm $Z_{CR/W}$ of Section 3.6.3 to initialize an appropriate amount of auxiliary shared memory required by the simulation. There is an additive expense in work of $O(N + P \log^2 P \log^3 N / (\log \log N)^2)$.

Finally, if the faulty processors are restarted in the simulations so that they are re-synchronized at the beginning of the individual simulated PRAM steps then the simulations results apply as well. The bounds on memory access concurrency for simulations with undetectable restarts is an open problem.

5.5   IMPROVING OBLIVIOUS SIMULATIONS

In addition to serving as the basis for oblivious simulations, any solution for the *Write-All* problem can also be used as a building block for custom transformations of efficient parallel algorithms into robust ones. Custom transformations are interesting because in some cases it is possible to improve on the work of the oblivious simulation. These improvements are most significant for fast algorithms when a *full range* of processors is used, i.e., when N processors are used to simulate N processors, because in this case the parallel slack cannot be taken advantage of.

Using oblivious techniques, if $S_{N,P}$ is the efficiency of solving a *Write-All* instance of size N using P processors, then a single N-processor PRAM step can be simulated using P fail-stop processors and work $S_{N,P}$. Thus if the *Parallel-time* × *Processors* of an original N-processor algorithm is $\tau \cdot N$, then the work of the fault-tolerant version of the algorithm will be no better than $O(\tau \cdot S_{N,P})$.

One immediate result that improves on the general simulations follows from the fact that algorithms V, W, X, and AW^T, by their definition, implement an associative operation on N values.

Proposition 5.5.1 For any associative operation $\oplus$ on integers, and an integer array $x[1..N]$, it is possible to robustly compute $\bigoplus_{i=1}^{N} x[i]$ using P fail-stop processors at a cost of a single application of any of the algorithms V, W, X or AW^T.

This saves a full $\log N$ factor for all simulations of parallel associative operation algorithms. This does not present a significant improvement for models with undetectable restarts because the simulations there are only polynomially efficient, however for the fail-stop model (with synchronous restarts), the savings are significant. The savings in this model are also possible for the prefix sums and pointer doubling algorithms that occur in solutions of several important problems.

5.5.1   Parallel Prefix

We now show how to obtain deterministic improvements in work for the prefix sums computation. The *prefix problem* is defined as follows: Given an associative operation $\oplus$ on a domain $\mathcal{D}$, and $x_1, \ldots, x_N \in \mathcal{D}$, compute, for each k, $(1 \leq k \leq N)$ the sum $\bigoplus_{i=1}^{k} x_i$.

According to the known lower bounds results, to compute the prefix sums of N values using N processors, at least $\log N / \log \log N$ parallel steps are required. Therefore an oblivious simulation of a prefix algorithm will require simulating at least $\log N / \log \log N$ steps. When using N processors with algorithm W (the most efficient as of this writing *Write-All* solution for stop-failures and synchronous restarts) whose work is $S_w = \Theta(N \frac{\log^2 N}{\log \log N})$, the work of the simulation will be $\Omega(S_w \cdot \log N / \log \log N) = \Omega(N \frac{\log^3 N}{(\log \log N)^2})$.

We can extend Theorem 5.5.1 to show a robust prefix algorithm whose work is asymptotically the same as that of algorithm W. In the fail-stop no-restart model we have the following result:

Theorem 5.5.2 Parallel prefix sums for N values can be computed using N processors subject to fail-stop failures without restarts (or with synchronous restarts) using $O(N)$ clear memory with work $S = O(N \log^2 N / \log \log N)$.

Proof: The prefix summation will be computed in two stages: (1) first a binary summation tree is computed, (2) then the individual prefix sums are computed from the summation tree obtained in the first stage. Each prefix sum requires no more than logarithmic number of additions.

Each stage can be performed in logarithmic time in parallel by up to N processors. To produce the robust version of the above algorithm, we use algorithm W

```
01 forall processors PID = 0..N parbegin
02     shared integer array sum[1..2N − 1];  -- summation tree
03     shared integer array prefix[1..N];  -- prefix sums
04     private integer j, j1, j2,  -- current/left/right indices
05                    h;  -- depth in the summation tree
06     j := 1;  -- begin at the root,
07     h := 0;  -- and at depth 0
08     prefix[PID] := 0;  -- initialize the sum
09     while h ≠ 0 do  -- traverse from root to leaf
10          h := h + 1
11          j1 := 2 * j  -- left index
12          j2 := j1 + 1  -- right index
13          if ⟨⟨PID⟩⟩ₕ  -- Is the sub-sum at this level included?
14          then prefix[PID] := prefix[PID] + sum[j1]  -- add the left sub-sum
15               j := j2  -- go down to the right
16          else j := j1  -- go down to the left
17          fi ;
18     od
19 parend
```

Figure 5.6 Second stage of robust prefix computation.

twice to implement these two stages. For each stage the controls of algorithm W are used with appropriate modifications as follows:

Stage 1: A binary summation tree is computed in bottom up traversals at the same time when the progress tree of algorithm W is being updated. This modification to the algorithm does not affect its asymptotic complexity.

Stage 2: This is the work phase of algorithm W modified to include the logarithmic time summation operations using the tree computed in stage 1.

In the code, shown in Figure 5.6, $\langle\langle i \rangle\rangle$ is a binary string representing the value i in binary, where most significant bit is bit number 0, and $\langle\langle i \rangle\rangle_h$ is the true/false value of the hth most significant bit of the binary string representing i. The loop in lines 09-18 is the top-down traversal of the summation tree. In lines 13-17 the appropriate subtree sum is added (line 14) at depth h only if the corresponding bit value of the processor PID is *true*. ∎

Since at least $\log N / \log\log N$ parallel time and at least $N \log N / \log\log N$ work will be required by N processors to compute the prefix sums in the absence of failures, the multiplicative overhead in work of our parallel prefix algorithm is only $\log N$.

```
01 forall processors PID=1..N parbegin
02   for 1..log(N)/loglog(N) do
03      -- Perform a single stage to double each pointer at least log(N) times
04      Phase W3: Each processor doubles its leaf's pointer log(N) times.
05      Phase W4: Bottom up traversal to (under)estimate the no. of leaves visited
06      while the underestimate of the visited leaves is not N do
07         Phase W1: Bottom up traversal to enumerate remaining processors
08         Phase W2: Top down traversal to reschedule work
09         Phase W3: Each processor doubles its leaf's pointers log(N) times.
10         Phase W4: Bottom up traversal to measure progress made
11      od
12   od
13 parend
```

Figure 5.7   A high level view of the robust pointer doubling algorithm

5.5.2   Pointer Doubling

Another important improvement for the fail-stop case is a robust *pointer doubling* operation that is a basic building block for many parallel algorithms.

Theorem 5.5.3 There is a robust list ranking algorithm for the fail-stop model with $S = O(\frac{\log N}{\log \log N} S_w(P, N))$, where N is the input list size and $S_w(N, P)$ is the complexity of algorithm W for the initial number of processors P, where $1 \le P \le N$.

Proof: The robust algorithm is implemented using the framework of algorithm W, GPA, and the standard list ranking algorithm that uses the pointer doubling operation. A high level algorithm description is given in Figure 5.7, where Phases W1 through W4 refer to the phases of algorithm W.

We associate each list element with a progress tree leaf. Phase W3 uses the GPA approach to double pointers and update distances. As before, we use two generation of the arrays representing the pointers, and the running ranks of the list elements – one is used as the *current* values, and the other as the *future* values being computed. Binary tags are used to determine which generation is *current*, and which is *future*. The generations alternate as the computation progresses.

The $\log N$ pointer doubling operations in phase W3 makes it sufficient for the outmost **for** loop to iterate $\log N / \log \log N$ times, and it does not affect the complexity of the approach in algorithm W, since Phases W1, W2 and W4 take $\Theta(\log N)$ time. This results in $S = O(\frac{\log N}{\log \log N} S_w(P, N))$. ∎

The technique of Theorem 5.5.3 for the list ranking algorithm achieves a log log N improvement in work over the simulations using algorithm W, i.e., instead of $S = O(\log N \cdot S_w)$ we achieve $S = O(\log N \cdot S_w / \log \log N)$. Thus, with Theorem 3.3.5 we have the following result:

Corollary 5.5.4 There is a N-processor robust list ranking algorithm for the fail-stop model (with synchronous restarts) with $S = O(N \log^3 N / (\log \log N)^2)$.

This improvement can be used with any algorithm that is based on pointer doubling or that is dominated by a pointer doubling computation.

Remark 5.6 *Robust list ranking in the absence of failures*: The robust list ranking algorithm can be tailored to yield $S = O(N \log N)$ in the absence of failures. This is accomplished by preceding the algorithm with $\log N$ pointer doubling operations and a phase W4. This results in $O(N \log N)$ *additive* overhead. Therefore, for the algorithms that are dominated by pointer doubling with a cost of $\Theta(N \log N)$, there is no asymptotic degradation in the absence of failures. □

5.6 A COMPLEXITY CLASSIFICATION

It is important for parallel algorithms to have efficient work both in the failure-free environment and when they are subject to failures. Even optimal simulations of parallel algorithms can be no more efficient than the algorithms themselves. Here we list some efficiency classes of fault-free PRAM algorithms and the extent to which the algorithm efficiency is preserved under the simulations on fault-prone parallel machine.

5.6.1 Efficient Parallel Computation

An existence of an efficient parallel algorithm for a problem can be used to show the problem's membership in the class $\mathcal{NC}$, the class of problems solvable in polylogarithmic time using polynomial number of processors (where the degree of the polynomial can be greater than 1). The inverse is not necessarily true, i.e., membership in $\mathcal{NC}$ is not a guarantee of efficiency in the use of available resources. This is because the algorithms in $\mathcal{NC}$ allow for polynomial inefficiency in work – the algorithms are fast (polylogarithmic time), but the computational agent can be large (polynomial) relative to the size of a problem.

A characterization of parallel algorithm efficiency can be made to take into account both the parallel time and the size of the computational resource. Complexity classes can be defined with respect to the time complexity $T(N)$ of the best sequential algorithm for a problem of size N – this is analogous to the definition of *robustness*. A class can be characterized in terms of *parallel time* $\tau(N)$ and *parallel work* $\tau(N) \cdot P(N)$. Several such classes have been proposed, and we consider six of them here. For our purposes, in defining the classes it is convenient to use the overhead ratio σ instead of failure-free work. For the failure-free case σ is simply $\tau(N) \cdot P(N)/T(N)$.

Let $T(N)$ be the sequential (RAM) time complexity of a certain problem. The problem belongs to a class given in the table below, if there exists a fault-free parallel algorithm that solves an N-size instance of the problem using $P(N)$ processors in $\tau(N)$ time and with the overhead ratio σ, such that $\tau(N) \in \tau_0$, the parallel time complexity of the class, and $\sigma \in \sigma_0$, the overhead ratio complexity of the class.

Complexity Class	Parallel time complexity τ_0	Overhead ratio complexity σ_0
ENC	$\log^{O(1)}(T(N))$	$O(1)$
EP	$T(N)^\varepsilon, (\varepsilon < 1)$	$O(1)$
ANC	$\log^{O(1)}(T(N))$	$\log^{O(1)}(T(N))$
AP	$T(N)^\varepsilon, (\varepsilon < 1)$	$\log^{O(1)}(T(N))$
SNC	$\log^{O(1)}(T(N))$	$T(N)^{O(1)}$
SP	$T(N)^\varepsilon, (\varepsilon < 1)$	$T(N)^{O(1)}$

Table 5.1   Complexity classes for fault-free parallel computation

The names of the classes are formed by concatenating two designators. The first (E, A or S) denotes work-efficiency (represented by the overhead ratio σ_0), where E stands for "efficient", A for "almost efficient", and S for "semi-efficient". The second part (NC or P) denotes time-efficiency, where NC stands for polylogarithmic running time, and P stands for polynomial running time.

5.6.2   Closures under Failures

We now define criteria for evaluating whether algorithm transformation preserves the efficiency of the algorithms for each of the classes above.

To use time complexity in comparisons, we need to introduce a measure of time for the fault-tolerant algorithms. In a fault-prone environment, a time metric is meaningful provided that a significant number of processors still are active. Here we use the worst case time provided a linear number of processors is active during the computation. This is our weak survivability assumption. In the absence of some such assumption, all one can conclude about the running time is that it is no better than the time of the best sequential algorithm, since the number of active processors might become quite small.

We are again using the full range of simulating processors to maximize speed-up – P fault-prone processors are used to simulate P fault-free processors. We are assuming P is a polynomial in N. Then $\log P = O(\log N)$. We now state the definition:

Definition 5.6.1 Let C_{τ_0,σ_0} be a class with parallel time in the complexity class τ_0 and the overhead ratio in the complexity class σ_0. We say that C_{τ_0,σ_0} is *closed* with respect to a fault-tolerant transformation ϕ if for the best P-processor parallel algorithm A for any problem in C_{τ_0,σ_0} we have:
(1) the competitive overhead σ' of $\phi(A)$ is such that $\sigma' \cdot \sigma_A \in \sigma_0$, where σ_A is the algorithm's overhead ratio, and
(2) when the number of active processors for $\phi(A)$ is always at least cP for a constant c ($0 < c \leq 1$), then the running time τ of $\phi(A)$ is such that $\tau \in \tau_0$.
$\square$

We now consider the closures for the classes using the available simulations.

Failures without restarts or with synchronous restarts

In the fail-stop model without restarts or with synchronous restarts, given any algorithm A, let $\phi_f(A)$ be the fault-tolerant algorithm that can be constructed as either a simulation or a transformation.

Using algorithm W, whose work in solving P-size *Write-All* using P processors is $S_w = O(N \log^2 / \log\log N)$, as the basis for transforming algorithms for fault-free processors, we have the following:

(1) The work per each simulated P-processor step is $O(P \log P^2 / \log\log P)$, and so the worst case competitive overhead σ' is $O(\log P^2 / \log\log P) = \log^{O(1)} N$.

(2) Algorithm W terminates in $S_w/cP = O(\log^2 P / \log\log P)$ time when at least cP processors are active, therefore if the parallel time of algorithm A is τ_A (such that $\tau_A \in \tau_0$ for the appropriate class), then the parallel time of execution for $\phi_f(A)$ using at least cP active processors is $O(\tau_A \cdot \log^2 P / \log\log P) = O(\tau_A \cdot \log^2 N / \log\log N)$.

Synchronous restarts are accommodated by synchronizing restarts with the start of each use of algorithm W in the simulations. The resulting closure properties for fail-stop transformation ϕ_f are obtained by consulting Definition 5.6.1 for each of the classes of Table 5.1. The results are given in Table 5.2.

Complexity Class	Time τ with $\geq cP$ processors is $O(\tau_A \log^2 N / \log\log N)$	Competitive overhead σ' is $O(\log^2 N)$	Closed under ϕ_f?
ENC	$\tau \in O(\log^{O(1)}(T(N)))$	$\sigma' \cdot \sigma \notin O(1)$	No
EP	$\tau \in O(T(N)^\varepsilon)$	$\sigma' \cdot \sigma \notin O(1)$	No
ANC	$\tau \in \log^{O(1)}(T(N))$	$\sigma' \cdot \sigma \in \log^{O(1)}(T(N))$	Yes
AP	$\tau \in O(T(N)^\varepsilon)$	$\sigma' \cdot \sigma \in \log^{O(1)}(T(N))$	Yes
SNC	$\tau \in \log^{O(1)}(T(N))$	$\sigma' \cdot \sigma \in T(N)^{O(1)}$	Yes
SP	$\tau \in O(T(N)^\varepsilon)$	$\sigma' \cdot \sigma \in T(N)^{O(1)}$	Yes

Table 5.2 Closures for transformations in the fail-stop model (with synchronous restarts).

Failures with detectable restarts

In the fail-stop model with detectable restarts, for any algorithm A, let $\phi_r(A)$ be the fault-tolerant algorithm constructed using any of our techniques. In this model we obtain closure properties by deploying algorithm AW^T from Section 3.5.1 that is used, for every $\varepsilon > 0$, to simulates P instructions with $O(P^{1+\varepsilon})$ work. We interleave algorithm AW with algorithm V to lower the competitive overhead σ', and we have the following:.

(1) The work per each simulated P-processor step, is $S = \min\{O(P^{1+\varepsilon}), O(P + P\log^2 P + |F|\log P)\}$ (Theorems 3.4.5 and 3.5.6)) So the worst case competitive overhead σ' is $S/(P + |F|) = O(\log P^2) = \log^{O(1)} N$.

(2) The simulation of each P-processor step terminates $S/cP = O(N^\varepsilon)$ time when at least cP processors are active, regardless of the size of the failure pattern. Therefore if the parallel time of algorithm A is τ_A, then the parallel time of execution for $\phi_r(A)$ with at least cP active processors is $\tau = O(\tau_A \cdot N^\varepsilon)$.

Table 5.3 gives the closure properties under the restartable fail-stop transformation.

Note that due to the logarithmic lower bound for the *Write-All* problem of Corollary 4.1.4, the entries that are marked "No" mean non-closure, while the "Unknown" result means that closure is not achieved with the known results.

Efficient deterministic simulations for undetectable restarts are subject to further research. For example, in Section 5.3.4 we presented deterministic simulations for asynchronous processors or for undetectable restarts that are only efficient for *NC*-fast algorithms. undetectable restarts asynchronous processors

Complexity Class	Time τ with $\geq cP$ processors is $O(\tau_A \cdot P^\varepsilon)$	Competitive overhead σ' is $O(\log^2 N)$	Closed under ϕ_r?
ENC	$\tau \notin \log^{O(1)}(T(N))$	$\sigma' \cdot \sigma \notin O(1)$	No
EP	$\tau \in O(T(N)^\varepsilon)$	$\sigma' \cdot \sigma \notin O(1)$	No
ANC	$\tau \notin \log^{O(1)}(T(N))$	$\sigma' \cdot \sigma \in \log^{O(1)}(T(N))$	Unknown
AP	$\tau \in O(T(N)^\varepsilon)$	$\sigma' \cdot \sigma \in \log^{O(1)}(T(N))$	Yes
SNC	$\tau \notin \log^{O(1)}(T(N))$	$\sigma' \cdot \sigma \in T(N)^{O(1)}$	Unknown
SP	$\tau \in O(T(N)^\varepsilon)$	$\sigma' \cdot \sigma \in T(N)^{O(1)}$	Yes

Table 5.3 Closures for transformations in the model with failures and detectable restarts.

5.7 OPEN PROBLEMS

Narrowing the gap between theory and practice is an area of continuing research. In particular, mapping the simulated PRAM computations onto existing or realizable parallel architectures is a major challenge.

The parallel architecture presented in Chapter 2 relies on the processor-memory interconnect that is only moderately scalable (polylogarithmic growth) given the state-of-the-art technology. The PRAM simulations provide fault-tolerance of processor failures to a greater extent than that provided by realistic fault-tolerant properties of the assumed interconnects. For example, while the simulations can tolerate up to $P-1$ out of P processors failures in arbitrary patterns, the interconnects assume more benign failure patterns, for example of up to N out of $N \log N$ components, in order to guarantee correctness and efficiency.

Despite the attractiveness of oblivious simulations that work for any algorithm, it may be desirable, where optimal simulations are not (yet) possible, to develop custom algorithm transformations that can be optimized by taking advantage of the semantics of the algorithms being transformed. Are there interesting algorithms that can be transformed so that the overhead in work is polylogarithmic in the models with unlimited restarts? It may be necessary to consider algorithms may are less computationally powerful than *Write-All*, since efficient *Write-All* would enable efficient simulations.

Another open problem is to determine the remaining closure properties for the complexity classes presented in Section 5.6. For some classes, closures with respect to fault-tolerant transformations is not achieved with the known results. For undetectable results it is still unknown whether deterministic simulations with polylogarithmic competitive overhead exist.

5.8 BIBLIOGRAPHIC NOTES

Simulations between fault-free PRAM models are discussed by Karp and Ra-machandran in [60]. Simulations of fault-free PRAM by other fault-free models are discussed by Leighton [74, Section 3.6], and in the survey by Harris [46].

The simulation technique in this chapter based on the *Write-All* paradigm and the use of *general parallel assignment* as the basic building block is due to Kanellakis and Shvartsman [56]. The use of these techniques for simulation of arbitrary PRAMs is presented by Kedem, Palem and Spirakis in [63] and Shvartsman [110]. Martel, Park and Subramonian deployed these techniques in a probabilistic setting [87]. When the probability is low that the tentative phase in a simulation is incorrect due to failures, Kedem, Palem, Raghunathan and Spirakis [62] show how to combine a series of potentially incorrect tentative steps with a complete definitive step that detects and rolls back incorrect computation steps. Simulations for initial faults and simulations with bounded concurrent memory access are due to Kanellakis, Michailidis and Shvartsman [54]. Computation with faulty parallel processors and memory was studied by Chlebus, Gąsieniec and Pelc [22].

Kedem, Palem and Spirakis [63] observed that in a simulations, P processors can only read $O(P)$ and write $O(P)$ shared memory cells in a single PRAM step. Therefore the overhead in shared memory to store the future generation of memory need only be $O(P)$ when processors have no local memory (Remark 5.2). Shvartsman [110] showed that fail-stop no-restart simulations of ARBITRARY, PRIORITY and STRONG CRCW PRAMs can be done using fail-stop PRAMs of the same type.

In the models with clear initial memory, Kanellakis and Shvartsman [56] showed how to save a factor of $\log N / \log \log N$ off of the pointer doubling simulations. This improvement can be used for several important robust algorithms that are based on pointer doubling, e.g., the algorithms for computing the tree functions of Tarjan and Vishkin [113] that have the same work complexity as robust pointer doubling. Prefix sums algorithm occurs in solutions of several important problems, see Bilardi and Preparata [17]. Efficient parallel algorithms and circuits for computing prefix sums were given by Ladner and Fischer in [71]. Using randomization and off-line adversaries, improvements were obtained by Martel, Subramonian and Park [84, 87] in expected work of parallel prefix and other transformed algorithms. Shvartsman [112] constructed the robust transformation for parallel prefix using an iterative version of the recursive algorithm of Lynch and Fischer [71]. An asynchronous PRAM model was extensively studied by Cole and Zajicek [26, 27] who developed a number of algorithms for the model and analyzed them using a rounds complexity measure. Cole and Zajicek observed that in many cases the algorithms developed directly for their model are more efficient than oblivious simulations of synchronous algorithms using barriers.

An interesting duality can be observed for sequential and parallel computations in the context of asynchronous parallel models. Baudet [14] showed how a *sequential* computation can be made faster on an asynchronous parallel machine by capitalizing on processors that are *faster* than others during certain parts of the computation. On the other hand, Dasgupta, Kedem and Rabin [33] observed that *parallel* computation can be made faster by essentially ignoring processors that are *slower* than others.

Robust computation in the failure models with undetectable restarts or asynchrony is similar to, but is distinct from the notion of wait-free computation. In particular, the impossibility results of Herlihy [47, 48, 49] and Loui and Abu-Amara [77] for consensus and wait-free data structures do not directly translate to any impossibility results for asynchronous simulations. One of the reasons is that the simulating processors do not start the computation with private values involved in any kind of agreement – any private values of the simulated processors are stored in well-known locations in shared memory. Additionally, in simulations processors operate essentially autonomously and are not involved in the maintenance of data structures used for synchronization – even when the termination of a certain stage is established by a processor, it may be the only processor that does so, or it may be the last processor to do so being far behind other processors. For a discussion of related issues, see the paper by Kedem, Palem, Rabin and Raghunathan [61].

The discussion of the class $\mathcal{NC}$ can be found in Pippenger [99]. A characterization of parallel algorithm efficiency that takes into account both the parallel time and the size of the computational resource is defined by Vitter and Simmons [118] and expanded on by Kruskal, Rudolph and Snir [69]. In Section 5.6 we dealt with the classes in [69] using definitions that are equivalent for fault-free environment, but that are more convenient for comparisons with fault-tolerant algorithms. Ajtai, Aspnes, Dwork and Waarts [7] formulated a framework for systematic competitive analysis of distributed algorithms using a measure similar to the overhead ratio σ and the competitive overhead ratio σ'.

SHARED MEMORY RANDOMIZED ALGORITHMS AND DISTRIBUTED MODELS AND ALGORITHMS

I N THIS final chapter[1] we give an overview of the research results in robust computation for shared memory randomized algorithms and for the message passing model of computation.

6.1 ASYNCHRONY AND SHARED MEMORY RANDOMIZED ALGORITHMS

Synchrony is one of the strongest assumptions made in the standard PRAM models. Processor synchrony is realistically achievable for bounded numbers of processors as is done in many systolic arrays and some parallel machines. However, the requirement of synchrony becomes unrealistic when the number of processors needs to scale as the size of the problems increase or when it is necessary to extend the notion of "processor" to include processes or virtual processors.

We presented several deterministic algorithms for fault-prone models of shared-memory parallel computation where an omniscient adversary is able to impose processor failures, restarts and delays. While these algorithms achieve high efficiency for most models, when we unleash the most powerful adversary, that is able to cause failures and undetectable restarts, essentially imposing asynchrony, the algorithms can achieve only the polynomial efficiency. Fortunately we do not encounter any impossibility results – as would have been the case, for example, if processors had to start the computation with private values and

---

[1] This part of the monograph was planned by Paris Kanellakis to contain a synthesis of the latest results for fault-tolerance randomized parallel algorithms and for distributed memory models. Here I present a bibliographic overview of the results in this area that we consider important and that Paris planned to examine in depth. [AAS]

consensus was required. Nevertheless in an asynchronous setting the deterministic algorithms fall somewhat short of reaching the goal of near-linear parallel speed-up.

Randomization is an important tool which has extensive and fruitful application to fault-tolerance. Randomization can be introduced in two areas. It can be used as an algorithmic technique, and it can be used to limit the power of the adversary. Several randomized approaches have been developed for solving the *Write-All* problem, and for simulating arbitrary PRAM algorithms in the presence of failures and delays. Using the average or the expected performance measures, such algorithms and simulations can be extremely efficient or even optimal.

When randomization is used as an algorithmic tool, probabilistic techniques play a key role in the analysis of randomized (and asynchronous) parallel algorithms. However, it is often hard to compare the analytical bounds of randomized algorithms with those of deterministic algorithms. This is because much of the randomized analysis is done using an off-line and/or oblivious adversary assumption. For example, an adversary may not be allowed to stop or delay a processor based on the outcome of the processor's coin toss. When randomized algorithms are exposed to the on-line omniscient adversary, then their work efficiency, whether worst case or average, incurs a linear, or worse, overhead. In some cases such overhead can be induced by even unsophisticated adversaries. However, randomized algorithms often achieve better practical performance than deterministic ones, even when their analytical bounds are similar.

When randomization is used in models of failures, the adversary is allowed to stop or delay processors only on the basis of the random choice. In the fail-stop no-restart model, the adversary may be restricted to cause failures randomly, but with a probability that is inversely proportional to the running time of the algorithm. Such adversaries are relatively benign, as they are incapable of consistently causing bursts of failures or failures that affect specific subsets of the processors. As with randomized algorithms, when deterministic algorithms, designed for randomized oblivious adversary, are exposed to an omniscient adversary, their performance can be degraded by a linear factor.

6.1.1   Asynchrony and Randomization

As we have already suggested, randomization yields improvements over deterministic algorithms for the asynchronous models of parallel computation. Such asynchronous models were introduced and studied by Cole and Zajicek [26, 27], Gibbons [44], Martel, Subramonian and Park [87, 84], and Nishimura [93].

Cole and Zajicek [27] showed that fundmental parallel operations, e.g., associative summations and pointer doubling, can be efficiently implemented on an asynchronous PRAM where a variety of delays can be randomly caused by the adversary. In this model, memory accesses are atomic, but the time required to execute an instruction is not constrained to be a single time unit as in the synchronous PRAM, but it varies during the execution. The complexity measures used by Cole and Zajicek to evaluate the efficiency of asynchronous PRAM algorithms are the number of processors used by the algorithm and the *rounds* complexity. Here a round is defined as the time during which each processor executes at least one instruction. Rounds complexity then is the maximum number of rounds possible for a computation. In this model it is possible to develop algorithms with efficient rounds complexity that do not rely on global synchronization. For example, there is a rounds-optimal $O(\log N)$ algorithm for summation of N numbers that uses $N/\log N$ processors. The basic idea of the algorithm is to use a binary tree with $N/\log N$ nodes, position one processor at each node and associating $\log N$ input values (originally stored in shared memory) with each processor. The processors first sum these $\log N$ values, and then each processor adds its partial sum to the two partial sums of its children as soon as the partial sums are available. After at most $\log N$ rounds each processor computes its local partial sums and after at most another $\log N$ rounds the root processor computes the sum of all N input values. The rounds complexity measure is comparable to the parallel time complexity measure for synchronous parallel algorithms when the time required by any processor to execute an instruction is bounded from above by some constant. Cole and Zajicek also introduced a variable speed asynchronous PRAM model with the time to execute an instruction varying probabilistically and being either bounded by some parameter or unbounded. They showed the existence of tree-based summation and pointer-doubling algorithms that are fast with high probability.

A different way of handling processor asynchrony was introduced by Gibbons [44]. In this version of asynchronous PRAM, each processor executes instructions according to its own internal clock, while the synchronization of processors, where necessary, is achieved by an explicit step using a synchronization barrier. The cost, $B(p)$, of using the synchronization step depends on the number of processors p, participating in the synchronization step, and is parameterized using a function $B()$. This function is chosen to model the synchronization characteristics of a particular multiprocessor architecture for which an algorithm may be targeted. For example, $B()$ may be proportional to the diameter of the network interconnecting the processors.

Nishimura [93] showed that many synchronous parallel algorithms can be transformed to execute on asynchronous PRAM with minimal additive slow-down when the adversary is restricted to random selections of possible execution schedules.

Martel, Park and Subramonian [87] developed several optimal randomized algorithms for completely asynchronous PRAMs [84] and PRAMs with bounded asynchrony [87]. They developed randomized solutions for the *Write-All* problem and deployed their algorithms in general simulations.

With introduction of randomization, the lower bounds for the *Write-All* problem need to be reexamined to take into account the power of the adversary. All lower bounds we presented in Chapter 4 also hold for randomized algorithms subject to omniscient adversary. This adversary uses no knowledge about the methods that the algorithms employ in solving the *Write-All* problem. Therefore the worst case behavior caused by such adversaries applies to the algorithms using the stronger IDEAL PRAM model of Beame and Høastad [15], but also to the randomized algorithms. However, when the adversary is oblivious, it is not clear whether the bounds still hold.

For the CRCW model, Martel and Subramonian [86] have extended the logarithmic lower bound in Theorem 4.1.3 in Chapter 4 (due to Kedem, Palem, Ragunathan and Spirakis [62]) to randomized algorithms against oblivious adversaries, and they gave an optimal randomized CRCW algorithm for *Write-All*.

The power of randomization turns out to be an enabling factor for general PRAM simulations on the CREW variant of PRAM. We have shown in Chapter 4 (Theorem 4.1.5) that deterministic *Write-All* on CREW PRAM requires quadratic work for omniscient adversaries [56]. Martel and Subramonian [86] showed that in the presence of asynchrony, *Write-All* cannot be solved at all on the CREW PRAM. However, for synchronous CREW PRAMs, the quadratic lower bound does not apply to randomized algorithms against oblivious adversary — Martel and Subramonian show an optimal randomized CREW *Write-All* algorithm and use it to produce PRAM simulations on fault-prone CREW PRAMs.

6.1.2   Logical Clocks and Information Dispersal

Randomized approaches to asynchronous parallel computation have been examined in depth by Aumann and Rabin [11], Aumann, Kedem, Palem and Rabin [12], and Kedem, Palem, Rabin and Raghunathan [61]. These analyses involve randomness in a central way. They are mostly about off-line or oblivious adversaries, which cause faults during the computation but pick the times of these faults before the computation.

In [62], the algorithm simulation or transformation approach of [63] and [110] (covered in Chapter 5) was improved for randomized settings by combining probabilistic and deterministic *Write-All* algorithms to obtain extremely efficient program transformations. The sophisticated approach in [61] addresses the problems of variables being overwritten (*clobbered*) by slow asynchronous processors by using *information dispersal* (Rabin [104]), and *evasive* writes to random locations are used to dramatically reduce the probability of irrepairable damage being done by clobbering to a dispersed variable. The approach also provides a *logical clock* that maintains the step number being currently executed by processors and that is also resilient to clobbers [11]. This randomized approach requires a logarithmic overhead in memory, thus, it is more general and more space-efficient than our deterministic approach in Section 5.3.4. With dispersed variables, there is still a possibility of the variable being clobbered. In that case the computation will need to be rolled back and restarted at some prior point. The authors show that since the probability of this is very small, a simpler approach can be used in such case, with the increased costs readily amortized. Additional improvements for large-grained parallel programs is presented in [12].

6.2 DISTRIBUTED MEMORY MODELS AND ALGORITHMS

The *Write-All* problem, although stated in terms of writing to N locations in shared memory, was defined to capture the computational progress necessary by P processors to perform N units of work in the presence of failures. The general problem of performing N tasks reliably using P processors, whether in the shared-memory or the message-passing computation paradigm, is one of the fundamental issues in distributed computation. Abstracting away from shared-memory paradigm, we can generalize this problem in terms of *Do-All*:

Perform a set of N tasks using P fault-prone processors.

This problem was considered for the message-passing model by Dwork, Halpern and Waarts in their pioneering work [35]. They developed several efficient algorithms for *Do-All* in the setting where the processors are subject to fail-stop (or crash) failures and where the tasks can be performed using the *at-least-once* execution semantics (i.e., the tasks can be made idempotent). Their model of computation assumes a synchronous system of processors, such that in one time unit a processor can perform a local computation and complete one task, and perform one round of communication consisting of sending and receiving messages.

Algorithmic techniques for distributed *Do-All* are motivated with the help of an observation that there is a qualitative duality between the shared-memory and the message-passing settings. In a shared-memory algorithm, a key datum, say reflecting an important component of the state of the computation, can be stored in a shared memory cell, and P processors can learn the value stored by performing P reads. In a message-passing algorithm, the only way to propagate information, stored anywhere, to P processors, is to do so by means of at least $P - 1$ messages. Thus in message-passing algorithms, one sees a multicast or diffusion of a value to a subset of processors as a dual of these processors reading the value from a location in shared memory.

For the distributed message-passing models, one has to consider the costs of a computation in terms of the total work performed by the processors, and in terms of the number of messages sent by the processors. In the shared-memory models we have covered thus far, the algorithm efficiency was determined primarily by the *available processor steps* measure S. Since in the worst case each instruction involves a constant number of memory accesses, the measure S is also the measure of the number of memory accesses (i.e., the communication cost) performed by the computation. The one-to-one cost correspondence between work and communication does not apply to the message-passing models, since the number of messages sent and received by one processor in one round of communication can be 0, or it can be comparable to P when broadcasts are enabled.

To measure the communication efficiency of distributed algorithms, the number of messages sent by the processors is counted. One can also consider the total number of bits sent when the messages can vary in size or can be large. Measuring the work of a computation depends on the interpretation of the relative costs associated with different processing steps. Specifically, one needs to consider the costs associated with local processing and the costs associated with doing the tasks in solving the *Do-All* problem.

6.2.1   Optimizing Task-Oriented Work

In the setting of Dwork, Halpern and Waarts [35], the local computation, whether performing low-level administrative tasks (such as maintaining the local clock) or idling, is considered to be negligible compared to the costs of performing the *Do-All* tasks, where processors may need to do constant size, but significant processing, or the costs of communication with external systems. This approach is consistent with the accepted accounting of costs in distributed algorithms. Additionally, Dwork, Halpern and Waarts consider *processes*, a notion that can be more general than *processors*. For example, when we interpret processes as *threads of control*, such that several threads may co-exist on the same processor, then the idle "steps" taken by threads need not be accounted for, since during such idle steps the processor hosting the thread can be executing other steps on behalf of other threads. Thus idle thread steps do not constitute a waste of the computational resources, and it is reasonable to account only for work spent on the *Do-All* tasks.

Dwork, Halpern and Waarts define the *effort* of an algorithm as the sum of its work and message complexity. This is done under the assumption that the cost of performing a unit of work and sending a message are comparable. They observe that at least $P + N - 1$ units of work are necessary to solve the *Do-All* problem of size N using P processors. The goal then is the development of algorithms that perform $O(N + P)$ work, thus achieving work-optimality, while keeping the total effort reasonable. In this synchronous model, the running time of an algorithm is also a meaningful measure of efficiency, and in the analysis of algorithms this measure is also considered. The first two algorithms are sequential — at any point in time only one task is being performed, thus in these algorithms the redundancy of having multiple processors contributes to fault-tolerance, but not to speed-up. The third algorithm achieves fault-free time optimality, with graceful degradation of running time in the presence of failures.

One algorithm presented by the authors (protocol $\mathcal{B}$) has effort $O(N + P\sqrt{P})$, with work contributing the cost $O(N + P)$ towards the effort, and message complexity contributing the cost $O(P\sqrt{P})$. The running time of the algorithm is $O(N + P)$. The use of synchrony in the algorithm is limited to failure detection by means of time-outs. Such algorithms can be converted to asynchronous algorithms when the underlying system is equipped with failure detectors. In this algorithm the N tasks are divided into *chunks* and each of these is divided into *subchuncks*. Processors checkpoint their progress by multicasting the completion information to subsets of processors after performing a subchunk, and broadcasting to all processors after completing chunks of work.

Another algorithm in [35] (protocol $\mathcal{C}$) has effort $O(N + P \log P)$. This includes optimal work of $O(N + P)$, message complexity of $(P \log P)$, and time $O(P^2(N + P)2^{N+P})$. Thus the reduction in message complexity is traded-off for a significant increase in time.

The third work-optimal algorithm (protocol $\mathcal{D}$) is designed for maximum speedup, which is achieved with a more aggressive checkpointing strategy, thus trading-off time for messages. The message complexity is quadratic in P for the fault-free case, and in the presence of a failure pattern F, the message complexity degrades to $\Theta(|F| \cdot P^2)$.

One interesting application of the *Do-All* algorithms is to solving Byzantine agreement with crash failures. Dwork, Halpern and Waarts show that a *Do-All* algorithm with P processors and N tasks can be used to solve agreement for N processors and less than P failures [35]. In this application, the tasks performed by processors are sending messages to other processors informing them of the agreement value.

6.2.2   Optimizing Total Work

De Prisco, Mayer and Yung [34], following [35], also consider the *Do-All* problem. Their goal is the development of fast and message-efficient algorithms. The
work measure they consider is the available processor steps S, that accounts
for all steps taken by the processors, i.e., the steps involved in performing the
Do-All tasks and any other steps taken by the processors. Optimization of S
leads to fast algorithms whose performance degrades gracefully with failures.
The communication efficiency is gauged through the standard message complexity measure. The authors pursue efficiency in terms of what they call the
lexicographic optimization of complexity measures. This means firstly achieving
efficient work, then efficient communication complexity.

In the shared-memory paradigm, optimality cannot be achieved in solving the
Write-All problem with the full range of processors $P = N$ (as shown in Chapter 4). In [34] it is shown that in the message-passing paradigm solving the
Do-All problem is even harder — the work required to solve *Do-All* (measured
as available processor steps) becomes quadratic when P is comparable to N.
This is established by showing that at least one checkpoint involving all processors must be performed by any algorithm and that performing a checkpoint is
as hard as agreement. Since sub-quadratic work algorithms exist in the shared-
memory models, this result shows separation between the shared-memory and
message-passing models.

The authors [34] present an algorithm that has $S = O(N + (|F| + 1)P)$ and
message complexity $O((|F|+1)P)$. This algorithm can be used with any $P \leq N$.
However, due to the quadratic lower bound on work, substantial processing
slackness ($P \ll N$) is introduced. The algorithm proceeds iteratively, with each
iteration consisting of (1) the work-allocation phase, (2) the synchronization
phase, done concurrently with the work phase, and (3) the checkpoint phase.
The work phase uses the estimates of the remaining tasks and of the available
processors to balance the surviving processors' loads. Synchronization and
checkpoint phases are agreement protocols. Respectively, these determine the
time when the checkpoint is to start, and the set of active processors. This
algorithm achieves optimality in work with respect to the lower bound.

Galil, Mayer and Yung [43], working in the context of Byzantine agreement
with crash failures (for which they establish a message-optimal $O(N)$ solution),
improved the message complexity of [34] to $O(|F|P^\varepsilon + \min\{|F| + 1, \log P\}P)$
while maintaining work optimality. Their algorithms use message diffusion trees
providing a distributed analog of processor priority trees used in controlling
memory access concurrency in shared-memory algorithms.

Ἀλλὰ γὰρ ἤδη ὥρα ἀπιέναι,
ἐμοὶ μὲν ἀποθανουμένῳ, ὑμῖν δὲ βιωσομένοις·
ὁπότεροι δ' ἡμῶν ἔρχονται ἐπί ἄμεινον πρᾶγμα,
ἄδηλον παντὶ πλὶν ἢ τῷ θεῷ. [2]

---

[2] From Plato, *Apology of Socrates* [102]. Ending the farewell to his friends, Socrates says:

But now is the time to go,
for mine is to die and yours is to live.
Whose path is better is known only to God.

BIBLIOGRAPHY AND REFERENCES

[1] S. Abiteboul, G.M. Kuper, H.G. Mairson, A.A. Shvartsman and M.Y. Vardi, "In Memoriam: Paris C. Kanellakis", *ACM Computing Surveys*, vol. 28, no. 1, pp. 5-15, 1996.

[2] J.A. Abraham, P. Banerjee, C.-Y. Chen, W. K. Fuchs, S.-Y. Kuo, A.L. Narasimha Reddy, "Fault tolerance techniques for systolic arrays", *IEEE Computer*, Vol.20, No.7, pp. 65-76, 1987.

[3] G. B. Adams III, D. P. Agrawal, H. J. Seigel, "A Survey and Comparison of Fault-tolerant Multistage Interconnection Networks", *IEEE Computer*, 20, 6, pp. 14-29, 1987.

[4] Y. Afek, B. Awerbuch, E. Gafni, "Applying static network protocols to dynamic networks", in *Proc. of the 28th IEEE Symposium on Foundations of Computer Science*, pp. 358-370, 1987.

[5] Y. Afek, B. Awerbuch, S. Plotkin, M. Saks, "Local Management of a Global Resource in a Communication Network", *Proc. of the 28th IEEE Symposium on Foundations of Computer Science*, pp. 347-357, 1987.

[6] A. Aggarwal, A.K. Chandra and M. Snir, "On Communication Latency in PRAM Computations, in *Proc. of 1st ACM Symposium on Parallel Algorithms and Architectures*, pp. 11-21, 1989.

[7] M. Ajtai, J. Aspnes, C. Dwork, O. Waarts, "A Theory of Competitive Analysis for Distributed Algorithms", mansucript, 1996 (prelim. vers. appears as "The Competitive Analysis of Wait-Free Algorithms and its Application to the Co-operative Collect Problem", in *Proc. of the 35th IEEE Symp. on Foundations of Computer Science*, 1994).

[8] G. Almasi and A. Gottlieb, *Highly Parallel Computing*, Second Edition, Benjamin/Cummins, 1993.

[9] R.J. Anderson, H. Woll, "Algorithms for the Certified Write All Problem," to appear in *SIAM Journal of Computing*. Prel. version: "Wait-Free Parallel Algorithms for the Union-Find Problem", *Proc. of the 23rd ACM Symp. on Theory of Computing*, pp. 370-380, 1991.

[10] S.W. Apgar, "Interactive Animation of Fault-Tolerant Parallel Algorithms," Master's Thesis, Brown University, 1992.

[11] Y. Aumann and M.O. Rabin, "Clock Construction in Fully Asynchronous Parallel Systems and PRAM Simulation", in *Proc. of the 33rd IEEE Symposium on Foundations of Computer Science*, pp. 147-156, 1993.

[12] Y. Aumann, Z.M. Kedem, K.V. Palem, M.O. Rabin, "Highly Efficient Asynchronous Execution of Large-Grained Parallel Programs", in *Proc. of the 34th IEEE Symposium on Foundations of Computer Science*, pp. 271-280, 1993.

[13] B. Awerbuch, "On the effects of feedback in dynamic network protocols", *in Proc. of the 29th IEEE FOCS*, pp. 231-242, 1988.

[14] G. Baudet, "Asynchronous iterative methods for multiprocessors", *JACM*, vol. 25, no. 2, pp. 226-244, 1978.

[15] P. Beame and J. Høastad, "Optimal bounds for decision problems on the CRCW PRAM," *Journal of the ACM*, vol. 36, no. 3, pp. 643-670, 1989.

[16] P. Beame, M. Kik and M. Kutylowski, "Information broadcasting by Exclusive Read PRAMs", manuscript 1992.

[17] G. Bilardi and F.P. Preparata, "Size-Time Complexity of Boolean Networks for Prefix Computation," *Journal of the ACM*, vol. 36, no. 2, pp. 363-382, 1989.

[18] G. Birkhoff, S. MacLane, *A Survey of Modern Algebra*, 4th ed., Macmillan, 1977.

[19] R.P. Brent, The parallel evaluation of general arithmetic expressions, *J. of the ACM*, vol. 21, pp. 201–206, 1974.

[20] J. Buss, P.C. Kanellakis, P. Ragde, A.A. Shvartsman, "Parallel algorithms with processor failures and delays", *Journal of Algorithms*, vol. 20, pp. 45-86, 1996.

[21] M. Chean and J.A.B. Fortes, "A Taxonomy of Reconfiguration Techniques for Fault-Tolerant Processor Arrays," *IEEE Computer*, vol. 23, no. 1, pp. 55-69, 1990.

[22] B.S. Chlebus, L. Gąsieniec and A. Pelc, "Fast Determinsitic Simulation of Computations on Faulty Parallel Machines", in *Proc of the 3rd Annual European Symp. on Algorithms*, 1995.

[23] B.S. Chlebus, A. Gambin, and P. Indyk, "PRAM Computations Resilient to Memory Faults", in *Proceedings 2nd Annual European Symposium on Algorithms*, Springer Lecture Notes in Computer Science 855, pp. 401–412, 1994.

[24] B.S. Chlebus, A. Gambin, and P. Indyk, "Shared-memory Simulations on a Faulty-Memory DMM", in *Proceedings 23rd International Colloquium on Automata, Languages and Programming*, Springer Lecture Notes on Computer Science 1099, pp. 586–597, 1996.

[25] B. Chor, A. Israeli and M. Li, "On processor coordination using asynchronous hardware", in *Proc. of the 6th ACM Symp. on Principles of Distributed Computing*, pp. 86-97, 1987.

[26] R. Cole and O. Zajicek, "The APRAM: Incorporating Asynchrony into the PRAM Model," in *Proc. of the 1989 ACM Symp. on Parallel Algorithms and Architectures*, pp. 170-178, 1989.

[27] R. Cole and O. Zajicek, "The Expected Advantage of Asynchrony," in *Proc. 2nd ACM Symp. on Parallel Algorithms and Architectures*, pp. 85-94, 1990.

[28] S.A. Cook, "An Overview of Computational Complexity," in *Comm. of the ACM*, vol. 9, pp. 400-408, 1983.

[29] S.A. Cook, C. Dwork and R. Reischuk, "Upper and Lower Time Bounds for Parallel Random Access Machine without Simultaneous Writes, *SIAM Journal on Computing*, vol. 15, pp. 87-89, 1986.

[30] T.H. Cormen, C.E. Leiserson and R.L. Rivest, *Introduction to Algorithms*, MIT Press, 1990.

[31] F. Cristian, "Understanding Fault-Tolerant Distributed Systems", in *Communications of the ACM*, vol. 3, no. 2, pp. 56-78, 1991.

[32] D. Culler, R. Karp, D. Patterson, A. Sahay, K.E. Schauser, E. Santos, R. Subramonian and T. van Eicken, "LogP: Towards a Realistic Model of Parallel Computation", in *4th ACM PPOPP*, pp. 1-12, 1993.

[33] P. Dasgupta, Z. Kedem and M. Rabin, "Parallel Processing on Networks of Workstation: A Fault-Tolerant, High Performance Approach", in the *Proc. of the International Conference on Distributed Computer Systems*, pp. 467-474, 1995.

[34] R. De Prisco, A. Mayer, M. Yung, "Time-Optimal Message-Efficient Work Performance in the Presence of Faults", in *Proc. of the 13-th ACM Symposium on Principles of Distributed Computing*, pp. 161-171, 1994.

[35] C. Dwork, J. Halpern, O. Waarts, "Performing Work Efficiently in the Presence of Faults", to appear in *SIAM J. on Computing*, prelim. vers. appeared in *Proc. 11th ACM Symposium on Principles of Distributed Computing*, pp. 91-102, 1992.

[36] C. Dwork, D. Peleg, N. Pippenger and E. Upfal, "Fault Tolerance in Networks of Bounded Degree", *in Proc. of the 18th ACM Symposium on Theory of Computing*, pp. 370-379, 1986.

[37] D. Eppstein and Z. Galil, "Parallel Techniques for Combinatorial Computation", *Annual Computer Science Review*, 3 (1988), pp. 233-83.

[38] M.J. Fischer, "The consensus problem in unreliable distributed systems (a brief survey)", *Yale Univ. Tech. Rep.*, DCS/RR-273, 1983.

[39] M.J. Fischer and N. A. Lynch, "A lower bound for the time to assure interactive consistency", *IPL*, vol. 14., no. 4, pp. 183-186, 1982.

[40] M.J. Fischer, N. A. Lynch, M. S. Paterson, "Impossibility of distributed consensus with one faulty process", *JACM*, vol. 32, no. 2, pp. 374-382, 1985.

[41] M.J. Flynn, "Very High Speed Computing Systems", in *Proc. of IEEE*, vol. 54, no. 12, pp. 1901-1909, 1966.

[42] S. Fortune and J. Wyllie, "Parallelism in Random Access Machines", *Proc. the 10th ACM Symposium on Theory of Computing*, pp. 114-118, 1978.

[43] Z. Galil, A. Mayer and M. Yung, "Resolving the Message Complexity of Byzantine Agreement and Beyond", in *Proceedings of the IEEE Foundations of Computer Science FOCS*, 1995.

[44] P. Gibbons, "A More Practical PRAM Model," in *Proc. of the 1989 ACM Symposium on Parallel Algorithms and Architectures*, pp. 158-168, 1989.

[45] A. Gibbons and P. Spirakis, Eds., *Lectures on Parallel Computation*, Cambridge International Series on Parallel Computation: 4, Cambridge University Press, 1993.

[46] T.J. Harris, "A Survey of PRAM Simulation Techniques, *ACM Computing Surveys*, vol. 26, no. 2, pp. 187-206, 1994.

[47] M.P. Herlihy, "Wait-Free Synchronization", *ACM Trans. on Prog. Lang. and Systems*, vol. 4, no. 1, pp. 32-53, 1986.

[48] M.P. Herlihy, "Impossibility and universality results for wait-free synchronization", in *Proc. of the 7th ACM Symp. on Principles of Distributed Computing*, pp. 276-290, 1988.

[49] M.P. Herlihy, "Impossibility Results for Asynchronous PRAM", in *Proc. of the Third ACM Symposium on Parallel Algorithms and Architectures*, pp. 327-336, 1991.

[50] S.W. Hornick and F. P. Preparata, "Deterministic P-RAM: simulation with constant redundancy," in *Proc. of the 1989 ACM Symp. on Parallel Algorithms and Arch.*, pp. 103-109, 1989.

[51] *IEEE Computer*, "Interconnection Networks", special issue, vol. 20, no. 6, 1987.

[52] *IEEE Computer*, "Fault-Tolerant Systems", special issue, vol. 23, no. 7, 1990.

[53] C. Kaklamanis, A. Karlin, F. Leighton, V. Milenkovic, P. Raghavan, S. Rao, C. Thomborson, A. Tsantilas, "Asymptotically Tight Bounds for Computing with Arrays of Processors," in *Proc. of the 31st IEEE Symposium on Foundations of Computer Science*, pp. 285-296, 1990.

[54] P.C. Kanellakis, D. Michailidis, A.A. Shvartsman, "Controlling Memory Access Concurrency in Efficient Fault-Tolerant Parallel Algorithms", *Nordic J. of Computing*, vol. 2, pp. 146-180, 1995 (prel. vers. in *7th Int-l Work. on Distributed Algorithms*, pp. 99-114, 1993).

[55] P.C. Kanellakis, D. Michailidis, A.A. Shvartsman, "Concurrency = Fault-Tolerance in Parallel Computation", invited paper, *Proc. 5th Int-l Conf. on Concurrency Theory*, LNCS vol. 836, pp. 242-266, 1994.

[56] P.C. Kanellakis and A.A. Shvartsman, "Efficient Parallel Algorithms Can Be Made Robust", *Distributed Computing*, vol. 5, no. 4, pp. 201-217, 1992; prelim. vers. in *Proc. of the 8th ACM PODC*, pp. 211-222, 1989.

[57] P.C. Kanellakis and A.A. Shvartsman, "Efficient Parallel Algorithms On Restartable Fail-Stop Processors", in *Proc. of the 10th ACM Symposium on Principles of Distributed Computing*, 1991.

[58] P.C. Kanellakis and A.A. Shvartsman, "Robust Computing with Fail-Stop Processors", in *Proc. of the Second Annual Review and Workshop on Ultradependable Multicomputers*, Office of Naval Research, pp. 55-60, 1991.

[59] P.C. Kanellakis and A.A. Shvartsman, "Fault-Tolerance and Efficiency in Massively Parallel Algorithms", in *Foundations of Dependable Computing – Paradigms for Dependable Applications*, G. M. Koob and C. G. Lau, Eds., Kluwer Acad. Publ., pp. 125-154, 1994.

[60] R.M. Karp and V. Ramachandran, "A Survey of Parallel Algorithms for Shared-Memory Machines", in *Handbook of Theoretical Computer Science* (ed. J. van Leeuwen), vol. 1, North-Holland, 1990.

[61] Z.M. Kedem, K.V. Palem, M.O. Rabin, A. Raghunathan, "Efficient Program Transformations for Resilient Parallel Computation via Randomization," in *Proc. 24th ACM Symp. on Theory of Comp.*, pp. 306-318, 1992.

[62] Z.M. Kedem, K.V. Palem, A. Raghunathan, and P. Spirakis, "Combining Tentative and Definite Executions for Dependable Parallel Computing," in *Proc 23d ACM. Symposium on Theory of Computing*, pp. 381-390, 1991.

[63] Z. M. Kedem, K. V. Palem, and P. Spirakis, "Efficient Robust Parallel Computations," *Proc. 22nd ACM Symp. on Theory of Computing*, pp. 138-148, 1990.

[64] D.E. Knuth, *The Art of Computer Programming, vol. 3, Sorting and Searching*, Addison-Wesley Publ. Co., 1973.

[65] G.M. Koob and C.G. Lau, Eds., *Foundations of Dependable Computing: Paradigms for Dependable Applications*, Kluwer Academic Publishers, 1994.

[66] G.M. Koob and C.G. Lau, Eds., *Foundations of Dependable Computing: Models and Frameworks for Dependable Systems*, Kluwer Academic Publishers, 1994.

[67] G.M. Koob and C.G. Lau, Eds., *Foundations of Dependable Computing: System Implementaiton*, Kluwer Academic Publishers, 1994.

[68] C.P. Kruskal, L. Rudolph, M. Snir, "Efficient Synchronization on Multiprocessors with Shared Memory," in *ACM Trans. on Programming Languages and Systems*, vol. 10, no. 4, pp. 579-601 1988.

[69] C.P. Kruskal, L. Rudolph, M. Snir, "A Complexity Theory of Efficient Parallel Algorithms," *Theoretical Computer Science* **71**, pp. 95-132, 1990.

[70] H.T. Kung and C.E. Leiserson, "Algorithms for VLSI Processor Arrays", presented at the *Symp. on Sparse Matrix Computations and Their Applications*, Knoxville, TN, 1978.

[71] L.E. Ladner and M.J. Fischer, "Parallel Prefix Computation", *Journal of the ACM*, vol. 27, no. 4, pp. 831-838, 1980.

[72] L. Lamport and N.A. Lynch, "Distributed Computing: Models and Methods," in *Handbook of Theoretical Computer Science* (ed. J. van Leeuwen), vol. 1, North-Holland, 1990.

[73] L. Lamport, R. Shostak and M. Pease, "The Byzantine Generals Problem", *ACM TOPLAS*, vol. 4, no. 3, pp. 382-401, 1982.

[74] F. Thomson Leighton, *Introduction to Parallel Algorithms and Architectures: Array, Trees, Hypercubes*, Morgan Kaufman Publishers, San Mateo, CA, 1992.

[75] D.E. Lenoski and W.-D. Weber, *Scalabale Shared-Memory Multiprocessing*, Morgan Kaufmann Publishers, San Francisco, CA, 1995.

[76] M. Li and Y. Yesha, "New Lower Bounds for Parallel Computation," *Journal of the ACM*, vol. 36, no. 3, pp. 671-680, 1989.

[77] M. Loui and H. Abu-Amara, "Memory requirements for agreement among unreliable asynchronous processes," in *Advances in Computing Research*, F.P. Preparata, Ed., vol. 4, pp. 163-183, 1987.

[78] A. López-Ortiz, "Algorithm X takes work $\Omega(n \log^2 n / \log \log n)$ in a synchronous fail-stop (no restart) PRAM", unpublished manuscript, 1992.

[79] N.A. Lynch and M.J. Fischer, "On Describing the Behavior of an Implementation of Distributed Systems", *Theoretical Computer Science*, vol. 13, pp. 17-43, 1981.

[80] N.A. Lynch, *Distributed Algorithms*, Morgan Kaufman Publishers, San Mateo, CA, 1995.

[81] N.A. Lynch, "One Hundred Impossibility Proofs for Distributed Comuting", *Proc. of the 8th ACM Symposium on Principles of Distributed Computing*, pp. 1-27, 1989.

[82] N.A. Lynch, N.D. Griffeth, M.J. Fischer, L.J. Guibas, "Probabilistic Analysis of a Network Resource Allocation Algorithm", *Information and Control*, vol. 68, pp. 47-85, 1986.

[83] C. Martel, personal communication, March, 1991.

[84] C. Martel, A. Park, and R. Subramonian, "Work-optimal Asynchronous Algorithms for Shared Memory Parallel Computers," *SIAM Journal on Computing*, vol. 21, pp. 1070-1099, 1992

[85] C. Martel and A. Raghunathan, "Asynchronous PRAMs with Memory Latency", Tech. Report., U.C. Davis, 1992

[86] C. Martel and R. Subramonian, "On the Complexity of Certified Write-All Algorithms", *Journal of Algorithms*, vol. 16, no. 3., pp. 361-387, 1994 (a prel. version in the *Proc. of the 12th Conference on Foundations of Software Technology and Theoretical Computer Science*, New Delhi, India, December 1992).

[87] C. Martel, R. Subramonian, and A. Park, "Asynchronous PRAMs are (Almost) as Good as Synchronous PRAMs," in *Proc. 32d IEEE Symposium on Foundations of Computer Science*, pp. 590-599, 1990.

[88] R. McEliece, *The Theory of Information and Coding*, Addison-Wesley, 1977.

[89] C. Mead and L. Conway, *Introduction to VLSI Systems*, Addison-Wesley, Reading, MA, 1980.

[90] K. Mehlhorn and U. Vishkin, "Randomized and Deterministic Simulations of PRAMs by Parallel Machines with Restricted Granularity of Parallel Memories", *Acta Informatica*, vol. 21, no. 4, pp. 339-374, 1984.

[91] J. Naor, R.M. Roth, "Constructions of Permutation Arrays for Ceratin Scheduling Cost Measures", *Random Structures and Algorithms*, vol. 6, pp. 39-50, 1995.

[92] R. Negrini, M.G. Sami and R. Stefanelli, *Fault-Tolerance through Reconfiguration of VLSI and WSI Arrays*, the MIT Press, 1989.

[93] N. Nishimura, "Asynchronous Shared Memory Parallel Computation," in *Proc. 3rd ACM Symp. on Parallel Algor. and Architect.*, pp. 76-84, 1990.

[94] S. Owicki and D. Gries, "An Axiomatic Proof Technique for Parallel Programs I", *Acta Informatica*, vol. 6, pp. 319-340, 1976.

[95] C.H. Papadimitriou and M. Yannakakis, "Towards an Architecture-Independent Analysis of Parallel Algorithms", in *Proc. of the 20th Annual ACM Symp. on Theory of Computing*, pp. 510-513, 1988.

[96] D.A. Patterson and J.L. Hennessy, *Computer Architecture: A Quantitative Approach*, Morgan Kaufmann Publishers, San Mateo, CA, 1990.

[97] M. Pease, R. Shostak, L. Lamport, "Reaching agreement in the presence of faults", *JACM*, vol. 27, no. 2, pp. 228-234, 1980.

[98] A. Pietracaprina and F.P. Preparata, "A Practical Constructive Scheme for Deterministic Shared-Memory Access", Tech. Report CS-93-14, Brown University, 1993.

[99] N. Pippenger, "On Simultaneous Resource Bounds", in *Proc. of 20th IEEE Symposium on Foundations of Computer Science*, pp. 307-311, 1979.

[100] N. Pippenger, "On Networks of Noisy Gates", *Proc. of 26th IEEE Symposium on Foundations of Computer Science*, pp. 30-38, 1985.

[101] N. Pippenger, "Communications Networks," in *Handbook of Theoretical Computer Science* (ed. J. van Leeuwen), vol. 1, North-Holland, 1990.

[102] Πλατωνος, Απολογια Σωκρατους, quoted from L. Dyer (ed.), T.D. Seymour (rev.), *Plato, Apology of Socrates and Crito*, p. 114, 1905 (reprint, Demetrios & Victor, Booksellers, Los Angeles, 1973).

[103] F.P. Preparata, "Holographic Dispersal and Recovery of Information," in *IEEE Trans. on Info. Theory*, vol. 35, no. 5, pp. 1123-1124, 1989.

[104] M.O. Rabin, "Efficient Dispersal of Information for Security, Load Balancing and Fault Tolerance", *J. of ACM*, vol. 36, no. 2, pp. 335-348, 1989.

[105] A. Ranade, "How to Emulate Shared Memory", *Proc. of 28th IEEE Symposium on Foundations of Computer Science*, pp. 185-194, 1987.

[106] L. Rudolph, "A Robust Sorting Network", *IEEE Trans. on Computers*, vol. 34, no. 4, pp. 326-335, 1985.

[107] D.B. Sarrazin and M. Malek, "Fault-Tolerant Semiconductor Memories", *IEEE Computer*, vol. 17, no. 8, pp. 49-56, 1984.

[108] R.D. Schlichting and F.B. Schneider, "Fail-Stop Processors: an Approach to Designing Fault-tolerant Computing Systems", *ACM Transactions on Computer Systems*, vol. 1, no. 3, pp. 222-238, 1983.

[109] J. T. Schwartz, "Ultracomputers", *ACM Transactions on Programming Languages and Systems*, vol. 2, no. 4, pp. 484-521, 1980.

[110] A. A. Shvartsman, "Achieving Optimal CRCW PRAM Fault-Tolerance", *Information Processing Letters*, vol. 39, no. 2, pp. 59-66, 1991.

[111] A. A. Shvartsman, "Efficient Write-All Algorithm for Fail-Stop PRAM Without Initialized Memory", *Information Processing Letters*, vol. 44, no. 6, pp. 223-231, 1992.

[112] A. A. Shvartsman, *Fault-Tolerant and Efficient Parallel Computation*, Brown University, Tech. Rep. CS-92-23, 1992.

[113] R.E. Tarjan, U. Vishkin, "Finding biconnected components and computing tree functions in logarithmic parallel time", in *Proc. of the 25th IEEE FOCS*, pp. 12-22, 1984.

[114] E. Upfal, "An $O(\log N)$ Deterministic Packet Routing Scheme," in *Proc. 21st ACM Symposium on Theory of Computing*, pp. 241-250, 1989.

[115] E. Upfal and A. Widgerson, "How to Share Memory in a Distributed System," *J. of the ACM*, vol. 34, no. 1, pp. 116-127, 1987.

[116] L. Valiant, "General Purpose Parallel Architectures," in *Handbook of Theoretical Computer Science* (ed. J. van Leeuwen), vol. 1, North-Holland, 1990.

[117] L. Valiant, "A Bridging Model for Parallel Computation," *Communications of the ACM*, vol. 33, no. 8, pp. 103-111, 1990.

[118] J. S. Vitter, R. A. Simmons, "New Classes for Parallel Complexity: A Study of Unification and Other Complete Problems for $\mathcal{P}$," *IEEE Trans. Comput.*, vol. 35, no. 5, 1986.

[119] J. C. Wyllie, *The Complexity of Parallel Computation*, Ph.D. Thesis, Cornell University, TR 79-387, 1979.

[120] I-L. Yen, E.L. Leiss and F.B. Bastiani, "Exploiting Redundancy to Speed Up Parallel System", *IEEE Parallel and Distributed Technology*, vol. 1, no. 3, 1993.

AUTHOR INDEX

SUBJECT INDEX

A

Adversary, 13, 29, 31, 33, 40, 42, 160
  adaptive, 31
  dynamic, 31
  model, 13
  oblivious, 31–32, 160, 162
  off-line, 31, 160, 162
  omniscient, 31, 115
  on-line, 31, 115, 120
  worst-case, 125
Algorithm
  AW, 54, 90–**91**, 91, 94, 98
  AW^T, 54, **95**–97, 146
  $CR1$, 106
  $CR2$, 106
  CR/W, **104**
  CW, 102, 104
  E, 53, **55**, 142
  V, 53, 76–**77**, **81**, 144
  W, 53, 58–**59**, 72, 76, 102, 125, 129, 143
  W_{ave}, 53, **111**
  $W_{CR/W}$, 53, **106**, 108
  $W_{CR/W}^{opt}$, 53, **107**, 146
  W_{CW}, **102**
  W_{snap}, **125**
  X, 54, 76, 81, 84, 90
  X', **89**–90, 144
  Y, 54, **98**
  Z, 53, 73, **75**
  Z^{-1}, 53, **76**
  $Z_{CR/W}$, 54, **109**, 147

  heuristic, 98
  optimal, 4, 113, 115, 122
  optimized, 77
  parallel, 2, 5–6
  randomized, 48, 90, 159
  robust, 28, 47, 73, 120, 133
  sequential, 2, 12, 23, 29, 152–153, 165
  simulation, 12–14, 47, 61, 73, 76, 131, 162
    oblivious, 157
  transformation, xiii, 47, 61, 133, 152, 155, 162
  transformed, 76, 132, 147
Allocation paradigm
  global, 48
  hashed, 48, 90–91, 98
  hybrid, 90
  local, 48, 90
Available processor steps, 10–11, 15, **28**, 43

B

Block-step, 78, 125
Bootstrap procedure, 75–76

C

Clock, 23, 40, 78, 161
  external, 10
  global, 10
  internal, 10
  local, 11, 164
  logical, 163
Concurrency
  controlled write, 102

180

182